PRESIDENTIAL WAR POWER

PRESIDENTIAL WAR POWER

Louis Fisher

University Press of Kansas

Published by the University Press of Kansas (Lawrence, Kansas 66049), which was
organized by the Kansas Board of Regents and is operated and funded by Emporia State
University, Fort Hays State University, Kansas State University, Pittsburg State University, the
University of Kansas, and Wichita State University

Library of Congress Cataloging-in-Publication Data

Fisher, Louis.
  Presidential war power / Louis Fisher.
    p. cm.
  Includes bibliographical references and index.
  ISBN 0-7006-0690-4 (cloth)   ISBN 0-7006-0691-2 (pbk.)
    1. War and emergency powers—United States. 2. National security—
Law and legislation—United States. 3. United States—Foreign
relations—Law and legislation. I. Title.
  KF5060.F57 1995
  342.73′062—dc20
  [347.30262]   94-39353

British Library Cataloguing in Publication Data is available.

Printed in the United States of America

10 9 8 7 6 5 4 3 2

The paper used in this publication meets the minimum requirements of the American
National Standard for Permanence of Paper for Printed Library Materials Z39.48–1984.

To the republican principle
that reserves war-making
to the legislature

CONTENTS

PREFACE

During October 1993, when Congress was considering restrictions on the President's use of American forces in Somalia and Haiti, President Bill Clinton vigorously objected to any congressional interference: "I would strenuously oppose such attempts to encroach on the President's foreign policy powers."[1] While promising to *consult* with members of Congress, he claimed that "the Constitution leaves the President, for good and sufficient reasons, the ultimate decisionmaking authority."[2] Acknowledging that the President has an obligation to define and justify the use of U.S. force, Clinton said that "the President must make the ultimate decision."[3] In February 1994, while contemplating air strikes in Bosnia, he looked for authority not to Congress but to the UN Security Council and to NATO.[4] At a press conference on August 3, 1994, Clinton said he was not "constitutionally mandated" to receive approval from Congress before invading Haiti.[5]

This definition of executive power—to send troops anywhere in the world whenever the President likes—would have astonished the framers of the Constitution. Their structure of government very deliberately rejected the British models that gave the executive exclusive control over foreign affairs and the war power. Instead, the framers vested in Congress explicit control over the initiation and authorization of war, power over foreign commerce, approval of treaties, confirmation of ambassadors, power of the purse, and other authorities over external affairs.

The trend of presidential war power since World War II—the last congressionally declared war—collides with the constitutional framework adopted by the founding fathers. The period after 1945 created a climate in which Presidents have regularly breached constitutional principles and democratic values. Under these pressures (and invitations), Presidents have routinely exercised war powers with little or no involvement by Congress.

1. 29 Weekly Comp. Pres. Doc. 2097 (October 18, 1993).
2. Id. at 2101.
3. Id. at 2102.
4. 30 Weekly Comp. Pres. Doc. 219–20 (February 6, 1994).
5. Id. at 1616 (August 3, 1994).

The scope of presidential war powers climbed to such heights that Congress felt compelled to pass the War Powers Resolution in 1973. Later, in 1980 and 1991, it adopted new statutory procedures to tighten legislative controls over covert actions. The Iran-Contra Affair of the Reagan administration was not an aberration. It was merely a recent example of newly fashioned theories of executive power operating without effective checks from Congress, the judiciary, or the public. Numerous lawsuits, brought by members of Congress, were routinely sidestepped by federal judges who declined to place limits on presidential power.

So great is the magnitude of executive power that President Bush invaded Panama in 1989 without any involvement by Congress, and he threatened to take military action against Iraq in 1991 solely on the basis of resolutions adopted by the UN Security Council. Only at the eleventh hour did he obtain authority from Congress. The willingness of President Bush to use military force in 1991 without congressional authorization provoked a grave challenge to constitutional government.

To find a comparable threat we have to go back to 1950, when President Truman, on his own authority, ordered troops to Korea. Both Truman and Bush claimed they could send American troops into large-scale combat without first receiving authorization from Congress, and in each case they justified their actions largely on the basis of resolutions adopted by the UN Security Council. Although Congress did eventually authorize the use of armed force against Iraq, the circumstances reject the beguiling notion that the two branches worked in concert and the "constitution prevailed." Bush was ready and willing to act alone.

President Clinton inherited the commitment by President Bush to send U.S. troops to Somalia. Initially a humanitarian effort, over time this initiative acquired a military face. American forces, operating under the umbrella of the UN Security Council but without congressional authority, used military force and air attacks against a so-called warlord, Mohamed Farah Aideed. In these efforts, troops from the United States and other nations suffered substantial casualties. In 1993, President Clinton ordered the launching of cruise missiles against Baghdad, Iraq, in retaliation for an attempted assassination of George Bush. Clinton also deployed U.S. forces to Macedonia and to Haiti (two other UN operations) and contemplated sending American troops to Bosnia. All of these actions were taken unilaterally without any authorization from Congress.

The best that can be argued in support of presidential war power after World War II is that the language of the Constitution, the intent of the framers, and the republican values operating at that time are no longer relevant, having been superseded by twentieth-century conditions and pressures. Advocates of executive power state that ever since the early 1800s, in more than two hundred instances, Presidents have used military force without congressional authorization. In fact, the only significant precedent for Bush's contemplated action in Iraq is that of Truman in Korea. The two military actions demand close scrutiny, especially the claim that UN resolutions permitted Truman and Bush to act without congressional authority and that they now sanction military initiatives by Clinton.

What are the constitutional sources for presidential war power? At what point is prior authorization by Congress required? Why has Congress failed to protect its constitutional prerogatives over questions of war and peace? What role do the federal courts have in policing the limits of executive power? How do we keep presidential power consistent with the Constitution and the intent of the framers? Those questions, of fundamental interest to the liberties of American citizens, drive this book.

The entire manuscript was read by David Gray Adler and Loch Johnson, who offered a number of helpful suggestions. I appreciate their close reading and the many contributions they have made to the study of war powers over a period of years. Those people who read specific chapters include David Ackerman, Richard Best, Ellen Collier, Robert Gerber, Robert Goldich, Nancy Kassop, Leonard W. Levy, Robert Spitzer, and Duane Tananbaum. I gained much from their insights. Over the years I have kept in touch with other scholars, including Michael J. Glennon, Louis Henkin, Edward Keynes, Harold Hongju Koh, Jules Lobel, John Norton Moore, Richard M. Pious, and F. Robert Turner. They are not responsible for what I have written, but in many ways they have sharpened and deepened my understanding of the constitutional relationships between Congress and the President. I am delighted to publish once again with the University Press of Kansas, which has published and encouraged an outstanding list of books on constitutional aspects of the presidency. At each stage of production the staff members maintained a remarkable level of professionalism and competence.

A number of my articles, professional papers, and congressional testimony prepared the way for this book. In particular, I want to single out the following: "Foreign Policy Powers of the President and Congress," 499 The Annals 148 (1988); "How Tightly Can Congress Draw the Purse Strings?" 83 American Journal of International Law 758 (1989); "The Legitimacy of the Congressional National Security Role," in The Constitution and National Security (National Defense University, 1990); "War Powers: The Need for Collective Judgment," in Divided Democracy: Cooperation and Conflict between the President and Congress, ed. James A. Thurber (1991); "The Power of Commander in Chief," in The Presidency and the Persian Gulf War, ed. Marcia Lynn Whicker et al. (1993); "Historical Survey of the War Powers and the Use of Force," in The U.S. Constitution and the Power to Go to War: Historical and Current Perspectives, ed. Gary M. Stern and Morton H. Halperin (1994); testimony on covert spending on February 23, 1994, before the House Permanent Select Committee on Intelligence; "Congressional Responses to Military Initiatives," a paper presented at the annual meeting of the Society for Historians of American Foreign Relations (SHAFR), Bentley College, Waltham, Mass., June 23–26, 1994 (published under the title "Congressional Checks on Military Initiatives," *Political Science Quarterly* [1995]); and "The Korean War: On What Legal Basis Did Truman Act?" a paper presented at the Annual Meeting of the American Political Science Association, New York City, September 1–4, 1994 (published under the same title in *American Journal of International Law* [1995]). I have also spoken on the issue of war powers at the National Defense University, Ft. McNair, Washington, D.C.; the U.S. War College, Carlisle Barracks, Pa.; and the Center for National Security Law, Charlottesville, Va. In 1987, I served as Research Director of the House Iran-Contra Committee and wrote major sections of the final report dealing with institutional and constitutional issues.

NOTE ON CITATIONS

All court citations refer to published volumes whenever available: *United States Reports* (U.S.) for Supreme Court decisions, *Federal Reporter* (F.2d) for appellate decisions, and *Federal Supplement* (F.Supp.) for district court decisions. For cases not yet published in *United States Reports,* citations are to the *Supreme Court Reporter* (S.Ct.). There are also citations to *Opinions of the Attorney General* (Op. Att'y Gen.) and to *Opinions of the Office of Legal Counsel* (O.L.C.) in the Justice Department. Decisions that focus primarily on federal rules of civil and criminal procedure appear in *Federal Rules Decisions* (F.R.D.). Congressional legal sources are to the U.S. Statutes at Large (Stat.), the U.S. Code (U.S.C.), and United States Treaties and Other International Agreements (UST or TIAS). Several standard reference works are abbreviated as follows:

Elliot	Jonathan Elliot, ed., The Debates in the Several State Conventions, on the Adoption of the Federal Constitution, 5 vols. (Washington, D.C., 1836–1845)
Farrand	Max Farrand, ed., The Records of the Federal Convention of 1787, 4 vols. (New Haven, Conn.: Yale University Press, 1937)
FRUS	Foreign Relations of the United States, official documentary historical record, prepared by the Historian of the Department of State, beginning in 1863 (Washington, D.C.: Government Printing Office)
Journals of the Continental Congress	Journals of the Continental Congress, 1774–1789, 34 vols. (Washington, D.C.: Government Printing Office, 1904–1937)
Landmark Briefs	Landmark Briefs and Arguments of the Supreme Court of the United States: Constitutional Law, ed. Philip B. Kurland and Gerhard Casper (Bethesda, Md.: University Publications of America)
Richardson	James D. Richardson, ed., A Compilation of the Messages and Papers of the Presidents, 20 vols. (New York: Bureau of National Literature, 1897–1925)

Thorpe   Francis Newton Thorpe, ed., The Federal and State Con-
              stitutions, Colonial Charters and Other Organic Law, 7
              vols. (Washington, D.C.: Government Printing Office,
              1909)

Weekly Comp. Weekly Compilation of Presidential Documents, pub-
Pres. Doc.   lished each week by the Government Printing Office
              since 1965

1

THE CONSTITUTIONAL FRAMEWORK

When the framers assembled in Philadelphia in 1787 to draft the Constitution, existing models of government in Europe placed the war power securely in the hands of the monarch. The framers broke decisively with that tradition. Drawing on lessons learned at home in the American colonies and the Continental Congress, they deliberately transferred the power to initiate war from the executive to the legislature. The framers, aspiring to achieve the ideal of republican government, drafted a Constitution "that allowed only Congress to loose the military forces of the United States on other nations."[1] In their deliberations at the constitutional convention, the delegates held fast to the principle of collective judgment, shared power in foreign affairs, and "the cardinal tenet of republican ideology that the conjoined wisdom of many is superior to that of one."[2]

The British Models

The English Parliament gained the power of the purse in the 1660s to control the king. The power to initiate war, however, remained a monarchical prerogative. John Locke's *Second Treatise on Civil Government* (1690) spoke of three branches of government: legislative, executive, and "federative." The last consisted of "the power of war and peace, leagues and alliances, and all the transactions with all persons and communities without the commonwealth." The federative power (what we call foreign policy today) was "almost always united" with the executive. Separating the executive and federative powers, Locke warned, would invite "disorder and ruin."[3]

A similar model appeared in the *Commentaries* written by Sir William

1. Edwin B. Firmage, "War, Declaration of," in 4 Encyclopedia of the American Presidency 1573 (Leonard W. Levy and Louis Fisher, eds. 1994).
2. David Gray Adler, "Foreign Policy and the Separation of Powers: The Influence of the Judiciary," in Judging the Constitution: Critical Essays on Judicial Lawmaking 158 (Michael W. McCann and Gerald L. Houseman, eds. 1989).
3. John Locke, Second Treatise on Civil Government, secs. 146–48 (1690).

Blackstone, the great eighteenth-century jurist. He defined the king's prerogative as "those rights and capacities which the king enjoys alone."[4]
Some of the prerogatives he considered *direct*—those that are "rooted in
and spring from the king's political person," including the right to send
and receive ambassadors and the power to make war or peace.[5] By vesting
in the king the sole prerogative to make war, individuals entering society
gave up the private right to make war: "It would, indeed, be extremely
improper, that any number of subjects should have the power of binding
the supreme magistrate, and putting him against his will in a state of war."[6]

Through the exercise of Blackstone's prerogative the king could make
"a treaty with a foreign state, which shall irrevocably bind the nation."[7]
The king could issue letters of marque and reprisal (authorizing private
citizens to undertake military actions), and as Blackstone noted, that prerogative was "nearly related to, and plainly derived from, that other of
making war."[8] Blackstone considered the king "the generalissimo, or the
first in military command," who had "the sole power of raising and regulating fleets and armies."[9] Whenever the king exercised his lawful prerogative he "is, and ought to be absolute; that is, so far absolute, that there is
no legal authority that can either delay or resist him."[10]

These models of executive power were well known to the framers.
They knew that their forebears in England had committed to the executive the power to go to war. However, when they declared their independence from England, they vested *all* executive powers in the Continental
Congress. They did not provide for a separate executive or a separate judiciary. The ninth article of the first national constitution, the Articles of
Confederation, provided: "The United States, in Congress assembled,
shall have the sole and exclusive right and power of determining on peace
and war." The single exception to that principle lay in the sixth article,
which allowed states to engage in war if invaded by enemies or when
threatened with invasion by Indian tribes.

The authority of the Continental Congress extended to both "perfect"
and "imperfect" wars—to wars that were formally declared by Congress
and those that were merely authorized. As the Federal Court of Appeals
noted in 1782, a perfect war "destroys the national peace and tranquillity,

4. 2 William Blackstone, Commentaries on the Laws of England 238 (1803).
5. Id. at 239.
6. Id. at 257.
7. Id. at 251.
8. Id. at 258.
9. Id. at 262.
10. Id. at 250.

and lays the foundation of every possible act of hostility," whereas an imperfect war "does not entirely destroy the public tranquillity, but inter-
rupts it only in some particulars, as in the case of reprisals."[11] The power
over perfect and imperfect wars lay with the Continental Congress and
would remain with the U.S. Congress. The Constitution drafted in 1787
and ratified the next year not only empowered Congress to declare war
but authorized it to grant "Letters of Marque and Reprisal." Congressional
control over perfect and imperfect wars was recognized by the Supreme
Court in litigation growing out of the Quasi-War with France from 1798 to
1800 (see Chapter 2).

The states gave their governors broad power over the military, but that
power was directed to actions of self-defense. For example, the New
Hampshire Constitution of 1784 provided that the president of the state
"shall have full power" to lead and conduct the military forces

> to encounter, expulse, repel, resist and pursue by force of arms, as
> well as by land, within and without the limits of the state; and also to
> kill[,] slay, destroy, if necessary, and conquer by all fitting ways, enter-
> prize and means, all and every such person and persons as shall, at
> any time hereafter, in a hostile manner, attempt or enterprize the de-
> struction, invasion, detriment, or annoyance of the state; and to use
> and exercise over the army and navy, and over the militia in actual
> service, the law-martial in time of war, invasion, and also in rebellion,
> declared by the legislature to exist. . . .[12]

Clearly these executive powers were directed at defensive operations in
response to invasion from the outside or rebellion from the inside. Similar
authority was given to the governor of Massachusetts in the Constitution
of 1780.[13] The value of having states engage in self-defense is reflected in
the U.S. Constitution, which prohibits states from engaging in war "unless actually invaded, or in imminent Danger as will not admit of delay."[14]

Opposing Monarchical Powers

During their learned and careful debates at the Philadelphia convention,
the framers vested in Congress many of Locke's federative powers and

11. Miller v. The Ship Resolution, 2 Dall. (2 U.S.) 19, 20 (1782).
12. 4 Thorpe 2463–64.
13. 3 Thorpe 1901.
14. U.S. Const., Art. I, sec. 10.

Blackstone's royal prerogatives. Given the governmental systems operating worldwide in 1787, with power concentrated in the executive, the scope of power granted to Congress is extraordinarily progressive and democratic. The power to go to war was not left to solitary action by a single executive, but in collective decision making through parliamentary deliberations.

On numerous occasions the delegates to the constitutional convention emphasized that the power of peace and war associated with monarchy would not be given to the President. On June 1, 1787, Charles Pinckney said he was for "a vigorous Executive but was afraid the Executive powers of ⟨the existing⟩ Congress might extend to peace & war &c which would render the Executive a Monarchy, of the worst kind, towit an elective one."[15] John Rutledge wanted the executive power placed in a single person, "tho' he was not for giving him the power of war and peace."[16] Roger Sherman considered "the Executive magistracy as nothing more than an institution for carrying the will of the Legislature into effect."[17] James Wilson also preferred a single executive but "did not consider the Prerogatives of the British Monarch as a proper guide in defining the Executive powers. Some of these prerogatives were of a Legislative nature. Among others that of war & peace &c."[18]

Edmund Randolph worried about executive power, calling it "the foetus of monarchy." The delegates to the Philadelphia convention, he said, had "no motive to be governed by the British Governmt. as our prototype." If the United States had no other choice he might adopt the British model, but "the fixt genius of the people of America required a different form of Government."[19] Wilson agreed that the British model "was inapplicable to the situation of this Country; the extent of which was so great, and the manners so republican, that nothing but a great confederated Republic would do for it."[20]

In his lengthy speech on June 18, Alexander Hamilton set forth his principles of government. Although later associated with vigorous and independent presidential power, he too jettisoned the British model of executive prerogatives in foreign affairs and the war power. Explaining that in his "private opinion he had no scruple in declaring . . . that the British

15. 1 Farrand 64–65.
16. Id.
17. Id.
18. Id. at 65–66.
19. Id. at 66.
20. Id.

Govt. was the best in the world,"[21] he nonetheless discarded the Black-stonian and Lockean models. He proposed that the President would have "with the advice and approbation of the Senate" the power of making treaties, the Senate would have the "sole power of declaring war," and the President would be authorized to have "the direction of war when autho-rized or begun."[22]

By the time the framers completed their labors, the President had been stripped of the sole power to make treaties. Instead he shared that power with the Senate. As late as August 6, with about a month remaining at the convention, the constitutional draft gave the Senate exclusive power to make treaties and to appoint ambassadors. Only in early September was it agreed to include the President in these decisions.[23]

In *Federalist* no. 75, Hamilton noted that the act of making treaties "will be found to partake more of the legislative than of the executive character, though it does not seem strictly to fall within the definition of either of them." Treaties required legislative action because they were contracts with foreign nations with "the force of law." Although it might be appropriate in hereditary monarchies to vest the treaty-making power with the executive, "it would be utterly unsafe and improper to intrust that power to an elective magistrate of four years' duration." The history of mankind could not support transferring such power "to the sole dis-posal of a magistrate created and circumstanced as would be a President of the United States."

The framers rejected the British model for the appointment power, since the British monarch not only appointed officers but created the of-fices as well. The drafters at Philadelphia wanted to avoid that concentra-tion of power, with its potential for abuse and corruption. They granted the President the right to send and receive ambassadors but only after the Senate agreed to his nominations. He had no power to issue letters of marque and reprisal; that power was now vested exclusively in Congress. Although the President was made Commander in Chief, it was left to Con-gress to raise and regulate fleets and armies. The rejection of Locke and Blackstone was decisive.

The extent of this break with English precedents is set forth clearly in *The Federalist Papers*. In *Federalist* no. 69, Hamilton explained that the President has "concurrent power with a branch of the legislature in the formation of treaties," whereas the British king "is the *sole possessor* of

21. Id. at 288.
22. Id. at 292.
23. 2 Farrand 155, 169, 183, 297–98, 392–93, 495.

the power of making treaties." The royal prerogative in foreign affairs was deliberately shared with Congress, he noted. Hamilton contrasted the distribution of war powers in England and in the American Constitution. The power of the king "extends to the *declaring* of war and to the *raising* and *regulating* of fleets and armies." Unlike the king of England, the President "will have only the occasional command of such part of the militia of the nation *as by legislative provision may be called into the actual service of the Union*" (emphasis added). No such tether was attached to the king.

The Constitution grants to Congress a number of specific powers to control war and military affairs: to declare war; to raise and support armies and to provide and maintain a navy; the power to make regulations of the land and naval forces; the power to call forth the militia; and the power to provide for organizing, arming, and disciplining the militia.

Furthermore, the Constitution vests in Congress the power to regulate foreign commerce, an area with a direct relationship to the war power. Commercial conflicts between nations were often a cause of war. In *Gibbons* v. *Ogden* (1824), Chief Justice John Marshall said of the commerce power that "it may be, and often is, used as an instrument of war."[24] Guided by history, the framers placed that power with Congress. James Madison later remarked: "The constitution supposes, what the History of all Govts demonstrates, that the Ex. is the branch of power most interested in war, & most prone to it. It has accordingly with studied care, vested the question of war in the Legisl."[25]

Repelling Sudden Attacks

The debates at the Philadelphia convention reveal that the framers were determined to circumscribe the President's authority to take unilateral military actions. The early draft empowered Congress to "make war." Charles Pinckney objected that legislative proceedings "were too slow" for the safety of the country in an emergency, since he expected Congress to meet but once a year. Madison and Elbridge Gerry moved to insert "declare" for "make," leaving to the President "the power to repel sudden attacks." Their motion carried on a vote of 7 to 2. After Rufus King explained that the word "make" would allow the President to conduct war,

24. 22 U.S. (9 Wheat.) 1, 190 (1824).
25. 6 The Writings of James Madison 312 (Gaillard Hunt ed. 1900–1910) (letter of April 2, 1798, to Thomas Jefferson.)

which was "an Executive function," Connecticut changed its vote and the final tally became 9 to 1.[26]

There was little doubt about the limited scope of the President's war power. The duty to repel sudden attacks represents an emergency measure that permits the President to take actions necessary to resist sudden attacks either against the mainland of the United States or against American troops abroad. The President never received a general power to deploy troops whenever and wherever he thought best, and the framers did not authorize him to take the country into full-scale war or to mount an offensive attack against another nation. John Bassett Moore, a noted scholar of international law, made this observation:

> There can hardly be room for doubt that the framers of the constitution, when they vested in Congress the power to declare war, never imagined that they were leaving it to the executive to use the military and naval forces of the United States all over the world for the purpose of actually coercing other nations, occupying their territory, and killing their soldiers and citizens, all according to his own notions of the fitness of things, as long as he refrained from calling his action war or persisted in calling it peace.[27]

Reactions to the Madison-Gerry amendment reinforce the narrow grant of authority to the President. Pierce Butler wanted to give the President the power to make war, arguing that he "will have all the requisite qualities, and will not make war but when the Nation will support it." Roger Sherman objected: "The Executive shd. be able to repel and not to commence war."[28] Gerry said he "never expected to hear in a republic a motion to empower the Executive alone to declare war."[29] George Mason spoke "agst giving the power of war to the Executive, because not ⟨safely⟩ to be trusted with it; . . . He was for clogging rather than facilitating war."[30]

Similar statements were made at the state ratifying conventions. In Pennsylvania, James Wilson expressed the prevailing sentiment that the system of checks and balances "will not hurry us into war; it is calculated to guard against it. It will not be in the power of a single man, or a single body of men, to involve us in such distress; for the important power of

26. 2 Farrand 318–19.
27. 5 The Collected Papers of John Bassett Moore 196 (1944).
28. 2 Farrand 318.
29. Id.
30. Id. at 319.

declaring war is vested in the legislature at large."[31] In North Carolina, James Iredell compared the limited powers of the President with those of the British monarch. The king of Great Britain was not only the Commander in Chief "but has power, in time of war, to raise fleets and armies. He has also authority to declare war." By contrast, the President "has not the power of declaring war by his own authority, nor that of raising fleets and armies. These powers are vested in other hands."[32] In South Carolina, Charles Pinckney assured his colleagues that the President's powers "did not permit him to declare war."[33]

Separating Purse and Sword

The idea of keeping the purse and the sword in distinct hands was a bedrock principle for the framers. They were familiar with the efforts of English kings to rely on extraparliamentary sources of revenue for their military expeditions and other activities, with some of the payments coming from foreign governments. Because of these transgressions, England lurched into a civil war and Charles I lost both his office and his head.[34] The rise of democratic government is directly related to legislative control over all expenditures, including those for foreign and military affairs.

The U.S. Constitution attempted to avoid the British history of civil war and bloodshed by vesting the power of the purse squarely in Congress. Under Article I, Section 9, "No Money shall be drawn from the Treasury, but in Consequence of Appropriations made by Law." In *Federalist* no. 48, Madison explained that "the legislative department alone has access to the pockets of the people." In Article I, Section 8, Congress is empowered to lay and collect taxes, duties, imposts, and excises; to borrow money on the credit of the United States; and to coin money and regulate its value. This power of the purse, said Madison in *Federalist* no. 58, represents the "most compleat and effectual weapon with which any constitution can arm the immediate representatives of the people, for obtaining a redress of every grievance, and for carrying into effect every just and salutary measure."

The framers did more than place the power of the purse in Congress. They deliberately divided government by making the President the Commander in Chief while reserving to Congress the decision to finance mili-

31. 2 Elliot 528.
32. 4 Elliot 107.
33. Id. at 287.
34. Paul Einzig, The Control of the Purse 57–62, 100–106 (1959).

tary operations. Madison insisted on keeping the power of Commander in Chief at arm's length from the power to take the nation to war. To protect constitutional liberties, the latter had to be reserved to Congress:

> Those who are to *conduct a war* cannot in the nature of things, be proper or safe judges, whether *a war ought* to be *commenced, continued,* or *concluded*. They are barred from the latter functions by a great principle in free government, analogous to that which separates the sword from the purse, or the power of executing from the power of enacting laws.[35]

This understanding of the war power was widely held. Thomas Jefferson praised the transfer of the war power "from the executive to the Legislative body, from those who are to spend to those who are to pay."[36] At the Philadelphia convention, George Mason counseled that the "purse & the sword ought never to get into the same hands ⟨whether Legislative or Executive.⟩ "[37]

The fact that Congress was given express power to declare war did not mean that the President could prevail in undeclared wars. Whether declared or undeclared, the decision to initiate war was left to Congress. The framers were well aware that nations approved war either by declaration or authorization. In *Federalist* no. 25, Hamilton acknowledged that the "ceremony of a formal denunciation of war has of late fallen into disuse."

Commander in Chief

The framers empowered the President to be Commander in Chief, but that title must be understood in the context of military responsibilities that Congress authorizes. The language in the Constitution reads: "The President shall be Commander in Chief of the Army and Navy of the United States, and of the Militia of the several States, when called into the actual Service of the United States." Congress, not the President, does the calling. Article I gives to Congress the power to provide "for calling forth the Militia to execute the Laws of the Union, suppress Insurrections and repel invasions."

In *Federalist* no. 74, Hamilton explained part of the purpose for mak-

---

35. 6 The Writings of James Madison 148 (emphasis in original).
36. 5 The Writings of Thomas Jefferson 123 (Paul Leicester Ford ed. 1892–1899).
37. 1 Farrand 139–40.

ing the President Commander in Chief. The direction of war "most peculiarly demands those qualities which distinguish the exercise of power by a single head." The power of directing war and emphasizing the common strength "forms a usual and essential part in the definition of the executive authority." In *Federalist* no. 69, Hamilton offered a modest definition of commander-in-chief powers, claiming that the office "would amount to nothing more than the supreme command and direction of the military and naval forces, as first general and admiral of the Confederacy." He knew better than that. As Washington's aide during the revolutionary war, Hamilton understood that "command and direction" are more than clerical tasks. They can be powerful forces in determining the scope and duration of a war.

Designating the President as Commander in Chief represented an important technique for preserving civilian supremacy over the military. The person leading the armed forces would be the civilian President, not a military officer. One of the complaints included in the Declaration of Independence was that King George III had "affected to render the Military independent of and superior to the Civil Power." General Thomas Gage, British commander during the war of independence, issued orders to prevent his officers from interfering with the civil administration.[38]

Attorney General Edward Bates later explained in 1861 that the President is Commander in Chief not because he is "skilled in the art of war and qualified to marshal a host in the field of battle." He is Commander in Chief for a different reason. Whatever soldier leads U.S. armies to victory against an enemy, "he is subject to the orders of the *civil magistrate*, and he and his army are always 'subordinate to the civil power.' "[39] In 1895, the Supreme Court noted that the purpose of the commander-in-chief clause "is evidently to vest in the President the supreme command over all the military forces,—such supreme and undivided command as would be necessary to the prosecution of a successful war."[40]

Scholars have long disagreed whether the term Commander in Chief merely confers a title or implies additional powers for the President. Justice Robert Jackson underscored the elusive nature of this power by remarking that the commander-in-chief clause implies "something more than an empty title. But just what authority goes with the name has plagued presidential advisers who would not waive or narrow it by non-

38. Clarence E. Carter, "The Office of Commander in Chief: A Phase of Imperial Unity on the Eve of the Revolution," in The Era of the American Revolution 209–10 (Richard B. Morris ed. 1971).

39. 10 Op. Att'y Gen. 74, 79 (1861); (emphasis in original).

40. United States v. Sweeny, 157 U.S. 281, 284 (1895).

assertion yet cannot say where it begins or ends."[41] He noted that the commander-in-chief clause is sometimes put forth "as support for any presidential action, internal or external, involving use of force, the idea being that it vests power to do anything, anywhere, that can be done with an army or navy."[42] To this proposition he said that nothing would be "more sinister and alarming than that a President whose conduct of foreign affairs is so largely uncontrolled, and often even is unknown, can vastly enlarge his mastery over the internal affairs of the country by his own commitment of the Nation's armed forces to some foreign venture."[43]

Some studies would construe the commander-in-chief clause narrowly. Raoul Berger concluded: "How narrowly the function was conceived may be gathered from the fact that in appointing George Washington Commander-in-Chief, the Continental Congress made sure . . . that he was to be 'its creature . . . in every respect.'" Berger notes that instructions drafted by the Continental Congress in 1775 told Washington "punctually to observe and follow such orders and directions, from time to time, as you shall receive from this, or a future Congress of these United Colonies, or committee of Congress."[44]

Citing these precedents is misplaced for two reasons. First, they ignore the extensive delegations that the Continental Congress soon found necessary. For example, three days later the Congress gave these liberal instructions to General Washington: "whereas all particulars cannot be foreseen, nor positive instructions for such emergencies so before hand given but that many things must be left to your prudent and discreet management, as occurrences may arise upon the place, or from time to time fall out, you are therefore upon all such accidents or any occasions that may happen, to use your best circumspection."[45] Second, the precedents are drawn from the wrong period. The office of President in 1787 was created as a separate, coequal, and independent branch, unlike its status under the Continental Congress (a mere agent of Congress).

The constitutional framework adopted by the framers is clear in its basic principles. The authority to initiate war lay with Congress. The President could act unilaterally only in one area: to repel sudden attacks. Anyone who scans the war-power provisions of the Constitution is likely to

41. Youngstown Co. v. Sawyer, 343 U.S. 579, 641 (1952).
42. Id. at 641–42.
43. Id. at 642.
44. Raoul Berger, Executive Privilege 62 (1974); 2 Journals of the Continental Congress 96 (1905).
45. 2 Journals of the Continental Congress 101 (1905).

agree with Taylor Reveley that "the text tilts decisively toward Congress."[46] That impression is reinforced by reading the debates at the Philadelphia convention, the state ratification conventions, and the *Federalist Papers*. John Norton Moore, who supports a broad reading of presidential power in foreign affairs, nevertheless concluded that it "seems reasonably clear from the debates at the Federal Constitutional Convention that most of the framers sought to place the major war power in Congress and to leave the President only the right to repel sudden attacks."[47]

Over the next two centuries, a number of incidents were invoked by Presidents and their supporters to expand the President's potential for *making* war over the formal power of Congress for *declaring* war. In the nineteenth century, Presidents resorted to military force for the announced purpose of protecting American lives and property—actions that would be cited as a legal source for enlarging executive power. The concept of "defensive war" was stretched to justify presidential war-making throughout the world. Other developments in the twentieth century, including military security treaty provisions and the UN Charter, were used to inflate the President's war power beyond the intentions of the framers and beyond the control of Congress and the public.

46. W. Taylor Reveley III, War Powers of the President and Congress: Who Holds the Arrows and Olive Branch? 29 (1981).

47. John N. Moore, "The National Executive and the Use of the Armed Forces Abroad," 21 Naval War College Rev. 28, 29 (1969).

2

PRECEDENTS FROM 1789 TO 1900

Presidential use of force during the first few decades after the Philadelphia Convention conformed closely to the expectations of the framers. The decision to go to war or to mount offensive actions was reserved to Congress. Presidents accepted that principle for all wars: declared or undeclared. At first narrowly confined, the scope of presidential action gradually widened. Presidential movement of troops and vessels could provoke war, as in Mexico, and Presidents began to use force abroad to "protect American lives and property." Gradually the executive branch claimed for the President the power to initiate war and determine its magnitude and duration.

Indian Wars

The first exercise of the commander-in-chief clause involved actions by President Washington against certain Indian tribes, actions explicitly authorized by Congress. On September 29, 1789, Congress passed legislation "for the purpose of protecting the inhabitants of the frontiers of the United States from the hostile incursions of the Indians." To provide that protection, Congress authorized the President "to call into service from time to time, such part of the militia of the states respectively, as he may judge necessary for the purpose aforesaid."[1] In 1790 and again in 1791, Congress passed new authorizations to protect the inhabitants in the frontiers.[2]

In response to the 1789 authorization, President Washington wrote to Governor Arthur St. Clair and gave him instructions to implement the statute. Washington's first preference was to arrange a cessation of hostilities and a peace treaty. If that could not be arranged St. Clair was to call upon the nearest counties of Virginia and Pennsylvania for detachments of militia.[3] Two years later St. Clair's troops suffered a disastrous loss to the Indians. President Washington promptly notified Congress, promising

1. 1 Stat. 96, sec. 5 (1789).
2. 1 Stat. 121, sec. 16 (1790); 1 Stat. 222 (1791).
3. 30 The Writings of George Washington 430 (John C. Fitzpatrick ed. 1939).

a further communication "of all such matters as shall be necessary to enable the Legislature to judge of the future measures which it may be proper to pursue."[4]

St. Clair's defeat precipitated the first major congressional investigation. On March 27, 1792, the House of Representatives considered a resolution to request President Washington "to institute an inquiry into the causes of the late defeat of the army under the command of Major General St. Clair."[5] After debating the resolution, it was decided that the House, as "the grand inquest of the nation," should conduct the inquiry and not the President.[6] The resolution requesting the President to institute the inquiry was defeated, 35 to 21. Congress authorized the appointment of a committee to inquire "into the causes of the failure of the late expedition under Major General St. Clair; and that the said committee be empowered to call for such persons, papers, and records, as may be necessary to assist their inquiries."[7]

According to the account of Thomas Jefferson, President Washington convened his Cabinet to determine the extent to which the House could call for papers from the executive branch. The Cabinet considered and agreed that the House "was an inquest, and therefore might institute inquiries . . . [and] might call for papers generally." Moreover, the President "ought to communicate such papers as the public good would permit, and ought to refuse those, the disclosure of which would injure the public: consequently were to exercise a discretion." Having laid the seeds of executive privilege, the Cabinet then decided that there was not a paper "which might not be properly produced."[8] The congressional committee examined papers furnished by the executive branch, listened to explanations from department heads and other witnesses, and received a written statement from General St. Clair.[9]

Throughout this period the executive branch understood that its military operations against Indians were limited to defensive actions. Secretary of War Henry Knox wrote to Governor William Blount on October 9, 1792: "The Congress which possess the powers of declaring War will assemble on the 5th of next Month—Until their judgments shall be made

4. Id. at 442.
5. Annals of Cong., 2d Cong., 1–2 Sess. 490 (1792).
6. Id. at 491.
7. Id. at 493.
8. 1 The Writings of Thomas Jefferson 303–5 (Albert Ellery Bergh, ed. 1903).
9. Annals of Cong., 2d Cong., 1–2 Sess. 601–2, 877, 895, 907, 1052–59, 1106–13, 1309–17 (1792–1793).

known it seems essential to confine all your operations to defensive measures."[10] The following month Knox wrote again to Blount:

All your letters have been submitted to the President of the United States. Whatever may be his impression relatively to the proper steps to be adopted, he does not conceive himself authorized to direct offensive operations against the Chickamaggas. If such measures are to be pursued they must result from the decisions of Congress who solely are vested with the powers of War.[11]

President Washington consistently held to this policy. Writing in 1793, he said that any offensive operations against the Creek Nation must await congressional action: "The Constitution vests the power of declaring war with Congress; therefore no offensive expedition of importance can be undertaken until after they have deliberated upon the subject, and authorized such a measure."[12]

In 1795, Knox informed Blount that President Washington had waited for the results of congressional deliberations on Indian policy, and that Congress had appropriated $50,000 for opening trade with the Indians and $130,000 for defensive protection of the frontiers. "All ideas of offensive operations," said Knox, "are therefore to be laid aside and all possible harmony cultivated with the Indian Tribes."[13] When Blount suggested that Congress might order an army to "humble, if not destroy the Creek Nation," Knox told him firmly that Congress was determined to avoid a direct or indirect war with the Creeks: "Congress alone are competent to decide upon an offensive war, and congress have not thought fit to authorize it."[14]

This sensitivity to congressional prerogatives is reflected in other executive documents during this early period. In a message to Congress on November 16, 1818, President Monroe reviewed the military conflicts involving Indians in the Floridas. He described a number of battles, constituting self-defense, and why it was sometimes necessary to exceed boundaries while pursuing the enemy.[15] He also explained his instructions to Major-General Andrew Jackson to enter Florida in pursuit of the Semi-

---

10. 4 The Territorial Papers of the United States 195 (Clarence Edwin Carter ed. 1936).
11. Id. at 220–21.
12. 33 The Writings of George Washington 73.
13. 4 The Territorial Papers of the United States 387.
14. Id. at 389. See also Francis Paul Prucha, The Sword of the Republic: The United States Army on the Frontier, 1783–1846 46–47 (1969), and Wiley Sword, President Washington's Indian War: The Struggle for the Old Northwest, 1790–1795 (1985).
15. 2 Richardson 610–11.

noles without encroaching on the rights of Spain. On one occasion, however, Jackson found it necessary to seize Spanish posts with war materials to prevent their use by the Indians.[16] Monroe emphasized that in entering Florida "no idea was entertained of hostility to Spain." To preserve amicable relations between the United States and Spain, the posts were returned. Monroe recognized that the decision to go from peace to war belonged to Congress: "By ordering the restitution of the posts those relations are preserved. To a change of them the power of the Executive is deemed incompetent; it is vested in Congress only."[17]

The Whiskey Rebellion

The Whiskey Rebellion of 1794 marks the first time a President called out the militia to suppress a domestic insurrection. President Washington acted expressly on authority delegated to him by Congress. Legislation in 1792 provided that whenever the United States "shall be invaded, or be in imminent danger of invasion from any foreign nation or Indian tribe," the President may call forth the state militias to repel such invasions and to suppress insurrections.[18] The statute introduced a novel way of monitoring and checking presidential actions. Whenever the laws of the United States were opposed and their execution obstructed in any state, "by combinations too powerful to be suppressed by the ordinary course of judicial proceedings, or by the powers vested in the marshals by this act," the President would have to be first notified of that fact by an Associate Justice of the Supreme Court or by a federal district judge. Only after that notice could the President call forth the militia of the state to suppress the insurrection.[19]

After Congress enacted a federal excise tax on distilled whiskey in 1791, farmers in western Pennsylvania resorted to violence to resist the revenue measure. There was fear that the rebellion would spread to other states. In a proclamation issued September 15, 1792, President Washington warned those who were resisting the law that it was his duty "to take care that the laws be faithfully executed" and directed all courts, magistrates, and officers to see that the laws were obeyed.[20] In 1794 he issued another proclamation, itemizing a long list of abuses against federal agents

16. Id. at 611.
17. Id. at 612.
18. 1 Stat. 264, sec. 1 (1792).
19. Id., sec. 2.
20. 1 Richardson 116–17.

and stating that he had put into effect the procedures established by the militia statute of 1792. President Washington gave Justice James Wilson the evidence needed to verify the rebellion and received from Justice Wilson a certification that ordinary legal means were insufficient to execute national law.[21] Washington called forth the militias of four states to put down the rebellion. District Judge Richard Peters joined Alexander Hamilton and District Attorney William Rawle in accompanying the troops. Hamilton and Rawle conducted hearings before Peters to identify the instigators, who were later tried in Philadelphia.[22]

Quasi-War with France

Much has been made of the President's authority to engage the country in undeclared wars, such as the "quasi-war" with France in 1798–1800. In a major legal defense of the Vietnam War, the State Department in 1966 remarked: "Since the Constitution was adopted there have been at least 125 instances in which the President has ordered the armed forces to take action or maintain positions abroad without obtaining prior congressional authorization, starting with the 'undeclared war' with France (1798–1800)."[23] Many of those "instances" will be analyzed in subsequent chapters, but the reference to the war with France is clearly false. Congress debated the prospect of war openly and enacted a number of bills to put the country on a war footing.

President John Adams did not decide that he could, on his own authority, go to war against France. He asked Congress to prepare the country for war. While pledging to pursue negotiations toward a peaceful resolution, political conditions abroad compelled him to recommend to Congress "effectual measures of defense."[24] Congress carefully debated these bills, enacting several dozen to support military action by the President. A series of statutes granted supplemental funds for a naval armament, increased the number of ships, authorized another regiment of artillerists and engineers, reinforced the defense of ports and harbors, funded additional cannons, arms, and ammunition, empowered the President to raise a provisional army and seize French ships, and suspended commerce with France. Congress also terminated the 1778 treaty of amity and com-

21. Id. at 150–52.
22. Homer Cummings and Carl McFarland, Federal Justice 43–45 (1937).
23. 54 Dep't of State Bull. 474, 484 (1966).
24. 1 Richardson 226.

merce with France.[25] Although war was never formally declared, no one doubted that Congress had acted to authorize war. During the debates in 1798, Congressman Edward Livingston (D-N.Y.) considered the country "now in a state of war; and let no man flatter himself that the vote which has been given is not a declaration of war."[26]

Alexander Hamilton, always protective of executive authority, understood the limits of presidential power in the Quasi-War. Congress passed legislation on May 28, 1798, authorizing the President to seize armed French vessels.[27] He was asked what American ship commanders could do prior to the enactment of that bill. Hamilton was "not ready to say that [the President] has any other power than merely to employ" ships with authority "to *repel* force by *force,* (but not to capture), and to repress hostilities within our waters including a marine league from our coasts." Any actions beyond those measures "must fall under the idea of *reprisals* & requires the sanction of that Department which is to declare or make war."[28]

By prompting several important judicial decisions, the Quasi-War with France clarified the prerogatives of Congress over war and the deployment of military force. In 1800 and 1801 the Supreme Court recognized that Congress could authorize hostilities in two ways: either by a formal declaration of war or by statutes that authorized an undeclared war, as had been done against France. Military conflicts could be "limited," "partial," and "imperfect," without requiring Congress to make a formal declaration. In the first case Justice Samuel Chase noted: "Congress is empowered to declare a general war, or congress may wage a limited war; limited in place, in objects, and in time. . . . congress has authorised hostilities on the high seas by certain persons in certain cases. There is no authority given to commit hostilities on land."[29] In the second case, Chief Justice John Marshall wrote for the Court: "The whole powers of war being, by the constitution of the United States, vested in congress, the acts of that body can alone be resorted to as our guides in this inquiry."[30]

Those cases do not imply that once Congress authorizes war, the President is at liberty to choose the time, location, and scope of military activities. In authorizing war, Congress may place limits on what Presidents may and may not do. Part of the legislation in the 1798–1800 period au-

---

25. 1 Stat. 547–611 (1798).

26. 8 Annals of Congress 1519 (1798).

27. 1 Stat. 561 (1798).

28. 21 The Papers of Alexander Hamilton 461–62 (Harold C. Syrett ed. 1974); (emphasis in original).

29. Bas v. Tingy, 4 U.S. 37, 43 (1800).

30. Talbot v. Seeman, 5 U.S. 1, 28 (1801).

thorized the President to seize vessels sailing *to* French ports. President Adams acted contrary to this statute by issuing an order directing American ships to capture vessels sailing *to or from* French ports. Captain George Little followed Adams's order by seizing a Danish ship sailing from a French port. He was sued for damages and the case came to the Supreme Court.

Chief Justice Marshall, writing for the Court, admitted that the case gave him much difficulty. He confessed that the "first bias" of his mind was very strongly in favor of the opinion that although the instructions from President Adams "could not give a right, they might yet excuse [a military officer] from damages." Initially, Marshall assumed an "implicit obedience, which military men usually pay to the orders of their superiors, which indeed is indispensably necessary to every military system." That system of military hierarchy seemed to Marshall to justify the actions of Captain Little, "who is placed by the laws of his country in a situation which in general requires that he should obey them." And yet on further reflection Marshall decided that Captain Little could be sued for damages: "I have been convinced that I was mistaken, and I have receded from this first opinion. I acquiesce in that of my brethren, which is, that the instructions [by Adams] cannot change the nature of the transaction, or legalize an act which, without those instructions, would have been a plain trespass."[31]

In short, congressional policy announced in a statute necessarily prevails over inconsistent presidential orders and military actions. Presidential orders, even those issued as Commander in Chief, are subject to restrictions imposed by Congress.

In the case of Captain Little, Congress later decided that he should not have been liable for following a presidential order and in 1807 passed a private bill to reimburse him for the damages awarded against him.[32] The legislative history provides no reasons for the congressional action.[33] Congress may have concluded that federal law failed to adequately distinguish between lawful orders and unlawful orders. In 1789, Congress had directed military officers "to observe and obey the orders of the President of the United States."[34] Legislation in 1799 provided that any officer "who shall disobey the orders of his superior . . . on any pretense whatsoever"

31. Little v. Barreme, 6 U.S. (2 Cr.) 169, 179 (1804).
32. 6 Stat. 63 (1807).
33. Annals of Cong., 9th Cong., 2d Sess., 230–31 (1806), 253, 260–61, 29, 30, 31, 32 (1807).
34. 1 Stat. 96, sec. 3 (1789).

shall be subject to death or other punishment.[35] Not until 1800, after Captain Little had seized the vessel, did Congress clarify the duty of military officers. They were not to carry out any and all commands. Instead, they were specifically prohibited from executing "unlawful orders" issued by superior officers.[36]

Neutrality Act Prosecutions

At about this same time, the federal courts decided a Neutrality Act case that further restricted presidential war power. President Washington had issued his Proclamation of Neutrality in 1793 because he was concerned that military initiatives by private citizens might embroil the United States in the war between France and England.[37] Such private actions would undermine the constitutional powers of Congress. As Jefferson noted in private correspondence:

> . . . if one citizen has a right to go to war of his own authority, every citizen has the same. If every citizen has that right, then the nation (which is composed of all its citizens) has a right to go to war, by the authority of its individual citizen. But this is not true either on the general principles of society, or by our Constitution, which gives that power to Congress alone. . . .[38]

Washington's proclamation raised a delicate issue: did it encroach upon the power of Congress to decide questions of war and peace? Washington asked his Cabinet whether he should call Congress back in special session to deal with this issue, but they advised against it.[39] His Secretary of the Treasury, Alexander Hamilton, responded to the legal attacks directed against the proclamation. Writing under the pseudonym "Pacificus," Hamilton argued that the management of foreign affairs was vested in the President, who is "the *organ* of intercourse between the nation and foreign nations [and] the *interpreter* of the national treaties."[40] To say the

35. 1 Stat. 711, sec. 24 (1799).

36. 2 Stat. 47 (1800) (Art. 14).

37. 32 The Writings of George Washington 416, letter to Secretary of the Treasury Alexander Hamilton, April 12, 1793.

38. 9 The Writings of Thomas Jefferson 189, letter to Gouverneur Morris, August 16, 1793.

39. Id. at 420–21 n.14.

40. 4 The Works of Alexander Hamilton 437 (Henry Cabot Lodge ed. 1904); (emphasis in original).

proclamation represented the enactment of new law was "entirely erroneous," Hamilton insisted. It only announced a fact and informed citizens of what previous laws required.[41] Hamilton's position was modest: the President could proclaim neutrality to keep the peace, waiting until Congress decided to change a condition of peace to a state of war.

In a series of essays signed "Helvidius," James Madison rebuked Hamilton for borrowing a theory of government based on British royal prerogatives. Under Hamilton's theory of executive power, Madison warned, "no citizen could any longer guess at the character of the government under which he lives."[42] Madison was particularly disturbed by some of the implications in Hamilton's argument regarding presidential power:

> In no part of the constitution is more wisdom to be found, than in the clause which confides the question of war and peace to the legislature, and not to the executive department. . . . War is in fact the true nurse of executive aggrandizement. In war, a physical force is to be created; and it is the executive will, which is to direct it. In war, the public treasures are to be unlocked; and it is the executive hand which is to dispense them. In war, the honours and emoluments of office are to be multiplied; and it is the executive patronage under which they are to be enjoyed. It is in war, finally, that laurels are to be gathered; and it is the executive brow they are to encircle. . . .
>
> Hence it has grown into an axiom that the executive is the department of power most distinguished by its propensity to war: hence it is the practice of all states, in proportion as they are free, to disarm this propensity of its influence.[43]

Washington's attempt at lawmaking contained a built-in check: enforcement of the proclamation needed statutory backing. When Gideon Henfield was prosecuted for violating the proclamation, he was acquitted because jurors rebelled against the idea of convicting someone for a crime established by a proclamation.[44] With no statute to cite, the government dropped other prosecutions.[45] After Congress returned in December, Washington told the two Houses that it rested with "the wisdom of Congress to correct, improve, or enforce" the policy his proclamation had es-

41. Id. at 444.
42. 6 The Writings of James Madison 152 (Gaillard Hunt ed. 1900–1910).
43. Id. at 174.
44. Francis Wharton, State Trials of the United States during the Administrations of Washington and Adams 84–85, 88 (1849).
45. 2 John Marshall, The Life of George Washington 273 (1832).

tablished. It would be expedient "to extend the legal code" and the jurisdiction of federal courts in order to have effective enforcement, he
added.[46]

In short, he needed law from the legislative branch. Congress responded by passing the Neutrality Act of 1794, giving the administration
the firm legal footing it needed to prosecute violators. The Neutrality Act
prohibited the exportation of any articles of war. Prohibited articles
found on board a vessel would be forfeited, and if articles of war were ex-
ported to a foreign country, the vessel could be seized and the captain
fined.[47] Congress also prohibited American citizens from accepting a commission to serve "a foreign prince or state in war by land or sea."[48] Nor
could persons within the United States provide ships of war to be used by
a foreign prince or state "to cruise or commit hostilities upon the subjects, citizens or property of another foreign prince or state with whom
the United States are at peace."[49] Furthermore, persons within the territory or jurisdiction of the United States were prohibited from providing
assistance to "any military expedition or enterprise to be carried on from
thence against the territory or dominions of any foreign prince or state
with whom the United States are at peace."[50]

President Jefferson recognized the extreme danger of allowing private
citizens to decide by themselves to deploy armed forces. In his fourth annual message he referred to complaints that persons residing within the
United States had armed merchant vessels and forced a commerce in defiance of the laws of other countries: "That individuals should undertake to
wage private war, independently of the authority of their country, can not
be permitted in a well-ordered society."[51] The tendency, he said, was "to
produce aggression on the laws and rights of other nations and to endanger the peace of our own."[52]

Numerous violations of the Neutrality Act were brought before the federal courts. In one of the significant cases defining the power of Congress
to restrict presidential action, a circuit court in 1806 reviewed the indictment of Colonel William S. Smith for engaging in military actions against
Spain. He claimed that his military enterprise "was begun, prepared, and
set on foot with the knowledge and approbation of the executive depart-

---

46. Annals of Cong., 3d Cong., 1–2 Sess. 11 (1793).
47. 1 Stat. 369–70 (1794).
48. Id. at 381–82.
49. Id. at 382, sec. 3.
50. Id. at 384, sec. 5.
51. 1 Richardson 358.
52. Id.

ment of our government."[53] The court repudiated his claim that a President or his assistants could somehow authorize military adventures that violated congressional policy. The court described the Neutrality Act as "declaratory of the law of nations; and besides, every species of private and unauthorized hostilities is inconsistent with the principles of the social compact, and the very nature, scope, and end of civil government."[54]

As to Smith's claim that he acted with the knowledge and approbation of the executive branch, the court rejected the proposition that the Neutrality Act allowed executive officials to waive statutory provisions: "if a private individual, even with the knowledge and approbation of this high and preeminent officer of our government [the President], should set on foot such a military expedition, how can he expect to be exonerated from the obligation of the law?" The court continued:

> Supposing then that every syllable of the affidavit is true, of what avail can it be on the present occasion? Of what use or benefit can it be to the defendant in a court of law? Does it speak by way of justification? The President of the United States cannot control the statute, nor dispense with its execution, and still less can he authorize a person to do what the law forbids. If he could, it would render the execution of the laws dependent on his will and pleasure; which is a doctrine that has not been set up, and will not meet with any supporters in our government. In this particular, the law is paramount. Who has dominion over it? None but the legislature; and even they are not without their limitation in our republic. Will it be pretended that the President could rightfully grant a dispensation and license to any of our citizens to carry on a war against a nation with whom the United States are at peace?[55]

The circuit court said that even if the President had known about the expedition and approved of it, "it would not justify the defendant in a court of law, nor discharge him from the binding force of the act of congress." The court put the matter flatly: "Does [the President] possess the power of making war? That power is exclusively vested in congress."[56] If a nation invaded the United States the President would have an obligation to resist with force. But there was a "manifest distinction" between going to war with a nation at peace and responding to an actual invasion: "In

53. United States v. Smith, 27 Fed. Cas. 1192, 1229 (C.C.N.Y. 1806) (No. 16,342).
54. Id.
55. Id. at 1230.
56. Id.

the former case, it is the exclusive province of congress to change a state of peace into a state of war."[57]

Barbary Powers

From the precedents established by George Washington and John Adams, Thomas Jefferson was well aware when taking office in 1801 that the decision to initiate military action lay with Congress. One of the problems he inherited was the U.S. practice of paying annual bribes ("tributes") to four states of North Africa: Morocco, Algiers, Tunis, and Tripoli. Regular payments were made so that they would not interfere with American merchantmen. A variety of local chieftains—with the titles of Beys, Deys, and Pashas—grew wealthy from this custom. Over a ten-year period, Washington and Adams paid nearly $10 million in tributes.[58]

In 1790, in his capacity as Secretary of State, Jefferson had identified for Congress a variety of alternatives for dealing with the demands of the Barbary powers. The policy was to be established by Congress and implemented by the President:

> Upon the whole, it rests with Congress to decide between war, tribute, and ransom, as the means of re-establishing our Mediterranean commerce. If war, they will consider how far our own resources shall be called forth, and how far they will enable the Executive to engage, in the forms of the constitution, the co-operation of other Powers. If tribute or ransom, it will rest with them to limit and provide the amount; and with the Executive, observing the same constitutional forms, to make arrangements for employing it to the best advantage.[59]

On March 3, 1801, one day before Jefferson took office as President, Congress passed legislation to provide for a "naval peace establishment." Of the frigates to be retained and kept in constant service, six "shall be officered and manned as the President of the United States may direct."[60] On May 20, the State Department issued a directive to Captain Richard Dale of the U.S. Navy, calling attention to this statute. "Under this author-

57. Id.
58. Raymond Walters, Jr., Albert Gallatin: Jeffersonian Financier and Diplomat 150 (1957).
59. 1 American State Papers: Foreign Relations 105 (Walter Lowrie and Matthew St. Clair Clarke, eds. 1832).
60. 2 Stat. 110, sec. 2 (1801).

ity," Jefferson directed that a squadron should be sent to the Mediterranean. In the event the Barbary powers declared war on the United States, the American vessels were ordered to "protect our commerce & chastise their insolence—by sinking, burning or destroying their ships & Vessels wherever you shall find them."[61] Having issued that order, based on congressional authority, Jefferson also wrote that it was up to Congress to decide what policy to pursue in the Mediterranean: "The real alternative before us is whether to abandon the Mediterranean or to keep up a cruise in it, perhaps in rotation with other powers who would join us as soon as there is peace. But this Congress must decide."[62]

The Pasha of Tripoli, insisting on a larger tribute, declared war on the United States. On December 8, 1801, Jefferson informed Congress about the arrogant demands of the Pasha. Unless the United States paid tribute, the Pasha threatened to seize American ships and citizens. Jefferson sent a small squadron of frigates to the Mediterranean to protect against the attack and then asked Congress for further guidance, stating he was "unauthorized by the Constitution, without the sanction of Congress, to go beyond the line of defense." It was up to Congress to authorize "measures of offense also." Jefferson gave Congress all the documents and communications it needed so that the legislative branch, "in the exercise of this important function confided by the Constitution to the Legislature exclusively," could consider the situation and act in the manner it considered most appropriate.[63]

Alexander Hamilton, writing under the pseudonym "Lucius Crassus," issued a strong critique of Jefferson's message to Congress. Hamilton believed that Jefferson had defined executive power too narrowly, deferring excessively to congressional prerogatives. But even Hamilton, always pushing the edge of executive power, never argued that the President had full power to make war on other nations. He merely argued that when a foreign nation declares war on the United States, the President may respond to that fact without waiting for congressional authority:

The first thing in [the President's message], which excites our surprise, is the very extraordinary position, that though *Tripoli had de-*

---

61. 1 Naval Documents Relating to the United States Wars with the Barbary Powers 467 (1939).

62. 8 The Writings of Thomas Jefferson 63–64 (Paul Leicester Ford ed. 1897).

63. 1 Richardson 315. Earlier in the year, during Cabinet deliberations, Secretary of the Treasury Albert Gallatin argued that although the President "cannot put us in a state of war . . . if we be put into that state either by the decree of Congress or of the other nation, the command and direction of the public force then belongs to the Executive." The Complete Anas of Thomas Jefferson 213 (Franklin B. Sawvel ed. 1903).

clared war in form against the United States, and had enforced it by actual hostility, yet that there was not power, for want of *the sanction of Congress,* to capture and detain her cruisers with their crews.

. . . [The Constitution] has only provided affirmatively, that, "The Congress shall have power to declare War;" the plain meaning of which is, that it is the peculiar and exclusive province of Congress, *when the nation is at peace* to change that state into a state of war; whether from calculations of policy, or from provocations, or injuries received: in other words, it belongs to Congress only, *to go to War.* But when a foreign nation declares, or openly and avowedly makes war upon the United States, they are then by the very fact *already at war,* and any declaration on the part of Congress is nugatory; it is at least unnecessary.[64]

Recent studies by the Justice Department and statements made during congressional debate imply that Jefferson took military measures against the Barbary powers without seeking the approval or authority of Congress.[65] In fact, in at least ten statutes, Congress explicitly authorized military action by Presidents Jefferson and Madison. Congress passed legislation in 1802 to authorize the President to equip armed vessels to protect commerce and seamen in the Atlantic, the Mediterranean, and adjoining seas. The statute authorized American ships to seize vessels belonging to the Bey of Tripoli, with the captured property distributed to those who brought the vessels into port.[66] Additional legislation in 1804 gave explicit support for "warlike operations against the regency of Tripoli, or any other of the Barbary powers."[67] Duties on foreign goods were placed in a "Mediterranean Fund" to finance these operations.[68]

Jefferson often distinguished between defensive and offensive military operations, permitting presidential initiatives for the former but not the latter. In 1805, he notified Congress about a conflict with the Spanish along the eastern boundary of the Louisiana Territory (West Florida). After detailing the problem, he noted: "Considering that Congress alone is constitutionally invested with the power of changing our condition from

64. 7 The Works of Alexander Hamilton 745–47 (John C. Hamilton ed. 1851).

65. 4A O.L.C. 187 (1980); 140 Cong. Rec. S10666 (daily ed. August 5, 1994) (statement of Senator McClain, first column). The opinion by the Office of Legal Counsel was placed in the Congressional Record in 1993: 139 Cong. Rec. S14046 (daily ed. October 21, 1993).

66. 2 Stat. 129 (1802).

67. 2 Stat. 291 (1804).

68. Id. at 292, sec. 2; Annals of Cong., 8th Cong., lst Sess. 1203, 1210–24 (1804). See also 2 Stat. 206 (1803); 2 Stat. 391 (1806); 2 Stat. 436 (1807); 2 Stat. 456 (1808); 2 Stat. 511 (1809); 2 Stat. 614 (1811); 2 Stat. 675 (1812); 2 Stat. 809 (1813).

peace to war, I have thought it my duty to await their authority for using force in any degree which could be avoided."[69]

For purely defensive operations, Jefferson retained the right to act first and seek congressional approval later. After Congress had recessed in 1807, a British vessel fired on the American ship *Chesapeake*. Jefferson ordered military purchases for the emergency, reporting his action to Congress after it convened. "To have awaited a previous and special sanction by law," he said, "would have lost occasions which might not be retrieved."[70]

He later observed that fidelity to the written law is "doubtless *one* of the high duties of a good citizen, but it is not the *highest*." The laws of necessity, self-preservation, and "of saving our country when in danger" deserved a higher priority. He concluded: "To lose our country by a scrupulous adherence to written law, would be to lose the law itself, with life, liberty, property, and all those who are enjoying them with us; thus absurdly sacrificing the end to the means."[71] Jefferson was not opening the door to any and all presidential initiatives. He had something specific in mind: presidential actions in response to emergencies that threatened the survival of the nation, after which he would seek congressional approval. Future Presidents would attempt to justify U.S. military interventions in areas of the world (such as Grenada, Libya, Nicaragua, and Haiti) that posed no genuine threat to national security and without seeking the retroactive sanction of Congress.

Problems with the Barbary pirates persisted after Jefferson left office. The Dey of Algiers continued to make warfare against U.S. citizens trading in the Mediterranean and kept some in captivity. With the conclusion of the War of 1812 with England, Madison recommended to Congress in 1815 that it declare war on Algiers.[72] Instead of a declaration, Congress passed legislation "for the protection of the commerce of the United States against the Algerine cruisers." The first line of the statute read: "Whereas the Dey of Algiers, on the coast of Barbary, has commenced a predatory warfare against the United States." The legislative branch gave Madison authority to use armed vessels for the purpose of protecting the commerce of U.S. seamen on the Atlantic, the Mediterranean, and adjoining seas. U.S. vessels (both government and private) could "subdue, seize,

69. 1 Richardson 377.
70. Id. at 416.
71. 5 The Writings of Thomas Jefferson 542 (H. A. Washington ed. 1861); (emphasis in original).
72. 2 Richardson 539.

and make prize of all vessels, goods and effects of or belonging to the Dey of Algiers."[73]

An American flotilla set sail for Algiers, where it captured two of the Dey's ships and forced him to stop the piracy, release all captives, and renounce the practice of annual tribute payments. Similar treaties were obtained from Tunis and Tripoli.[74] By the end of 1815, Madison could report to Congress on the successful termination of the war with Algiers.[75]

The War of 1812

After two decades of congressionally authorized military actions against Indians, France, and the Barbary pirates, Congress declared its first war in 1812. Much like President Adams had done in the Quasi-War with France, President Madison submitted a message to Congress on November 5, 1811, alerting it to a number of hostile and discriminatory actions by England that required Congress to prepare for war. Explaining the British measures that "trampl[ed] on rights which no independent nation can relinquish," Madison suggested that Congress "will feel the duty of putting the United States into an armor and an attitude demanded by the crisis, and corresponding with the national spirit and expectations."[76] Congress responded by passing legislation to raise additional military forces, organize a volunteer military corps, and augment the navy.[77]

Madison's message to Congress on June 1, 1812, identified a variety of "injuries and indignities": British impressment of American seamen, their violation of U.S. rights to neutral seas and the blockade of U.S. ports, England's refusal to revoke the Orders of Council (discriminatory economic measures against America) and its provocation of Indian raids against frontier settlements. Although these practices amounted to "a state of war against the United States," Madison left to Congress the issue of declaring war, "a solemn question which the Constitution wisely confides to the legislative department of the Government."[78]

The House Foreign Relations Committee acted quickly by strongly advocating a declaration of war: "The mad ambition, the lust of power, and commercial avarice of Great Britain have left to neutral nations an alternative

73. 3 Stat. 230 (1815).
74. Robert Allen Rutland, The Presidency of James Madison 192–93 (1990).
75. 2 Richardson 547.
76. Id. at 479.
77. 2 Stat. 671, 676, 683, 685, 695, 699, 704 (1812).
78. 2 Richardson 490.

only between the base surrender of their rights, and a manly vindication of them."[79] On June 4 the House voted—79 to 49—to support the declaration of war. The Senate considered limiting the war to the high seas.[80] After a select committee had reported the bill to declare war, a motion was made to return the bill to committee to merely authorize warships and privateers to make reprisals against Britain. That motion carried by a 17 to 13 vote.[81] When the modified bill was reported to the floor for final action, a motion to accept the committee's changes failed by a tie vote, 16 to 16.[82] Other attempts to limit the war to the high seas also failed.[83] Finally, on June 17, the Senate approved the declaration of war, 19 to 13. Both chambers debated in secret. The declaration of war, dated June 18, 1812, authorized the President to use "the whole land and naval force of the United States."[84]

"Mr. Madison's war" lasted thirty months, producing heavy losses along the Canadian front, a costly British embargo of the eastern seaboard, and the burning of Washington, D.C. (including the Capitol, the White House, and most of the executive department buildings). So severe were the economic conditions in the northeast that several states assembled at the Hartford Convention to discuss the merits of seceding from the Union. A peace treaty was ratified by the Senate after which Madison, on February 18, 1815, issued a proclamation of peace.

In prosecuting the War of 1812, President Madison called on the state militia pursuant to authority given him by Congress. A legal dispute reached the Supreme Court in 1827. The Court said there could be no question of Congress passing legislation that gave the President the right to call up state militia to repel invasion from abroad or to suppress internal insurrections. The Court concluded that "the authority to decide whether the exigency has arisen, belongs exclusively to the president, and that his decision is conclusive upon all other persons."[85]

The Mexican War

The power of Commander in Chief is at its low point when there is no standing army because a President cannot deploy troops until Congress

---

79. Donald R. Hickey, The War of 1812 44 (1989).
80. Id. at 45.
81. Id. at 46; Annals of Cong., 12th Cong., 1st Sess. 266–67 (1812).
82. Annals of Cong., 12th Cong., 1st Sess. 270–71 (1812).
83. Hickey, The War of 1812, at 46.
84. 2 Stat. 755 (1812).
85. Martin v. Mott, 25 U.S. (12 Wheat.) 19, 28 (1827).

raises them. But when a standing army does exist, ready to move at the President's command, the balance of power can shift decisively. Such was the case with the Mexican War.

After Texas won its independence from Mexico in 1836, both Houses of Congress passed resolutions stating "that the independence of Texas ought to be acknowledged by the United States whenever satisfactory information should be received that it had in successful operation a civil government capable of performing the duties and fulfilling the obligations of an independent power." President Andrew Jackson hesitated to recognize the independence of Texas, fearing that such action could result in war with Mexico and invade the prerogatives of Congress. He advised Congress: "It will always be considered consistent with the spirit of the Constitution, and most safe, that [the power of recognition] should be exercised, when probably leading to war, with a previous understanding with that body by whom war can alone be declared, and by whom all the provisions for sustaining its perils must be furnished."[86]

In 1845, after almost a decade of negotiation, Texas was annexed to the United States. As President Polk noted in his first annual message that year: "This accession to our territory has been a bloodless achievement. No arm of force has been raised to produce the result. The sword has had no part in the victory."[87] A year later, Polk would not hesitate to use military force to gain additional territory from Mexico—and to do so without Jackson's concern about the war prerogatives of Congress.

During the autumn of 1845, Polk relied on the diplomatic efforts of John Slidell "to purchase for a pecuniary consideration" Upper California and New Mexico from Mexico.[88] Polk feared that Great Britain "had her eye" on California and "intended to possess it if she could." In asserting the Monroe Doctrine against foreign encroachment, Polk "had California & the fine bay of San Francisco as much in view as Oregon."[89] On February 13, 1846, he learned from a Spanish visitor that any government or administration in Mexico that agreed to sell Mexican territory to the United States would provoke "another revolution by which they would be overthrown. He said they must appear to be forced to agree to such a proposition." The visitor recommended that U.S. forces should be marched from Corpus Christi to the Del Norte and that a strong naval force should be assembled at Veracruz. Since it was "well known" that the

---

86. 4 Richardson 1486.
87. 5 Richardson 2237.
88. 1 The Diary of James K. Polk 34 (M. Quaife ed. 1910).
89. Id. at 71.

Mexican government had no funds to pay the amounts due to U.S. citizens, when the Mexicans "saw a strong force ready to strike on their coasts and border, they would . . . feel their danger and agree to the boundary suggested."[90]

Polk related this story to his cabinet, adding that "it would be necessary to take strong measures towards Mexico before our difficulties with that Government could be settled." He proposed that Slidell be instructed to demand an early decision of the Mexican government, and that if the government refused to receive him or refused to pay the amounts due to American claimants without unreasonable delay, Slidell should board one of the U.S. war vessels at Veracruz. In that event Polk would send a "strong message" to Congress authorizing him to make another demand and if that were refused, "to confer authority on the Executive to take redress into our own hands by aggressive measures."[91] Secretary of State James Buchanan objected to this course of action but eventually produced some drafts for the instruction to Slidell.[92]

Polk delayed in sending the dispatch, and modifications were still being made on March 12.[93] On April 7, the President and his cabinet continued to debate what to do if Mexico refused to receive Slidell.[94] After Slidell was rejected the Polk administration hesitated again.[95] From April 18 to May 3, Polk discussed the Mexican problem with his cabinet on repeated occasions, promising to send a strong message to Congress, even to the point of recommending a declaration of war for Mexico's failure to redress U.S. complaints.[96] On April 28 he directed Buchanan to prepare from the archives "a succinct history of these wrongs as a basis of a message to Congress, at his earliest convenience."[97]

Meanwhile, Polk had ordered General Zachary Taylor to occupy disputed territory along the Texas-Mexico border. On May 5, Polk and the cabinet talked about "the possibility of a collision between the American & Mexican forces."[98] On May 8, Slidell told Polk that only one course remained and that was "to take the redress of the wrongs and injuries which we had so long borne from Mexico into our own hands, and to act with

90. Id. at 228–29.
91. Id. at 233–34.
92. Id. at 234–36.
93. Id. at 238–39, 287.
94. Id. at 319.
95. Id. at 325–26.
96. Id. at 337, 343, 354.
97. Id. at 363.
98. Id. at 379.

promptness and energy." Polk agreed.[99] At the cabinet meeting on May 9, all concurred that if the Mexican forces committed any act of hostility on General Taylor's forces, Polk should immediately send a message to Congress recommending a declaration of war.[100] The cabinet adjourned about 2 P.M., and some four hours later learned there had been a military clash between American and Mexican forces.[101]

Despite the legal uncertainties of the disputed land, Polk told Congress on May 11 that Mexico "has passed the boundary of the United States, has invaded our territory and shed American blood upon the American soil." He notified Congress that "war exists."[102] Senator John Calhoun tried to resist the stampede in Congress to rush blindly and mechanically toward a declaration of war, as though all other options had been removed by Polk:

> . . . I agree . . . that the President has announced that there is war; but according to my interpretation, there is no war according to the sense of our Constitution. I distinguish between hostilities and war, and God forbid that, acting under the Constitution, we should ever confound one with the other. There may be invasion without war, and the President is authorized to repel invasion without war. But it is *our* sacred duty to make war, and it is for us to determine whether war shall be declared or not. If we have declared war, a state of war exists, and not till then.[103]

Other Senators echoed Calhoun's sentiments.[104] Senator John Middleton Clayton "condemned" the conduct of President Polk: "I do not see on what principle it can be shown that the President, without consulting Congress and obtaining its sanction for the procedure, has a right to send an army to take up a position, where, as it must have been foreseen, the inevitable consequence would be war."[105]

Similar points were made during debate in the House of Representatives. Congressman Isaac E. Holmes said legislators knew nothing more than that two armies had collided in disputed territory, "and I deny that war is absolutely, necessarily, the result of it."[106] Congressman Robert Rhett insisted that President Polk "has not made war; he does not recom-

99. Id. at 382.
100. Id. at 384.
101. Id. at 386.
102. 5 Richardson 2292.
103. Cong. Globe, 29th Cong., 1st Sess. 784 (1846); (emphasis in original).
104. Id. (Senators Morehead and Archer).
105. Id. at 786.
106. Id. at 792.

mend us to make war. Not a state of war exists, but a state of hostilities."[107] Yet those two legislators joined with others on May 11 to form a 174 to 14 majority in support of war against Mexico.[108] The Senate voted 40 to 2 in favor of war.[109] Congress declared war on May 13, recognizing that "a state of war exists."[110]

Polk offered some intriguing justifications for going to war. In part he pointed to "grievous wrongs perpetrated by Mexico upon our citizens throughout a long period of years" that remained unredressed.[111] As his critics in the Whig Party noted, England, France, Spain, Holland, Naples, and Denmark had all engaged in offenses against the United States without an automatic resort to war.[112] Polk also said that Mexico "is too feeble a power to govern these Provinces, lying as they do at a distance of more than 1,000 miles from her capital."[113] He warned that a failure by the United States to relinquish Upper California would invite European nations to possess it, either by conquest or by purchase. New Mexico, according to Polk, "has never been of any considerable value to Mexico."[114] Furthermore, Mexico was "too feeble" to prevent depredations by Indians against the inhabitants of New Mexico and other northern states of Mexico, and it "would be a blessing to all these northern States to have their citizens protected against them by the power of the United States."[115] Later, in submitting a treaty of peace to Congress (a treaty signed in 1848), Polk described the "valuable territories ceded by Mexico" but concluded that in the hands of Mexico they would have remained "almost unoccupied, and of little value to her or to any other nation, whilst as a part of our Union they will be productive of vast benefits to the United States, to the commercial world, and the general interests of mankind."[116] That line of argument would be used in subsequent decades by American Presidents to intervene in neighboring countries.

On May 13, the same day that Congress declared war, Buchanan prepared a dispatch to be sent to U.S. ministers in London, Paris, and other foreign courts, explaining that "our object was not to dismember Mexico

107. Id. at 793.

108. Id. at 795.

109. Id. at 804.

110. 9 Stat. 9 (1846).

111. 5 Richardson 2291.

112. "The President's Message: The War," 5 The American Review: A Whig Journal 1, 10 (1847).

113. 5 Richardson 2389.

114. Id. at 2390.

115. Id. at 2390–91.

116. Id. at 2430.

or to make conquests" and that in going to war it was not the intention "to acquire either California or New Mexico or any other portion of the Mexican territory." Polk objected to this language, saying that it was "unnecessary and improper" to send such a statement. Although the United States had not gone to war for conquest, "it was clear that in making peace we would if practicable obtain California and such other portion of the Mexican territory as would be sufficient to indemnify our claimants on Mexico, and to defray the expenses of the war which that power by her long continued wrongs and injuries had forced us to wage." Polk told Buchanan that "it was well known that the Mexican Government had no other means of indemnifying us."[117]

Polk's action was censured by the House of Representatives in 1848 on the ground that the war had been "unnecessarily and unconstitutionally begun by the President of the United States."[118] This language was approved by a vote of 85 to 81. One of the members voting for the censure was Abraham Lincoln, who later wrote to a friend:

Allow the President to invade a neighboring nation, whenever *he* shall deem it necessary to repel an invasion, and you allow him to do so, *whenever he may choose to say* he deems it necessary for such purpose—and you allow him to make war at pleasure. . . . This, our Convention understood to be the most oppressive of all Kingly oppressions; and they resolved to so frame the Constitution that *no one man* should hold the power of bringing the oppression upon us.[119]

During the war between the United States and Mexico, U.S. authorities acting under presidential orders conquered the port of Tampico. The Supreme Court offered this important limit on presidential power: "As commander-in-chief, he is authorized to direct the movements of the naval and military forces placed by law at his command, and to employ them in the manner he may deem most effectual to harass and conquer and subdue the enemy."[120] Notice the language: placed *by law* at his command. The power of Commander in Chief, necessarily broad, must adhere to the policy declared by Congress in law.

117. 1 The Diary of James K. Polk 397.
118. Cong. Globe, 30th Cong., 1st Sess. 95 (1848).
119. 1 The Collected Works of Abraham Lincoln 451–52 (Roy Basler, ed. 1953); (emphasis in original).
120. Fleming v. Page, 50 U.S. (9 How.) 603, 615 (1850).

Bombarding Greytown

Although the Constitution does not expressly direct the President to protect American life and property in foreign countries, Presidents have sent U.S. forces abroad for that purpose on many occasions. They base such actions not on legislative authority but rather on inherent or implied executive responsibilities.

In 1854, an American ship was ordered to the Nicaraguan port of Greytown (now San Juan del Norte) to compel local authorities to make amends for an affront to an American diplomat. American firms in that area had also complained about property losses. When the commander of the American *Cyane* decided that the local authorities had failed to make appropriate amends, he proceeded to bombard the town from nine in the morning to mid-afternoon, pausing periodically to see whether town officials would yield. American forces subsequently went ashore to destroy by fire whatever remained of the town.[121] President Pierce, reporting this incident to Congress, seemed to regard the commander's operation as a model of due process:

[The commander] warned them by a public proclamation that if they did not give satisfaction within a time specified he would bombard the town. By this procedure he afforded them opportunity to provide for their personal safety. To those also who desired to avoid loss of property in the punishment about to be inflicted on the offending town he furnished the means of removing their effects to boats of his own ship and of a steamer which he procured and tendered to them for that purpose.[122]

A resident of Greytown sued for damages to his property, but in 1860 a federal circuit court upheld the commander's actions on the basis of the President's duty to protect lives and property in other countries. As the head of the executive branch, the President "is made the only legitimate organ of the general government, to open and carry on correspondence or negotiations with foreign nations, in matters concerning the interests of the country or its citizens." It is to the President that citizens abroad "must look for protection of person and of property." The court continued: "Now, as it respects the interposition of the executive abroad, for the

121. Milton Offutt, "The Protection of Citizens Abroad by the Armed Forces of the United States," Johns Hopkins University Studies in Historical and Political Science, ser. 44, no. 4 (1928), 32–34.
122. 6 Richardson 2816.

protection of the lives or property of the citizen, the duty must, of necessity, rest in the discretion of the president. Acts of lawless violence, or of threatened violence to the citizens or his property, cannot be anticipated and provided for; and the protection, to be effectual or of any avail, may, not infrequently, require the most prompt and decided action."[123]

The court did not attempt to explore the extent to which the President could destroy foreign property or commit acts of violence while protecting American interests. James Buchanan, American minister to the Court of St. James at the time of Greytown bombardment, told the British government that he believed the American commander had acted without express authority and that his action would be disavowed by the American government. Instructed to the contrary by Secretary of State Marcy, Buchanan had to switch positions and defend the bombardment.[124]

After becoming President in 1857, Buchanan had an opportunity to express his own views about presidential power and the Greytown precedent. In a message to Congress on December 6, 1858, he stated that the executive branch "in its intercourse with foreign nations is limited to the employment of diplomacy alone. When this fails it can proceed no further." The President "can not legitimately resort to force without the direct authority of Congress, except in resisting and repelling hostile attacks." Turning now to the specific situation in Nicaragua, Buchanan said that the President would "have no authority to enter the territories of Nicaragua even to prevent the destruction of the transit and protect the lives and property of our own citizens on their passage."[125]

Buchanan reiterated the same principles in 1859. He told Congress that the "executive governments" of Great Britain, France, and other countries, "possessing the war-making power," could use military force to rectify outrages against the life and property of their subjects. "Not so the executive government of the United States." If the President ordered a vessel of war to any port to demand prompt redress of an outrage committed,

> the offending parties are well aware that in case of refusal the commander can do no more than remonstrate. He can resort to no hostile act. . . . The remedy for this state of things can only be supplied by Congress, since the Constitution has confided to that body alone the

123. Durand v. Hollins, 8 Fed. Cas. (Cir. Ct. S.D. N.Y. 1860) (Case No. 4,186), p. 1123.
124. Charles C. Tansill, "The President and the Initiation of Hostilities: The Precedents of the Mexican and Spanish-American Wars," reprinted in The President's War Powers: From the Federalists to Reagan 86 (Demetrios Caraley ed. 1984).
125. 7 Richardson 3047.

power to make war. Without the authority of Congress the Executive can not lawfully direct any force, however near it may be to the scene of difficulty, to enter the territory of Mexico, Nicaragua, or New Granada for the purpose of defending the persons and property of American citizens.[126]

A few years later, Congress had an opportunity to revisit the use of presidential power abroad in protecting lives and property. A more measured and pacific policy was promoted by legislation in 1868 (still in effect) directing the President to demand from a foreign government the reason for depriving any American citizen of liberty. If it appeared wrongful and in violation of the rights of American citizenship, the President was to demand the citizen's release. If the foreign government delayed or refused, the President could use such means "not amounting to acts of war" as he thought necessary and proper to obtain the release.[127]

An early version of this bill gave the President the power to suspend commercial relations with a government that arrested and detained an American citizen. Senator Charles Sumner rebelled against this grant of power: "Here is a way to make war easy. To the President is given this alarming power. In Europe war proceeds from the sovereign; in England from the queen in council; in France from Louis Napoleon. This is according to the genius of monarchies. By the Constitution of our Republic it is Congress alone that can declare war. And yet by this bill One Man, in his discretion, may do little short of declaring war. He may hurl one of the bolts of war, and sever the commercial relations of two great Powers."[128] Another portion of the draft bill empowered the President—as an act of reprisal—to arrest and detain a citizen of a foreign country. Senator Oliver Morton objected to this provision because he was "not willing to place in the hands of the President of the United States the power to bring on war in any contingency."[129] The section on suspending commercial relations was eliminated on a vote of 30 to 7,[130] and the President's explicit power to retain foreigners as an act of reprisal was deleted also. In the end, the

126. Id. at 3070.
127. 15 Stat. 223 (1868); 22 U.S.C. 1732 (1988). For a legislative history of this statute, see Abner J. Mikva and Gerald L. Neuman, "The Hostage Crisis and the 'Hostage Act'," 49 U. Chi. L. Rev. 292 (1982). Legislation in 1989 inserted "and not otherwise prohibited by law" after "acts of war." 103 Stat. 1900, sec. 9 (1989).
128. Cong. Globe, 40th Cong., 2d Sess. 4205 (1868).
129. Id. at 4235.
130. Id. at 4330.

President was authorized to use such means "not amounting to acts of war."

The Civil War

Lincoln's vote in 1848 to censure Polk for "unnecessarily and unconstitutionally" beginning the Mexican War may appear to be hypocritical. During his own years as President he exercised military force without first obtaining authority from Congress. In April 1861, with Congress in recess, he issued proclamations calling forth the state militia, suspending the writ of habeas corpus, and placing a blockade on the rebellious states.

There are crucial differences between the actions of Polk and Lincoln. Polk's initiatives helped precipitate war with a foreign nation while Lincoln confronted a genuine internal emergency of civil war. Polk had some discretion over his actions; Lincoln was compelled to use force to put down an internal rebellion. Moreover, Lincoln had genuine doubts about the legality of his actions, particularly the suspension of the writ of habeas corpus, and openly requested statutory authority from Congress.

When Lincoln's blockade was upheld by the Supreme Court in 1863, Justice Robert Grier said that the President as Commander in Chief "has no power to initiate or declare a war either against a foreign nation or a domestic State." In the event of foreign invasion, however, the President was not only authorized "but bound to resist force by force. He does not initiate the war, but is bound to accept the challenge without waiting for any special legislative authority."[131] The President had no choice but to meet the crisis in the shape it presented itself "without waiting for Congress to baptize it with a name; and no name given to it by him or them could change the fact."[132]

Unlike Truman, Bush, and Clinton, Lincoln never claimed that he possessed full authority to act as he did. In fact, he admitted to exceeding the constitutional boundaries established for the President and thus needed the sanction of Congress. When Congress returned he explained that his actions, "whether strictly legal or not, were ventured upon under what appeared to be a popular demand and a public necessity, trusting then, as now, that Congress would readily ratify them."[133] Lincoln did not claim to act outside the Constitution. He acted under his powers and probably also those of Congress, believing that his actions (especially suspending

131. The Prize Cases, 67 U.S. 635, 668 (1863).
132. Id. at 669.
133. 7 Richardson 3225.

the writ of habeas corpus) were not "beyond the constitutional competency of Congress."[134]

Lincoln therefore invoked each stage of the executive prerogative: acting in the absence of law and sometimes against it; explaining to the legislature what he had done, and why; and requesting the legislative body to authorize his actions. The superior law-making body was Congress, not the President. Congress debated this request at length, with members supporting the President on the explicit assumption that his acts were illegal.[135] Congress eventually passed legislation "approving, legalizing, and making valid all the acts, proclamations, and orders of the President, etc., as if they had been issued and done under the previous express authority and direction of the Congress of the United States."[136]

Lincoln's proclamation emancipating the slaves proceeded through a number of drafts, at first relying on statutory authority but later invoking the power of Commander of Chief. The first draft, citing statutory authority, also noted that the proclamation was "a fit and necessary military measure" for ending slavery. He would, as Commander in Chief, declare on January 1, 1863, that all slaves in rebellious states "shall then, thenceforward, and forever, be free."[137] A subsequent draft relied on the commander-in-chief clause while also "calling attention" to previous statutes on the subject of abolishing slavery.[138] The final Emancipation Proclamation made no mention of congressional statutes, grounding itself entirely on the President's power as Commander in Chief. At the conclusion of this document, Lincoln said he regarded the proclamation "sincerely to be an act of justice, warranted by the Constitution, upon military necessity."[139]

In one notable instance, Lincoln's exercise of the war power collided with the judiciary. Lincoln's suspension of the writ of habeas corpus was opposed by Chief Justice Roger Taney, sitting as circuit judge. Taney ruled that since the President had no power under the Constitution to suspend the writ, the prisoner, John Merryman, should be set free. Merryman was suspected of being the captain of a secession troop and of having assisted in destroying railroads and bridges to prevent federal troops from reaching Washington, D.C. When Taney attempted to serve a paper at the prison, to free Merryman, prison officials refused to let Taney's marshal

---

134. Ibid.
135. Cong. Globe, 37th Cong., lst Sess. 393 (1861) (Senator Howe).
136. 12 Stat. 326 (1861).
137. 5 The Collected Works of Abraham Lincoln 336–37 (Roy Basler ed. 1953).
138. Id. at 433–36.
139. 6 id. at 30.

carry out his duty. Avoiding a direct confrontation with Lincoln, which the judiciary could not afford, Taney merely noted:

> I have exercised all the power which the constitution and laws confer upon me, but that power has been resisted by a force too strong for me to overcome. . . . I shall, therefore, order all the proceedings in this case, with my opinion, to be filed and recorded in the circuit court of the United States for the district court of Maryland, and direct the clerk to transmit a copy, under seal, to the president of the United States. It will then remain for that high officer, in fulfillment of his constitutional obligation to "take care that the laws be faithfully executed," to determine what measures he will take to cause the civil process of the United States to be respected and enforced.[140]

Not until the war was over and Lincoln in his grave did the Court, in 1866, breathe some life into the privilege of the writ of habeas corpus. The Court then held that military courts could not function in states where federal courts had been open and operating.[141] In response to this ruling, Congress passed legislation to limit the Court's jurisdiction to hear cases involving martial law and military trials. Although cases were already pending with regard to the conduct of U.S. officials during and immediately after the war, Congress gave indemnity to all officials who implemented presidential proclamations from March 4, 1861, to June 30, 1866, with respect to martial law and military trials. The statute provided: "And no civil court of the United States, or of any State, or of the District of Columbia, or of any district or territory of the United States, shall have or take jurisdiction of, or in any manner reverse any of the proceedings had or acts done as aforesaid."[142]

Lincoln's military actions during the Civil War were reviewed by the Joint Committee on the Conduct of the War. Triggered initially by the disasters of Bull Run and other defeats, members of Congress introduced legislation to create a committee to investigate military operations.[143] Committee members were criticized for some of their procedures and operations, but "they brought speed and energy into the conduct of the war; . . . ferreted out abuses and put their fingers down heavily upon governmental inefficiency; . . . [and] labored, for a time at least, to preserve a balance and effect a cooperation between the legislative and executive

---

140. Ex parte Merryman, 17 Fed. Case No. 9,487 (1861), 153.
141. Ex parte Milligan, 71 U.S. (4 Wall.) 2 (1866).
142. 14 Stat. 432, 433 (1867).
143. Cong. Globe, 37th Cong., 2d Sess. 16–17, 29–32, 40 (1861).

departments."[144] The committee also strengthened Lincoln's hand against the eventual removal of General George B. McClellan, prepared the groundwork for abolishing slavery, uncovered corruption and inefficiency, and served as a "splendid propaganda agency" in furthering the war effort.[145]

Spanish-American War

Aside from Polk's initiatives in Mexico and Lincoln's emergency actions during the Civil War, the power of war in the nineteenth century remained basically in the hands of Congress and Presidents recognized the rule of legislative supremacy in matters of going to war. In a case decided by the Supreme Court in 1889, England had called upon the United States to supply naval forces in a military action against China. The Court made it clear that offensive operations had to be authorized by Congress, not the President: "As this proposition involved a participation in existing hostilities, the request could not be acceded to, and the Secretary of State in his communication to the English government explained that the war-making power of the United States was not vested in the President but in Congress, and that he had no authority, therefore, to order aggressive hostilities to be undertaken."[146] Significantly, the Court spoke not merely of the congressional power to declare war but of a broader power: *war-making*. The decision to spill the nation's blood and treasure was left to Congress, not the President. The lack of a declaration of war could not be a pretext for the executive branch to use armed force against another nation. That fundamental decision lay with Congress.

Congress would declare war in 1898 for a third time in response to Cuban rebellions against Spanish rulers. American sentiment, strongly favoring the rebels, prepared the way for U.S. intervention. The insurrection had destroyed sugar and tobacco plantations, affecting the interests of a number of American exporters and investors. The United States supplied about half of Cuban imports, while almost 90 percent of Cuban exports went to the United States.

Congress passed a concurrent resolution in 1896 offering the "friendly offices" of the United States to Spain for the recognition of an indepen-

144. William Whatley Pierson, Jr., "The Committee on the Conduct of the Civil War," 23 Am. Hist. Rev. 550, 575–76 (1918).

145. Hans L. Trefousse, "The Joint Committee on the Conduct of the War," 10 Civil War Hist. 5, 7–9 (1964).

146. The Chinese Exclusion Case, 130 U.S. 581, 591 (1889).

dent Cuba.[147] Spain rejected the offer. Some members of Congress itched for war. An associate of President Cleveland was once present when a delegation from Congress arrived at the White House to announce: "We have about decided to declare war against Spain over the Cuban question. Conditions are intolerable." Cleveland responded bluntly: "There will be no war with Spain over Cuba while I am President." A member of Congress protested that the Constitution gave Congress the right to declare war, but Cleveland countered by saying that the Constitution also made him Commander in Chief and "I will not mobilize the army." Cleveland said that the United States could buy Cuba from Spain for $100 million, whereas a war "will cost vastly more than that and will entail another long list of pensioners. It would be an outrage to declare war."[148] This standoff raises the intriguing possibility that a President, presented with a declaration of war from Congress, could veto it on the ground that intelligence obtained from diplomatic sources demonstrated that war was unnecessary. In such situations, one would assume that this information would be shared with Congress and derail efforts to declare war.

William McKinley entered the White House in March 1897 and devoted much of that year to passing the Dingley Tariff Act. However, in a message to Congress at the end of that year, McKinley's focus had begun to shift: "The most important problem with which this Government is now called upon to deal pertaining to its foreign relations concerns its duty toward Spain and the Cuban insurrection."[149]

On February 15, 1898, the American battleship *Maine* was destroyed while sitting in the Havana harbor. Two officers and 264 members of the crew died. McKinley ordered an investigation to determine the cause of the blast. In a message to Congress on April 11, he said that the destruction of the ship "was caused by an exterior explosion—that of a submarine mine."[150] By implication, Spain was responsible for the blast and the loss of American lives. Subsequent studies (released after the war) concluded that the explosion came from the *interior* of the ship.[151]

McKinley's message to Congress said that the right to intervene in Cuba "may be justified by the very serious injury to the commerce, trade, and business of our people and by the wanton destruction of property and devastation of the island."[152] Military intervention, however, was a matter

147. 28 Cong. Rec. 2256–57 (1896).
148. 2 Robert McElroy, Grover Cleveland 249–50 (1923).
149. 13 Richardson 6254.
150. Id. at 6290.
151. Lewis L. Gould, The Spanish-American War and President McKinley 35 (1982).
152. 13 Richardson 6289.

for Congress to decide. He asked legislators "to authorize and empower the President to take measures to secure a full and final termination of hostilities between the Government of Spain and the people of Cuba."[153]

Congress passed a joint resolution on April 20 stating that the people of Cuba "are, and of right to be, free and independent" and that Spain should "at once relinquish its authority and government in the Island of Cuba and withdraw its land and naval forces from Cuba and Cuban waters." Congress empowered President McKinley "to use the entire land and naval forces of the United States, and to call into the actual service of the United States the militia of the several States, to such extent as may be necessary to carry these resolutions into effect."[154] The House majorities were large: 325 to 19 and 311 to 6.[155] The Senate was more divided, supporting the war 42 to 35.[156] On April 22, Congress increased the size of the military establishment to prepare for war.[157] Three days later Congress declared war, stating that war "has existed since the twenty-first day of April."[158]

The war lasted but a few months, and on August 12, Spain accepted an armistice. As a result of the war, Cuba gained its independence and the United States acquired the Philippines, Puerto Rico, and Guam. The peace treaty, ratified on February 6, 1899, extended American territory to the Pacific, despite Congress's previous disclaimer of any intention to exercise control over Cuba, much less over other territories. U.S. aims in Cuba could most likely have been secured by diplomatic rather than by military means. Shortly after war had been declared, Senator John Coit Spooner wrote to a friend that "possibly the President could have worked out the business without war, but the current was too strong, the demagogues too numerous, and the fall elections too near."[159]

In a speech delivered in Boston in 1899, McKinley observed that the war power has a momentum of its own, often spiraling beyond the control of either Congress or the President: "What nation was ever able to write an accurate program of the war upon which it was entering, much less decree in advance the scope of its results? Congress can declare war, but a higher power decrees its bounds and fixes its relations and responsi-

153. Id. at 6292.
154. 30 Stat. 738–39 (1898).
155. 31 Cong. Rec. 3820–21, 4063–64 (1898).
156. Id. at 4040.
157. 30 Stat. 361–63.
158. Id. at 364.
159. Spooner to C. W. Porter, May 2, 1898; Spooner Papers, Container 135, page 224, Library of Congress.

bilities. The President can direct the movements of soldiers on the field and fleets upon the sea, but he can not foresee the close of such movements or prescribe their limits.[160]

McKinley was too modest about his influence, suggesting that he was largely a pawn in world affairs. Once war broke out between the United States and Spain, it was McKinley who cabled Admiral Dewey: "Proceed at once to Philippine Islands. Commence operations at once, particularly against the Spanish fleet. You must capture vessels or destroy."[161] A war begun in Cuba and authorized by Congress quickly spread to the Far East because of a presidential decision. On April 20, Congress recognized the independence of Cuba and directed the President to use land and naval forces to carry this resolution into effect.[162] Two days later Congress increased the military establishment.[163] McKinley's cable to Dewey is dated April 24, one day before the declaration of war (stating that "war has existed since the twenty-first day of April").

After the peace treaty with Spain was ratified, rebels in the Philippines remained at war against U.S. forces and were not subdued until 1906. Scattered hostilities continued as late as 1913.[164] The Senate held hearings in 1902 to examine charges of American atrocities against Filipinos, receiving testimony from American commanders who admitted to the burning and destruction of homes and shacks. When one Senator noted that the punishment fell "mainly upon the women and little children" and asked whether such conduct by U.S. troops were within the ordinary rules of civilized warfare, an American general replied: "These people are not civilized."[165]

160. Home Market Club Banquet, Boston, Mass., 1899, McKinley Papers, Library of Congress, 7–8.

161. 1 John D. Long, The New American Navy 181–82 (1903).

162. 30 Stat. 738 (1898).

163. Id. at 361–63.

164. R. Ernest Dupuy and William H. Baumer, The Little Wars of the United States 65–99 (1968).

165. Hearings before the Senate Committee on the Philippines in Relation to Affairs in the Philippine Islands, 57th Cong., 1st Sess. 559 (1902); Richard E. Welch, Jr., "American Atrocities in the Philippines: The Indictment and the Response," 43 Pac. Hist. Rev. 233 (1974).

3

AMERICA STEPS OUT: 1900–1945

By the time the nineteenth century closed, America's empire stretched far beyond the narrow confines of the eastern seaboard familiar to the founding fathers. To continental America was now added the Louisiana Purchase, the Floridas (East and West), Texas, territory from the Mexican War (California, Arizona, Nevada, New Mexico, and Utah), the Pacific northwest (Idaho, Oregon, and Washington), Alaska, and Hawaii. The war with Spain in 1898 extended the arm of America to Cuba and Puerto Rico in the Atlantic and to the Philippines and Guam in the Pacific.

President Theodore Roosevelt, in his fourth annual message in 1904, underscored America's long-term interest in its newly acquired empire. The people in the Philippines, he said, "are utterly incapable of existing in independence at all or of building up a civilization of their own."[1] The strategic value of this region was readily acknowledged. "I do not overlook the fact," said Roosevelt, "that in the development of our interests in the Pacific Ocean and along its coasts, the Philippines have played and will play an important part; and that our interests have been served in more than one way by the possession of the islands."[2]

In the early decades of the twentieth century, America intervened regularly in other countries to "protect lives and property." The two world wars (especially the second) shifted major international responsibilities to the United States. Because of mutual security treaties, including NATO and SEATO, the United States joined with other countries in collective security pacts. Despite legislative history to the contrary, executive officials would cite these treaties as an additional source of unilateral presidential authority. The United Nations Charter added to these expectations, triggering expansive (and misguided) definitions of presidential power when operating under the umbrella of a UN operation.

1. 14 Richardson 6928.
2. Id.

Protecting Life and Property

On numerous occasions Presidents invoked the right to protect American lives and property abroad as justification for military intervention in foreign countries. Although "life and property" was the ostensible reason, these military adventures always served some larger purpose of American foreign policy. Presidents based military action not on legislative authority but on inherent executive responsibilities. A prominent example from the nineteenth century was the U.S. bombardment of Greytown (see Chapter 2).

Various studies attempted to identify these life-and-property actions. In 1928, Milton Offutt compiled a list of 76 instances between 1813 and 1927,[3] and in a 1945 study James Grafton Rogers collected 148 examples of U.S. military operations abroad. The latter list, however, includes many declared wars as well as actions taken by President Franklin D. Roosevelt before Pearl Harbor: the destroyers/bases agreement with Great Britain, the U.S. occupation of Greenland, and the armed convoy ordered by President Roosevelt.[4]

The twentieth century began with presidential use of force in China. In the spring of 1900, in the midst of the presidential campaign in the United States, an antiforeign group of Chinese revolutionists (called "the Boxers") demanded that foreigners be expelled from the country. Foreign legations in Peking were placed under siege and American lives were threatened. With Congress in recess, President McKinley hastily dispatched 5,000 U.S. troops from the Philippines as part of an international expeditionary force including Great Britain, Russia, Germany, France, and Japan. The *Philadelphia Times* called the action "an absolute declaration of war by the executive without the authority or knowledge of Congress, and it is without excuse because it is not a necessity."[5]

When Congress returned, McKinley described in detail the actions that he had taken[6] and explained that his actions "involved no war against the Chinese nation."[7] Troops were used to rescue Americans from the imperiled legation, obtain redress from wrongs committed, secure the safety of

---

3. Milton Offutt, "The Protection of Citizens Abroad by the Armed Forces of the United States," Johns Hopkins University Studies in Historical and Political Science, ser. 44, no. 4 (1928).

4. James Grafton Rogers, World Policing and the Constitution (1945).

5. Lewis L. Gould, The Presidency of William McKinley 221–22 (1980).

6. 13 Richardson 6417–25 (December 3, 1900).

7. Id. at 6423.

American life and property, and prevent a spread of the disorders or their recurrence.[8]

A court case raised the question of whether the Boxer Uprising was a "war." Fred Hamilton, a U.S. serviceman charged with murder and found guilty by a military court, was tried and convicted under the fifty-eighth article of war, which requires that a general court-martial be assembled in "time of war." A circuit court in Kansas noted that Congress had increased the pay of military personnel fighting in China to the amount paid in "time of actual war." On the basis of that statutory action, including the occupation of Chinese territory by U.S. troops and the many military conflicts, there prevailed in China "a condition of war, within the spirit and intent" of the fifty-eighth article of war.[9]

The customary justification for using American forces to protect life and property expanded in 1904 when President Theodore Roosevelt explained America's policy toward other nations in the Western Hemisphere. No nation, he said in his fourth annual message to Congress, need fear U.S. interference in its internal affairs—provided that it act with "reasonable efficiency and decency in social and political matters . . . [and] if it keeps order and pays its obligations." Yet if through mismanagement these nations failed to meet their foreign obligations, thereby inviting European nations to intervene in South America and the Caribbean to protect their interests, the United States would have to act first. "Chronic wrongdoing," he warned, "or an impotence which results in a general loosening of the ties of civilized society," might compel America to intervene.[10] The United States would interfere "only in the last resort" and "only if it became evident that their inability or unwillingness to do justice at home and abroad had violated the rights of the United States or had invited foreign aggression to the detriment of the entire body of American nations."[11]

This policy became known as the "Roosevelt Corollary" to the Monroe Doctrine. In a message to Congress on December 2, 1823, Monroe had warned European nations not to intervene in American waters: "We should consider any attempt on their part to extend their system to any portion of this hemisphere as dangerous to our peace and safety."[12] In announcing this policy, Monroe made no claim that he could use military

8. Id.
9. Hamilton v. M'Claughry, 136 Fed. 445, 451 (C.C. Kan. 1905).
10. 14 Richardson 6923.
11. Id. at 6924.
12. 2 Richardson 787.

power on his own authority to enforce it. Enforcement actions would depend on Congress.

On the basis of this policy of noninterference from other nations, Theodore Roosevelt now justified presidential power to intervene in this region. Troops would be sent abroad not to protect American lives and
property but to promote American foreign policy. He had already given
this new doctrine a trial run in 1903, responding to Colombia's refusal to
ratify a treaty giving the United States a canal right-of-way in Panama (then
a province of Colombia). In a draft message to Congress Roosevelt considered taking possession of the isthmus "without any further parley" with
Colombia, but events made it unnecessary to deliver the message.[13] After
encouraging a revolt by Panamanians, he dispatched U.S. warships to prevent Colombia from suppressing the insurrection.[14] For authority to intervene he cited the Treaty of New Granada of 1846, which he said guaranteed "free and open right of way or transit across the Isthmus of
Panama."[15] The actual treaty language provided that the government of
New Granada guaranteed to the United States that the right-of-way or
transit across the isthmus "shall be open and free to the government and
citizens of the United States."[16]

A treaty agreed to by a President and the Senate cannot be the basis for
recognizing a unilateral power by the President to use military force, a
result that would exclude the House of Representatives from its constitutionally assigned duties in matters of war and peace. Nevertheless,
Roosevelt promptly recognized Panama as an independent republic and
used force to gain control of the canal zone. He justified his action by
pointing to past revolutions, rebellions, insurrections, riots, and other
outbreaks that had occurred in Panama: "In short, the experience of over
half a century has shown Colombia to be utterly incapable of keeping order on the Isthmus. Only the active interference of the United States has
enabled her to preserve so much as a semblance of sovereignty."[17]
Roosevelt's logic is interesting: the United States had to intervene to protect another country's sovereignty.

After the new Republic of Panama offered to negotiate a treaty with the
United States, Roosevelt submitted the treaty to the Senate, which ratified

13. George E. Mowry, The Era of Theodore Roosevelt and the Birth of Modern America,
1900–1912, 151 (1958).

14. Lewis L. Gould, The Presidency of Theodore Roosevelt 96–97 (1991).

15. 14 Richardson 6807. See also statement by Secretary of State Hay, reproduced in
"The Panama Revolution," 27 Literary Digest 649 (1903).

16. 9 Stat. 898 (1846).

17. 14 Richardson 6812.

it in 1904. Roosevelt boasted: "I took the canal zone and let Congress de-bate, and while the debate goes on the canal does also."[18] His actions were so flagrant that the United States later agreed to make amends. The Thompson-Urrutia Treaty of 1922 gave Colombia special canal rights and a cash grant of $25 million to compensate, in effect, for Roosevelt's heavy-handed tactics. The original version of the treaty contained an expression of "sincere regret" for America's action in 1903,[19] but the final version merely said that the United States and Colombia were "desirous to re-move all the misunderstandings growing out of the political events in Pan-ama in November 1903."[20]

Roosevelt implemented his "corollary" when he intervened in the Do-minican Republic to set up a fiscal protectorate. The Dominican Republic had built up more than $32 million in debts, primarily to European inves-tors.[21] In 1904 Roosevelt began negotiating an agreement with the Domin-ican Republic, but Congress insisted that a presidential agreement would not be legally binding. A treaty would be required.[22] Opposition in the Senate, coming primarily from Democrats, spelled defeat for his treaty. Early in 1905 an Italian cruiser sailed to the Dominican Republic to collect a debt. Roosevelt responded with military intervention and further nego-tiation, hoping that the Senate would approve the treaty when Congress returned in December. However, opponents in the Senate held firm, and the treaty was never brought to a vote.[23] Only after Roosevelt drafted a new treaty in 1907, taking into account the objections raised by legisla-tors, did the Senate approve the pact.[24]

President William Howard Taft continued the Roosevelt Corollary by intervening twice in Nicaragua and once each in Honduras and Cuba.[25] Taft responded in part to pressure from American financial interests.[26] Al-though he used force against these smaller countries, in 1911 he defined his power as Commander in Chief narrowly when it came to intervening in Mexico to protect American lives and property. He then told Congress

18. Henry F. Pringle, Theodore Roosevelt 330 (1931).

19. Robert K. Murray, The Harding Era: Warren G. Harding and His Administration 340 (1969).

20. 42 Stat. 2122 (1922).

21. Gould, The Presidency of Theodore Roosevelt, at 175.

22. W. Stull Holt, Treaties Defeated by the Senate 214 (1933).

23. Id. 219–22.

24. Id. at 228; 35 Stat. 1880 (1907).

25. Offutt, "The Protection of Citizens Abroad by the Armed Forces of the United States" 104, 107, 109, 111–13.

26. R. Ernest Dupuy and William H. Baumer, The Little Wars of the United States 158 (1968).

that it was his duty as Commander in Chief to place troops "in sufficient number where, if Congress shall direct that they shall enter Mexico to save American lives and property, an effective movement may be promptly made." He "seriously doubt[ed]" if he had the power "under any circumstances" to intervene on Mexican soil to protect American lives or property. Even if he had such authority he "would not exercise it without express congressional approval."[27]

President Wilson's Forays

Self-determination and nonintervention ranked high among the guiding principles of President Woodrow Wilson, at least in theory. Yet those tenets were often subordinated to his crusading determination to export American constitutionalism to other countries. Taking the Greytown bombardment of 1854 as an acceptable precedent, he ordered American forces to occupy Veracruz in 1914. In a message to a joint session of Congress he said that Mexican officials, under the leadership of President Victoriano Huerta, had arrested several Americans. Although they were released with apologies from the Mexican commander and an expression of regret from Huerta, Wilson was not satisfied. He wanted a formal salute of twenty-one guns to be given to U.S. naval vessels, a gesture Huerta declined to give. Other incidents convinced Wilson that Mexico had failed to show proper respect for America and that military action was necessary to preserve U.S. dignity and authority. He told Congress:

> No doubt I could do what is necessary in the circumstances to enforce respect for our Government without recourse to the congress, and yet not exceed my constitutional powers as President; but I do not wish to act in a manner possibly of so grave consequence except in close conference and co-operation with both the Senate and the House. I therefore come to ask your approval that I should use the armed forces of the United States.[28]

The House acted in one day to authorize the use of armed forces. The leader of the Republicans, James R. Mann, commented that if the reported incident had involved England, Germany, France, "or any other great power" there would be no clamor for a military response. But because Mexico "is weak, we think we have the moral right to declare practical

27. 15 Richardson 7659.
28. 16 Richardson 7936.

war against her."[29] After perfunctory debate the House voted 337 to 37 for this language: "That the President of the United States is justified in the employment of armed forces of the United States to enforce the demands made upon Victoriano Huerta for unequivocable amends to the Government of the United States for affronts and indignities committed against this Government by Gen. Huerta and his representatives."[30]

When Senators had the effrontery to pause for one day to think about what they were doing, Wilson went ahead and ordered landing operations by the marines. The following day—just two days after his request—Congress completed action on the joint resolution justifying the President's use of force. The resolution was based entirely on "the facts presented by the President." Although authorizing the use of force, the joint resolution curiously "disclaims any hostility to the Mexican people or any purpose to make war upon Mexico."[31] After beginning with a trivial incident involving U.S. seamen in Tampico, the dispute escalated to U.S. bombardment of Veracruz, American occupation of the town for seven months, and the downfall of Huerta.[32]

During the congressional debate, Senator George W. Norris deplored Wilson's demand for flag salutes by small countries: "This matter of saluting the flag is one of the relics that has come down to us through the ages; and a hundred years from now, when the world has advanced farther in civilization, this silly custom, this foolish rule, this international courtesy that has outlived its usefulness, will be forgotten and will be unknown, at least in practice."[33]

The following year Wilson intervened in Haiti to secure a government more acceptable to his administration. He confided to his Secretary of State: "I fear we have not the legal authority to do what we apparently ought to do."[34] Nevertheless, Wilson decided "there is nothing for it but to take the bull by the horns and restore order. A long programme . . . involves legislation and the cooperation of the Senate in treaty-making, and must therefore await the session of our Congress."[35] Unlike the Roosevelt Corollary, Wilson's action was not motivated by any threat of military in-

29. 51 Cong. Rec. 6937 (1914).
30. Id. at 6957–58.
31. 38 Stat. 770 (1914). The Senate supported the joint resolution on April 21, 1914, by a vote of 72 to 13; 51 Cong. Rec. 7014 (1914).
32. Robert E. Quirk, An Affair of Honor: Woodrow Wilson and the Occupation of Veracruz (1962).
33. 51 Cong. Rec. 6999 (1914).
34. Arthur S. Link, Wilson: The Struggle for Neutrality 536 (1960).
35. Id.

tervention by European powers,[36] although there was some concern about German influence.[37] American troops remained in Haiti until 1934.

President Wilson's intervention in the Dominican Republic in 1916 resulted in a military occupation that lasted eight years.[38] There appeared to be little financial or commercial interest behind this intervention; a desire for markets or raw materials was not a principal motive.[39] There was some concern that European nations, especially Germany, might gain an unwanted foothold in the area, and the Wilson administration was determined to preserve a U.S. hegemony over the Caribbean region.[40] As an unintended consequence of this invasion, Rafael Trujillo participated in the U.S.-controlled Guardia Nacional and used that group as a unified, military base to install himself as dictator for thirty-one years, from 1930 to his assassination in 1961. He was able to consolidate power in part because the U.S. occupation had weakened the countervailing forces of the regional leaders.[41]

Also in 1916, in a variation of the life-and-property prerogative, Wilson ordered General John J. Pershing in "hot pursuit" of Pancho Villa. The expedition penetrated 350 miles into Mexico, lasted almost a year, and came close to outright war with Mexico.[42] The Senate considered several joint resolutions authorizing military action in Mexico, but no floor votes were taken.[43]

Intervention in Nicaragua

Intervention by the Reagan administration in Nicaragua, one prong of the Iran-Contra affair, was merely the latest of many U.S. incursions in that region. From 1909 to 1933, the United States was rarely out of Nicaragua, moving in repeatedly under the customary banner of protecting lives and property.

In 1909, President Taft sent in marines as part of a policy to undermine the presidency of Jose Santos Zelaya, leader of the Liberty Party. After U.S.

36. Id. at 535.
37. Hans Schmidt, The United States Occupation of Haiti, 1915–1934, 57–60 (1971).
38. Link, Wilson: The Struggle for Neutrality, 543–49.
39. Id. at 549.
40. Bruce J. Calder, The Impact of Intervention: The Dominican Republic during the U.S. Occupation of 1916–1924, xii (1984).
41. Id. at xviii, 239.
42. Link, Wilson: The Struggle for Neutrality, 233–34, 456, 467, 489–91; see also Arthur S. Link, Wilson: Confusion and Crises 196–208, 216–17 (1964).
43. 53 Cong. Rec. 1189–96, 9748–49 (1916).

forces sided with a rebellion sponsored by the Conservative Party, an unstable coalition of Liberals and Conservatives tried to govern, eventually giving way to Conservative control by 1911. In response to a Liberal revolt in 1912, Taft ordered U.S. troops to crush the rebellion. A legation guard of 100 American troops remained in Managua, helping to secure U.S. control of political and economic conditions in Nicaragua. The Taft administration exerted influence in the election of 1912 to obtain a Nicaraguan president to its liking,[44] and in the election of 1916 the Wilson administration actively supported the candidacy of General Emiliano Chamorro, who was elected.[45]

The U.S. marines were not removed from Managua until August 4, 1925. Chamorro, who had been out of office, staged a coup d'etat and ousted President Carlos Solorzano. Under pressure from the United States and other Central American countries, Chamorro tried to name a successor but Adolfo Diaz was eventually named president. Diaz promptly appealed to the United States to aid him in the protection of the interests of Americans and other citizens. In response, President Calvin Coolidge sent war vessels to Nicaragua in 1926, citing the need to protect American lives and property.[46] He told Congress that U.S. military assistance was required because Mexico was supporting revolutionists in Nicaragua.[47]

This explanation, as well as other justifications for the intervention, provoked a skeptical response from Congress and major newspapers. In another effort to justify the use of American troops, the Coolidge administration released a memorandum suggesting that Mexico was trying to spread bolshevism in Nicaragua and Latin America. This account was discredited when Congress learned that the State Department had tried to conceal its role in disseminating this story in the newspapers.[48]

Senator John James Blaine (R-Wis.) led the charge to deny funds to the administration for its involvement in Nicaragua. His amendment read:

> Provided, That after December 25, 1928, none of the appropriations made in this act [naval appropriations] shall be used to pay any expenses incurred in connection with acts of hostility against a friendly foreign nation, or any belligerent intervention in the affairs of a foreign nation, or any intervention in the domestic affairs of any

44. Dana G. Munro, Intervention and Dollar Diplomacy in the Caribbean, 1900–1921, 160–216 (1964).
45. Stuart H. Graham, Latin America and the United States 361 (1943).
46. 68 Cong. Rec. 1324–25 (1927).
47. Id. at 1325.
48. Bryce Wood, The Making of the Good Neighbor Policy 17–20 (1961).

foreign nation, unless war has been declared by Congress or unless a state of war actually exists under recognized principles of international law.[49]

Although Blaine's amendment, as later modified, was defeated, the Senate debate on the President's power as Commander in Chief lasted day after day and signaled to the administration that its policy in Nicaragua faced a substantial opposition that would only get stronger.[50] Congressional and public criticism of the administration's involvement in Nicaragua continued. Finally, in 1932, Congress enacted this language in a naval appropriations bill: "No money appropriated in this Act shall be used to defray the expense of sending additional Marines to Nicaragua to supervise an election there."[51]

President Coolidge offered this reason for U.S. intervention: "We are not making war on Nicaragua any more than a policeman on the street is making war on passersby."[52] Constitutional scholar Edward S. Corwin puzzled over this explanation: "In other words, our armed forces has just as much right to be on Nicaragua soil as a policeman has to appear on the streets of his home town."[53] U.S. troops were finally removed from Nicaragua in 1933.

The lengthy and costly interventions in Nicaragua and Haiti created so much dissent in America—within Congress, the executive branch, and the public—that the United States did not again intervene (openly) in the Caribbean or Central America until President Lyndon B. Johnson dispatched U.S. troops to the Dominican Republic in 1965. He feared that there would be a Communist takeover, although later he explained that "99 percent of our reason for going in there was to try to provide protection for these American lives and for the lives of other nationals."[54] In addition to this public intervention, the United States engaged in a number of covert operations during this period, including Guatemala in 1954 and Cuba in 1961 (see Chapter 8).

World War I

Upon the outbreak of the European war in 1914, President Wilson issued proclamations of neutrality.[55] To ensure the enforcement of those proclamations, he issued an order to prohibit "from transmitting or receiving

49. 69 Cong. Rec. 6684 (1928).
50. Id. at 7192.
51. 47 Stat. 439 (1932).
52. Thomas A. Bailey, A Diplomatic History of the American People 678 (1969).
53. Edward S. Corwin, Total War and the Constitution 148 (1947).
54. Public Papers of the Presidents, 1965, II, 616.
55. 16 Richardson 7969–77.

for delivery messages of an unneutral nature, and from in any way rendering to any one of the belligerents any unneutral service, during the continuance of hostilities."[56] He later closed the Marconi Wireless Station at Siasconset, Massachusetts, because it had refused to comply with naval censorship regulations. Attorney General Thomas Gregory justified the action by stating that it was the President's right and duty, in the absence of any statutory restrictions, to close down or seize any plant "should he deem it necessary in securing obedience to his proclamation of neutrality."[57]

Wilson's initial policy of neutrality gave way gradually to a preference for England over Germany. Americans on the high seas were at risk after Germany announced that the waters around the British isles constituted a war zone and warned neutral ships to keep out of those waters. On May 1, 1915, the American tanker *Gulflight* was torpedoed, with the loss of two lives. A few days later another German torpedo sank the British steamer *Lusitania*. Of the 1,198 passengers who lost their lives, 124 were American. The *Lusitania* carried rifle cartridges, shrapnel, shell castings, and other war matériel.[58]

Wilson, assisted by Secretary of State William Jennings Bryan and counselor to the State Department Robert Lansing, drafted "notes" to be sent to Germany to articulate American policy on submarine warfare. Bryan believed that Germany had the right to prevent contraband from going to the Allies: "A ship carrying contraband should not rely upon passengers to protect her from attack—it would be like putting women and children in front of an army."[59] He also objected to the bias in American policy: "We unsparingly denounce the retaliatory methods employed by [Germany] without condemning the announced purpose of the allies to starve the non-combatants of Germany and without complaining of the conduct of Great Britain in relying on passengers, including men, women and children of the United States, to give immunity to vessels carrying munitions of war."[60] Nevertheless, Bryan acquiesced in Wilson's first note to Germany asking it to disavow the submarine attacks on neutral ships, to make reparation, and to prevent the recurrence of these incidents.[61]

Bryan urged Wilson to warn passengers against taking trips on vessels

56. Id. at 7962.
57. 30 Att'y Gen. 291, 293 (1914).
58. 33 Papers of Woodrow Wilson 135n (Arthur S. Link ed. 1980).
59. Id. at 134–35.
60. Id. at 166.
61. Id. at 177.

that carried contraband,[62] a policy Wilson found "both weak and futile."[63] Lansing pressed for a harder line, insisting that citizens of neutral countries should be able to traverse the high seas—even in ships carrying defensive armament—without fear of attack.[64] Preferring Lansing's position, Wilson drafted a second note that was more confrontational in tone.[65] Bryan tried to soften the language of the text.[66] When it became obvious that he had lost this battle within the administration and that he could not, in conscience, sign the second note, he resigned from office.[67]

Wilson took steps to prepare the nation for war. In an address delivered to Congress on December 7, 1915, he recommended an increase in the size of the army, acceleration of shipbuilding, and strengthening of the merchant marine.[68] Nevertheless, his reelection campaign in 1916 relied heavily on a promise to keep America out of war. Wilson's renomination at the Democratic convention was accompanied by shouts of "He Kept Us Out of War." On the eve of the election, on October 31, 1916, he announced: "I am not expecting this country to get into war."[69]

When Germany refused to abandon its policy of unrestricted submarine warfare, Wilson broke diplomatic relations on February 3, 1917. On February 26, he asked Congress for authority to arm American merchant ships to protect them from German submarine attacks. In stepping from neutrality to armed neutrality, he offered this analysis of his constitutional powers:

> I feel that I ought . . . to obtain from you full and immediate assurance of the authority which I may need at any moment to exercise. No doubt I already possess that authority without special warrant of law, by the plain implication of my constitutional duties and powers; but I prefer, in the present circumstances, not to act upon general implication. I wish to feel that the authority and the power of the Congress are behind me in whatever it may become necessary for me to do.[70]

---

62. Id. at 192.
63. Id. at 194.
64. Id. at 312–13.
65. Id. at 328–31.
66. Id. at 351–55.
67. Id. at 375–76.
68. 16 Richardson 8106–10.
69. Harvey A. DeWeerd, President Wilson Fights His War: World War I and the American Intervention 21 (1968).
70. 16 Richardson 8211.

The House passed the bill on March 1 by a vote of 403 to 13, but a number of Senators joined in a filibuster to block action on the proposal. Wilson denounced them as a "little group of wilful men, representing no opinion but their own."[71] After Congress adjourned without acting on Wilson's request, he proceeded to arm the vessels "for the sole purpose of defense." The administration's policy stipulated that no armed guard of any American merchant vessel "shall take any offensive action against any submarine of Germany or of any nation following the policy of Germany . . . unless the submarine is guilty of an unlawful act that jeopardizes the vessel, her passengers, or crew, or unless the submarine is submerged."[72]

It was Wilson, then, who made the basic policy decision to move from neutrality to armed neutrality and finally to a state of war with Germany. In his history of World War I, Harvey A. DeWeerd said that of all the American pressures operating to bring the country into war in April 1917, "the greatest force was that of the President. His position, his opinions, his decisions, and his actions were decisive."[73] On April 2, 1917, Wilson called Congress into extraordinary session to review the continued use of German submarines against neutral vessels. Concluding that armed neutrality "now appears [to be] impracticable,"[74] he asked Congress to declare war on Germany, a step it took four days later. The Senate supported the declaration 82 to 6; the vote in the House was 373 to 50.[75]

The *Curtiss-Wright* Case

In recent decades, presidential power in foreign affairs has drawn much of its legal support from a badly reasoned, badly grounded decision issued by the Supreme Court in 1936. In *United States* v. *Curtiss-Wright Corp.*, the Court had to decide whether Congress had delegated too broadly when it empowered the President to declare an arms embargo in South America. The statute allowed the President to impose an arms embargo whenever he found that it "may contribute to the reestablishment of peace" between belligerents. Did this give the President too much discretion?

The previous year, in two cases, the Court had struck down the delega-

71. Id. at 8218.
72. 41 Papers of Woodrow Wilson 395–96 (Arthur S. Link ed. 1983).
73. DeWeerd, President Wilson Fights His War, 7–8.
74. 16 Richardson 8227.
75. 55 Cong. Rec. 261, 412–13 (1917).

tion of *domestic* power to the President.[76] All that was necessary in *Curtiss-Wright* was for the Court to announce that Congress could delegate more broadly in international affairs than in domestic affairs. The issue was never the existence of independent presidential power. The Court was asked whether *Congress*, in determining the extent of *its* power, could grant the President more discretion than would be permissible for domestic policy. Instead, the Court went far beyond the bounds of the case to find extraconstitutional powers for the President. Seldom has a court reached so far with so little evidence to support its conclusion.

The author of *Curtiss-Wright*, Justice George Sutherland, had been a Senator from Utah and a member of the Senate Foreign Relations Committee. The decision closely tracks his article "The Internal and External Powers of the National Government" (printed as a Senate document in 1910) and his book, *Constitutional Power and World Affairs* (1919).[77] According to his biographer, Sutherland advocated "a vigorous diplomacy which strongly, even belligerently, called always for an assertion of American rights."[78]

There are many deficiencies in Sutherland's opinion. He insisted that foreign and domestic affairs are different "both in respect of their origin and their nature" because the powers of external sovereignty "passed from the Crown not to the colonies severally, but to the colonies in their collective and corporate capacity as the United States of America."[79] By transferring external or foreign affairs directly to the national government, and then linking foreign affairs to the executive, Sutherland supplied a powerful but deceptive argument for presidential power.

Sutherland's history is false. External sovereignty did not circumvent the colonies and the states and pass directly to an independent executive. In 1776, there was no President or separate executive branch. Only one branch of government functioned at the national level: the Continental Congress. It had to discharge all governmental duties, including legislative, executive, and judicial. Scholars, pointing out that the states in 1776 operated as sovereign entities and not as part of a collective body, have repudiated this part of Sutherland's opinion. The creation of a Continental Congress in 1776 did not disturb the sovereign power of the states to make treaties, borrow money, solicit arms, lay embargoes, collect tariff

---

76. Panama Refining Co. v. Ryan, 293 U.S. 388 (1935); Schechter Corp. v. United States, 295 U.S. 495 (1935).

77. S. Doc. No. 417, 61st Cong., 2d Sess. (1910).

78. Joel Francis Paschal, Mr. Justice Sutherland: A Man Against the State 93 (1951).

79. 299 U.S. 304, 315–16 (1936).

duties, and conduct separate military campaigns.[80] The Supreme Court has recognized that the American colonies, upon their separation from England, acquired certain elements of sovereignty.[81]

Even if the power of external sovereignty had somehow passed intact from the Crown to the "United States," the Constitution allocates that power both to Congress and the President. The President and the Senate share the treaty power. The President receives ambassadors from other countries, but U.S. ambassadors must be approved by the Senate. Congress has the power to declare war, to raise and support the military forces, to make rules for their regulation, to provide for the calling up of the militia to suppress insurrections and repel invasions, and to provide for the organization and disciplining of the militia. The Constitution also explicitly grants to Congress the power to lay and collect duties on foreign trade, to regulate commerce with foreign nations, and to establish a uniform rule of naturalization. Sutherland was also simplistic in drawing such a bright line between external and internal affairs and in assuming that the President's latitude was inordinately broad whenever he acted in foreign or international matters. The framers made no such distinction and world events since 1936 have increased the overlap between foreign and domestic affairs.[82] In 1991 President Bush remarked: "I guess my bottom line . . . is you can't separate foreign policy from domestic."[83]

Sutherland spoke strongly about the President's independent power to negotiate agreements with other countries: "He *makes* treaties with the advice and consent of the Senate; but he alone negotiates. Into the field of negotiation the Senate cannot intrude; and Congress itself is powerless to invade it."[84] But the power to negotiate is not the power to make foreign policy unilaterally. Edwin Borchard, a specialist in international law, said that the power discussed by Sutherland "does not give the President carte blanche to do anything he pleases in foreign affairs, for it is limited to 'negotiation and inquiry.' "[85]

---

80. Charles Lofgren, "*United States* v. *Curtiss-Wright Export Corporation*: An Historical Reassessment," 83 Yale L. J. 1 (1973); David M. Levitan, "The Foreign Relations Power: An Analysis of Mr. Justice Sutherland's Theory," 55 Yale L. J. 467 (1946); Claude H. Van Tyne, "Sovereignty in the American Revolution: An Historical Study," 12 Am. Hist. Rev. 529 (1907).

81. United States v. California, 332 U.S. 19, 31 (1947); Texas v. White, 74 U.S. 700, 725 (1869).

82. Bayless Manning, "The Congress, the Executive and 'Intermestic' Affairs: Three Proposals," 55 Foreign Affairs 306 (1977).

83. 27 Weekly Comp. Pres. Doc. 1853 (December 17, 1991).

84. 299 U.S. at 319; (emphasis in original).

85. Edwin Borchard, "The Attorney General's Opinion on the Exchange of Destroyers for Naval Bases," 34 Am. J. Int'l L. 690, 691 (1940).

Sutherland wrote eloquently about "this vast external realm, with its important, complicated, delicate and manifold problems." As a consequence, he said, legislation over the international field must often accord to the President "a degree of discretion and freedom from statutory restrictions which would not be admissible were domestic affairs alone involved."[86] He then went beyond this position (based on *statutory* grants of power) to argue for inherent presidential power. He claimed that the exercise of presidential power does not depend solely on an act of Congress because of the "very delicate, plenary and exclusive power of the President as the sole organ of the federal government in the field of international relations."[87] Sutherland searched for powers outside the Constitution.[88]

The magic term "sole organ" suggests that when it comes to foreign policy, the President is the exclusive policymaker. The language carries special weight because John Marshall used it in a speech in 1800 while serving in the House of Representatives. Given Marshall's elevation a year later to become Chief Justice of the Supreme Court, Sutherland seemed to be drawing from an impeccable, authoritative source, but Sutherland wrenched Marshall's statement from context to imply a position Marshall never advanced. At no time, either in 1800 or later, did Marshall suggest that the President could act unilaterally to make foreign policy. Quite the contrary.

During the debate in 1800, opponents of President John Adams argued for his impeachment because he had agreed to turn over to England someone charged with murder. Because the case was already pending in an American court, some members of Congress recommended that Adams be impeached for encroaching upon the judiciary and violating the doctrine of separation of powers. At this point Marshall intervened to say that there was no basis for impeachment. Adams, merely carrying out an extradition treaty entered into between England and the United States, was not attempting to make national policy single-handedly. He was carrying out a policy made jointly by the President and the Senate (for treaties). Only after the policy had been formulated through the collective effort of the executive and legislative branches (by treaty or by statute) did the President emerge as the "sole organ" in *implementing* national policy. It was here that Marshall said that the President "is the sole organ of the nation in its

86. 299 U.S. at 319, 320.
87. Id. at 320.
88. Louis Henkin, Foreign Affairs and the Constitution 22 (1972).

external relations and its sole representative with foreign nations."[89] The President merely *announced* policy; he did not *make* it.

As Justice Robert Jackson later observed, the most that can be drawn from *Curtiss-Wright* is the intimation that the President "might act in external affairs without congressional authority, but not that he might act contrary to an act of Congress."[90] Jackson noted that "much of the [Sutherland] opinion is dictum"—comments extraneous to the issue before the Court.[91] In 1981 a federal appellate court cautioned against placing undue reliance on "certain dicta" in Sutherland's opinion: "To the extent that denominating the President as the 'sole organ' of the United States in international affairs constitutes a blanket endorsement of plenary Presidential power over any matter extending beyond the borders of this country, we reject that characterization."[92]

Even though Sutherland's opinion is filled with historical and conceptual inaccuracies, *Curtiss-Wright* became a popular citation for Court decisions upholding presidential power. The case is frequently cited to support not only broad delegations of legislative power to the President but even the existence of independent, implied, and inherent powers for the President.[93]

Legislative Constraints in the 1930s

By passing the Neutrality Acts of 1935, 1937, and 1939, Congress attempted to keep the United States out of foreign wars. Even though this legislation initially enjoyed the backing of the executive branch, the Neutrality Acts would later be cited as evidence that members of Congress lack the sophistication to participate effectively in issues of foreign policy and national security. Also during the 1930s Congress debated the Ludlow Resolution, another legislative effort to restrict the ability of the national government to engage in war. This constitutional amendment

---

89. Annals of Congress, 6th Cong., 613 (1800).

90. Youngstown Co. v. Sawyer, 343 U.S. 579, 636 n.2 (1952).

91. Id.

92. American Intern. Group v. Islamic Republic of Iran, 657 F.2d 430, 438 n.6 (D.C. Cir. 1981).

93. For broad-delegation arguments, see Ex parte Endo, 323 U.S. 283, 298 n.21 (1944); Zemel v. Rusk, 381 U.S. 1, 17 (1965), and Goldwater v. Carter, 444 U.S. 996, 1000 n.1 (1979). Inherent powers are discussed in United States v. Pink, 315 U.S. 203, 229 (1942), Knauff v. Shaughnessy, 338 U.S. 537, 542 (1950), United States v. Mazurie, 419 U.S. 544, 566–67 (1975), and Dames & Moore v. Regan, 453 U.S. 654, 661 (1981).

would have required a referendum vote by the people before the United States could participate in foreign wars.

Although Congress would later receive the lion's share of criticism for the Neutrality Acts of the 1930s, executive officials also believed that this type of legislation would help insulate the United States from foreign wars. On January 11, 1933, President-elect Franklin D. Roosevelt said that he had "long been in favor of the use of embargoes on arms to belligerent nations, especially to nations which are guilty of making an attack on other nations . . . that is, against aggressor nations."[94] When the Chaco War in South America could not be resolved through negotiation, Roosevelt asked Congress in 1934 for authority to place an arms embargo on both belligerents and received that authority in a statute later upheld by the Supreme Court in *Curtiss-Wright.*[95]

A committee investigation by Senator Gerald P. Nye (R-N.Dak.) in 1934 popularized the theory that controls on the U.S. munitions industry would help keep the United States out of foreign wars. The Neutrality Act of 1935 provided for the prohibition of the export of arms, ammunition, and implements of war to belligerent countries. Under this legislation, "upon the outbreak or during the progress of war between, or among, two or more foreign states," the President would proclaim that fact and trigger the prohibition of war matériel to that region.[96] President Roosevelt signed the bill and called its purpose "wholly excellent" and "wholly good," cautioning that some "inflexible [embargo] provisions might drag us into war instead of keeping us out."[97] Some experts testified that the legislation created opportunities for presidential war-making.[98]

The outbreak of war in Spain in 1936 called attention to the fact that the neutrality legislation, confined to wars between nations, did not cover civil wars. Congress proceeded to pass separate legislation to prohibit the exportation of arms, ammunition, and implements of war from the United States to Spain.[99] In issuing a proclamation to comply with that statute, Roosevelt acknowledged that "the people of the United States and their representatives certainly were not prepared in 1937 to risk the

94. Edwin Borchard, Neutrality for the United States 308 (1973).
95. Id. at 313–14; 48 Stat. 811 (1934); United States v. Curtiss Wright, 299 U.S. 304 (1936).
96. 49 Stat. 1081 (1935).
97. 4 Public Papers and Addresses of Franklin D. Roosevelt 345 46 (1935 volume).
98. Borchard, Neutrality for the United States 327.
99. 50 Stat. 3 (1937).

slightest chance of becoming involved in a quarrel in Europe which had all the possibilities of developing into a general European conflict."[100]

Congress continued to pass other neutrality acts in 1937 and 1939. The 1937 statute carved out an exception for the Monroe Doctrine by providing that the neutrality policy "shall not apply to an American state or states, provided the American republic is not cooperating with a non-American state or state in such war."[101] The 1939 statute provided that either branch could find that a state of war existed in other counties. The President or Congress (acting by concurrent resolution) could declare the existence of war between foreign nations.[102]

Throughout 1939 Roosevelt criticized the embargo provisions of the Neutrality Acts and recommended their repeal, telling Congress that he now regretted signing the neutrality statutes in 1935 and 1937.[103] Although he objected to the use of arms embargoes and fought successfully for their removal from the 1939 bill, at the same time he announced: "Our acts must be guided by one single hard-headed thought—keeping America out of this war [in Europe].[104]

Also during this period Congress considered a constitutional amendment proposed by Louis Ludlow (D-Ind.) to subject a declaration of war to a popular vote in a referendum. Except in the event of an invasion of the United States or its territorial possessions and attacks upon U.S. citizens residing in those areas, "the authority of Congress to declare war shall not become effective until confirmed by a majority of all votes cast thereon in a Nationwide referendum."[105] Sufficient signatures were collected to discharge the amendment from the House Committee of Rules, but the House voted 209 to 188 against the effort to bring the measure to the floor for further debate and consideration.[106]

World War II

Even more than Wilson, Franklin Delano Roosevelt led the country from a state of neutrality to one of war. On September 8, 1939, after Germany

100. 6 Public Papers and Addresses of Franklin D., Roosevelt 192 (1937 volume).

101. 50 Stat. 124, sec. 4 (1937).

102. 54 Stat. 4, sec. (1a) (1939).

103. 8 Public Papers and Addresses of Franklin D. Roosevelt 516 (1939 volume). See also 3–4, 154–55, 381–88, 395–97.

104. Id. at 521.

105. 82 Cong. Rec. 250 (1937).

106. 83 Cong. Rec. 282–83 (1938). See also 82 Cong. Rec. 242–51, 1516–18 (1937); 83 Cong. Rec. 276–83 (1938); Buel W. Patch, "The Power to Declare War," 1 Editorial Research Reports 3–18, 398–99 (1938).

invaded Poland, Roosevelt proclaimed a state of limited emergency. In response to a Senate resolution, Attorney General Frank Murphy collected a list of statutes that became active upon the proclamation of a state of emergency or war. Murphy, without claiming to be presenting a complete list, referred to about fifty statutes granting powers that could be exercised by the President in time of national emergency or during a war in which the United States was neutral.[107]

The United States supplied war matériel to the Allies to help them in their struggle against Germany and Italy. In June 1940, when France requested additional assistance from the United States, Roosevelt expressed admiration for the "resplendent courage" of French armies resisting German invaders and pledged continuing assistance of airplanes, artillery, and munitions. But he cautioned: "I know that you will understand that these statements carry with them no implication of military commitments. Only the Congress can make such commitments."[108] At a speech in Charlottesville, Va., that same month, he promised to "extend to the opponents of force the material resources of this nation."[109]

When France asked for some old U.S. destroyers to strengthen its naval forces in the Mediterranean, Roosevelt claimed he had no such authority: "Any exchange for American destroyers probably inacceptable because of enormous sea area which must be patrolled by us and would require Congressional action which might be very difficult to get. Our old destroyers cannot be sold as obsolete as is proved by fact. All of them are now in commission and in use or are in process of being commissioned for actual use."[110] Nevertheless, some members of Congress heard of rumors that "destroyers in our Navy were being transferred, or that negotiations were under way for the transfer of these naval vessels."[111] In response, Congress enacted a statute on June 28, 1940, seeking to prohibit such transfers unless the Chief of Naval Operations or the Chief of Staff of the Army "shall first certify that such material is not essential to the defense of the United States."[112]

Prime Minister Winston Churchill pressed Roosevelt for used destroyers, and when Roosevelt presented the matter to his cabinet, White

107. Executive Powers Under National Emergency, S. Doc. No. 133, 76th Cong., 2d Sess. (October 5, 1939).

108. 9 Public Papers and Addresses of Franklin D. Roosevelt 267 (1940 volume).

109. Id. at 264.

110. Charles Callan Tansill, Back Door to War: The Roosevelt Foreign Policy, 1933–1941 591 (1952) (Roosevelt to Sumner Welles, June 1, 1940).

111. 86 Cong. Rec. 8775 (1940).

112. 54 Stat. 681, sec. 14 (1940).

House aides suggested ways of transferring the vessels without obtaining authority from Congress. The administration enlisted the assistance of retired General Pershing, who urged that the United States give England and Canada "at least fifty of the over-age destroyers which are left from the days of the World War."[113] Wendell Wilkie, Republican candidate for the presidency in 1940, assured the administration that he would not make an issue of the transfer in the campaign.[114]

With the ground thus softened up, President Roosevelt announced on September 3 an agreement to exchange fifty "over-age" destroyers with Britain in return for the right to use bases on British islands in the Atlantic and the Caribbean.[115] Made solely by executive agreement, the destroyers/bases deal circumvented congressional control. Attorney General Robert Jackson defended the constitutionality of the agreement by claiming that the President's function as Commander in Chief placed upon him a responsibility "to use all constitutional authority which he may possess to provide adequate bases and stations for the utilization of the naval and air weapons of the United States at their highest efficiency in our defense."[116] Jackson relied partly on Sutherland's opinion in *Curtiss-Wright*.[117]

Legal experts did not find Jackson's opinion convincing under domestic law or international law.[118] Concluded one expert: "The destroyers have by now been transferred; but let no one say that it was accomplished 'legally.' The supplying of these vessels by the United States Government to a belligerent is a violation of our neutral status, a violation of our national law, and a violation of international law."[119] Edward S. Corwin also attacked Jackson's opinion, regarding the destroyer deal as an invasion of Congress's power to define for the United States the requirements of international law respecting neutrality and an invasion of Congress's constitutional power to declare war.[120]

Jackson himself, sitting later as Associate Justice of the Supreme Court, did not find all of his earlier writings on presidential power convincing ei-

---

113. The New York Times, August 5, 1950, at 1.

114. Charles Callan Tansill, Back Door to War, at 597.

115. 9 Public Papers and Addresses of Franklin D. Roosevelt 391 (1940 volume).

116. 39 Op. Att'y Gen. 484, 486 (1940).

117. Id. at 486–87.

118. Quincy Wright, "The Transfer of Destroyers to Great Britain," 34 Am. J. Int'l L. 680 (1940); Edwin Borchard, "The Attorney General's Opinion on the Exchange of Destroyers for Naval Bases," 34 Am. J. Int'l L. 690 (1934).

119. Herbert W. Briggs, "Neglected Aspects of the Destroyer Deal," 34 Am. J. Int'l L. 569, 587 (1940).

120. Edward S. Corwin, "Executive Authority Held Exceeded in Destroyer Deal," The New York Times, October 13, 1940, sec. 4, at 6, 7.

ther. In the Steel Seizure Case of 1952, attorneys for President Truman cited Jackson's arguments on several occasions.[121] Jackson merely noted: "While it is not surprising that counsel should grasp support from such unadjudicated claims of power, a judge cannot accept self-serving press statements of the attorney for one of the interested parties as authority in answering a constitutional question, even if the advocate was himself."[122]

Similar to Wilson's promise to the American people in 1916, Roosevelt pledged to keep the nation out of war. On October 23, 1940, in Philadelphia, he vigorously denied that his administration "wishes to lead this country into war." He repeated the Democratic Party platform: "We will not participate in foreign wars and we will not send our army, naval or air forces to fight in foreign lands outside of the Americas except in case of attack."[123] On October 30, in Boston, Roosevelt told the crowd: "I have said this before, but I shall say it again and again and again: 'Your boys are not going to be sent into any foreign wars.' "[124]

After his election, Roosevelt could be more open about giving military weapons to England. In a news conference on December 17, Roosevelt used a down-home argument to justify additional assistance to Great Britain. Instead of building ships and other weapons to be sold to England, he suggested that it might make more sense to let England use those materials rather than keep them in storage in America. In that way, defending England would defend America. Through such techniques he was trying to "eliminate the dollar sign." Roosevelt then gave his famous analogy:

> Well, let me give you an illustration: Suppose my neighbor's home catches fire, and I have a length of garden hose four or five hundred feet away. If he can take my garden hose and connect it up with his hydrant, I may help him to put out his fire. Now, what do I do? I don't say to him before that operation, "Neighbor, my garden hose cost me $15; you have to pay me $15 for it." What is the transaction that goes on? I don't want $15—I want my garden hose back after the fire is over.[125]

Asked whether this concept would require congressional approval, Roosevelt responded: "Oh, yes, this would require various types of legis-

---

121. 48 Landmark Briefs 705, 755–57, 920–22, 927–28 (1975).
122. Youngstown Co. v. Sawyer, 343 U.S. 579, 647 (1952).
123. 9 Public Papers and Addresses of Franklin D. Roosevelt 494, 495 (1940 volume).
124. Id. at 517.
125. Id. at 607.

lation, in addition to appropriation."[126] On March 11, 1941, Congress passed the Lend-Lease Act, which authorized the President to manufacture any defense article and to "sell, transfer title to, exchange, lease, lend, or otherwise dispose of" the defense articles to any country whose defense he deemed vital to the defense of the United States.[127]

In an appeal to Congress on April 10, Roosevelt asked for legislation that would allow him to make use of foreign merchant vessels in American ports. About 80 foreign ships were lying idle in U.S. waters and another 150 vessels were idle in other ports of the Western Hemisphere. Roosevelt said that he lacked authority to use these ships.[128] Congress provided the necessary legislation.[129]

On April 11, Roosevelt signed an agreement with Denmark that pledged America's defense of Greenland (a Danish possession) in return for the right to construct and operate defense installations on the island.[130] Also in April, he announced his decision to extend American naval patrols halfway across the Atlantic. The Navy would search for German submarines and report their presence to British commanders.[131]

On May 27, Roosevelt proclaimed the existence of an unlimited national emergency.[132] Within two weeks he had signed another agreement with Iceland to permit U.S. forces to land there in order to prevent Germany from occupying that island and using it as a naval or air base against the Western Hemisphere.[133] Still operating on the basis of independent executive power, Roosevelt seized the North American Aviation plant in Inglewood, California, on June 7 and followed that with the seizure of several other defense facilities.[134] On June 14, Roosevelt ordered the freezing of all remaining assets of Germany, Italy, and Axis-controlled countries.[135] Three months before Pearl Harbor, he issued his "shoot-on-sight" order to U.S. forces in defense waters, warning that German and Italian vessels would enter those areas at their own risk.[136]

Following Japan's attack on Pearl Harbor on December 7, 1941,

---

126. Id. at 610.
127. 55 Stat. 31 (1941).
128. 10 Public Papers and Addresses of Franklin D. Roosevelt 94 (1941 volume).
129. 55 Stat. 242 (1941).
130. 10 Public Papers and Addresses of Franklin D. Roosevelt 96 (1941 volume).
131. Id. at 132–35.
132. Id. at 194.
133. Id. at 255.
134. Id. at 205.
135. Id. at 217.
136. Id. at 390–91.

Roosevelt asked Congress to declare war.[137] The Senate voted unanimously for the declaration, 82 to 0; the House vote was 388 to 1.[138] On December 11, Germany and Italy declared war on the United States. Congress promptly recognized a state of war with those nations.

In the autumn of 1942, President Roosevelt notified Congress that it had failed to enact two of his recommendations for inflation control. Now that four months had passed, the President told Congress that if it did not pass such legislation in the next month, authorizing him to stabilize the cost of living, he could be left with "an inescapable responsibility to the people of this country to see to it that the war effort is no longer imperiled by threat of economic chaos." In the event that Congress failed to act, "and act adequately, I shall accept the responsibility, and I will act."[139] Congress provided the additional inflation controls only one day after his deadline.

In that same address to Congress, Roosevelt said that when the war was over, "the powers under which I act automatically revert to the people—to whom they belong."[140] Yet those powers did not revert to the people when the war was over; presidential powers are not surrendered so easily. President Harry Truman announced the end of the war in Europe on May 8, 1945, and on August 14 he announced the surrender of Japan. Nevertheless, in May 1946 he seized certain bituminous coal mines under authority of the War Labor Disputes Act, which empowered the President to take possession of any plant, mine, or facility as may be required for the "war effort." That authority remained in force until the President proclaimed the "termination of hostilities," a step Truman did not take until December 31, 1946, more than sixteen months after Japan's surrender. By proclaiming that hostilities had terminated, Truman relinquished certain wartime powers but retained others that remained available during "a state of war" or a "state of emergency." Truman stressed that "a state of war still exists."[141]

The Supreme Court endorsed this consolidation of presidential power. The Housing and Rent Act of 1947 provided for an extension of wartime rent controls. In upholding this statute, the Court observed that the housing deficit, created by the demobilization of veterans and the reduction of residential construction during the war, had not yet been eliminated. The Court did concede that war in modern times affected the economy for

137. Id. at 515.
138. 87 Cong. Rec. 9506, 9536–37 (1941).
139. 11 Public Papers and Addresses of Franklin D. Roosevelt 364 (1942 volume).
140. Id. at 365.
141. Public Papers of the Presidents, 1946, 512–13.

years afterward and created a dangerous situation in which the war power "may not only swallow up all other powers of Congress but largely obliterate the Ninth and Tenth Amendments as well."[142]

In 1947 Congress terminated several "temporary" emergency war powers. Approximately 175 statutory provisions were involved, many dating back to World War I. Even with that action, 103 war or emergency statutes statutes remained in effect.[143] On April 28, 1952, Truman finally signed a statement terminating the state of war with Japan and the national emergencies proclaimed by Roosevelt in 1939 and 1941. Although actual hostilities had lasted for fewer than four years, Roosevelt and Truman exercised emergency and war powers for more than twelve.

142. Woods v. Miller, 333 U.S. 138, 146 (1948).
143. 61 Stat. 449 (1947); Public Papers of the President, 1947, 357.

4

THE UN CHARTER AND KOREA

In June 1950, President Truman ordered U.S. troops to Korea without first requesting congressional authority. For legal footing he cited resolutions passed by the United Nations Security Council, a beguiling but spurious source of authority. In 1990 the Bush administration tried the same tactic, using the Korean War as an acceptable precedent for taking offensive action against Iraq, again without seeking congressional approval. Like Truman, Bush claimed that UN resolutions were a sufficient base of authority. In Bosnia, too, President Clinton relied on UN resolutions and NATO agreements as sufficient authority to use military force without first seeking congressional approval. He cited a UN resolution as authority to invade Haiti.

UN machinery is not a legal substitute for congressional action. If that were possible, the President and the Senate, through treaty action, could strip from the House of Representatives its constitutional role in deciding questions of war. Following that same logic, the President and the Senate, through the treaty process, could rely on the United Nations to determine trade and tariff matters, again bypassing the prerogatives of the House of Representatives. The history of the United Nations makes it very clear that all parties in the legislative and executive branches understood that the decision to use military force through the United Nations required prior approval from both Houses of Congress.

The League of Nations

The need for congressional approval for UN-sanctioned military actions derives from the history of the Versailles Treaty and the League of Nations. The Senate defeated the Versailles Treaty in 1919 and again in 1920, largely because a number of Senators insisted that any commitments of U.S. troops to a world body (the League of Nations) first had to be approved by Congress. On that issue, and others, President Wilson refused to yield.

President Wilson submitted the treaty to the Senate on July 10, 1919, attaching to it the Covenant of the League of Nations. The Covenant pro-

vided for an assembly (giving each member nation an equal voice) and a
council (consisting of representatives from the United States, Great Britain, France, Italy, Japan, and four other nations elected by the assembly).
Members pledged to submit to the League all disputes threatening war and
to use military and economic sanctions against nations that threatened
war. In an emotional address to the Senate, Wilson called the League of
Nations a "practical necessity" and "indeed indispensable." He said that
statesmen saw it as "the hope of the world. . . . Shall we or any other free
people hesitate to accept this great duty? Dare we reject it and break the
heart of the world?"[1]

Senator Henry Cabot Lodge (R-Mass.) favored U.S. participation in the
League but proposed a number of "reservations" to protect American interests. The second of fourteen reservations concerned the congressional
prerogative to decide questions of war:

> The United States assumes no obligation to preserve the territorial
> integrity or political independence of any other country or to inter-
> fere in controversies between nations—whether members of the
> league or not—under the provisions of article 10, or to employ the
> military or naval forces of the United States under any article of
> the treaty for any purpose, unless in any particular case the Congress,
> which, under the Constitution, has the sole power to declare war or
> authorize the employment of the military or naval forces of the
> United States, shall by act or joint resolution so provide.[2]

Wilson opposed the Lodge reservations, claiming that they "cut out the
heart of this Covenant" and represented "nullification" of the treaty.[3]
Wilson's theory of the treaty process was a simple one: the President pro-
poses, the Senate acquiesces. There was no room in his philosophy of
government for independent Senate thinking or the offering of legislative
amendments and reservations.

Wilson's attitude toward the Senate and presidential power had been revealed crisply in two books. In *Congressional Government* (1883), he advocated unilateral presidential negotiation with complete exclusion of the
Senate. These executive initiatives would supposedly get the country
"into such scrapes, so pledged in the view of the world to certain courses
of action, that the Senate hesitates to bring about the appearance of dis-

1. 17 Richardson 8735.
2. 58 Cong. Rec. 8777 (1919).
3. 63 The Papers of Woodrow Wilson 451 (Arthur S. Link ed. 1990); 64 The Papers of
Woodrow Wilson 47, 51 (Link ed. 1991).

honor which would follow its refusal to ratify the rash promises or to support the indiscreet threats of the Department of State."[4] In *Constitutional Government in the United States* (1908), he reiterated the same line of argument:

> One of the greatest of the President's powers I have not yet spoken of at all: his control, which is very absolute, of the foreign relations of the nation. The initiative in foreign affairs, which the President possesses without any restriction whatever, is virtually the power to control them absolutely. The President cannot conclude a treaty with a foreign power without the consent of the Senate, but he may guide every step of diplomacy, and to guide diplomacy is to determine what treaties must be made, if the faith and prestige of the government are to be maintained. He need disclose no step of negotiation until it is complete, and when in any critical matter it is completed the government is virtually committed. Whatever its disinclination, the Senate may feel itself committed also.[5]

This legislative strategy, fully articulated in Wilson's writings, failed abysmally with the Treaty of Versailles. After excluding the Senate from the negotiating sessions, he tried to present Senators with a fait accompli. The result: a resounding political defeat for Wilson. He had never cultivated sufficient support among Senators to have his handiwork approved, and the treaty was rejected in November 1919 and again in March 1920. Wilson appealed to the public in an exhausting campaign across the country, which led to his physical and emotional collapse. The dismal experience of a President "going it alone" would remain seared in the nation's memory, casting a shadow over future efforts to create the United Nations.

Creating the UN Charter

America's entry into a world organization was revived in 1943 through a series of methodical steps: the Ball Resolution, the Connally and Fulbright Resolutions, and the Moscow Declaration. Those actions were followed by meetings at Dumbarton Oaks in 1944 and in San Francisco in 1945. The issue of which branch takes the nation to war—Congress or the President—was ignored at some of these meetings and addressed at others.

4. Woodrow Wilson, Congressional Government 233–34 (1885).
5. Woodrow Wilson, Constitutional Government in the United States 77–78 (1908).

The predominant view required prior authorization by Congress (both Houses) of any commitment of U.S. forces to the United Nations.

On March 16, 1943, Senator Joseph Hurst Ball (R-Minn.) introduced a resolution calling for the formation of the United Nations. Joined by Senators Lister Hill (D-Ala.), Harold Burton (R-Ohio), and Carl Hatch (D-N.Mex.), the bipartisan nature of the resolution commanded respectful attention. Senator Ball said that the "whole world, and our allies, know today that it is the United States Senate which will finally decide what will be the foreign policy of our country when the war ends." He noted that the Senate's constitutional power in the past had been used "negatively," reminding listeners of the rejection of the Treaty of Versailles. Senator Ball hoped that the decision on the United Nations would not become embroiled in partisan politics.[6] Senate debate on the Ball Resolution said nothing about which branch of government would commit U.S. troops.

On the day that Ball introduced his resolution, Walter Lippmann wrote an article on the Senate's role in giving advice and consent to treaties. Lippmann had long been identified as a defender of foreign policy formulated by elites and executive officials. In an article published in the *Washington Post*, he now urged that President Wilson's mistake with the Treaty of Versailles not be repeated. Ways and means had to be found of "enabling the Senate to participate in the negotiations."[7]

On September 20, the House debated a resolution introduced by J. William Fulbright (D-Ark.) to support the concept of a United Nations. The language was exceedingly brief: "*Resolved by the House of Representatives (the Senate concurring), That the Congress hereby expresses itself as favoring the creation of appropriate international machinery with power adequate to establish and to maintain a just and lasting peace, among the nations of the world, and as favoring participation by the United States therein.*"[8] Congressman Hamilton Fish, Jr. (R-N.Y.) proposed that Fulbright's resolution end with the language "favoring participation by the United States therein *through its constitutional processes.*"[9] Fish explained that the additional language meant that any commitment to join the United Nations, made either by agreement or by treaty, "must go through in a constitutional way, either by a two-thirds vote of the Senate or by the approval of the entire Congress."[10] He warned that a number of members of Congress were prepared to oppose the Fulbright Resolution

6. 89 Cong. Rec. 2031 (1943).
7. Id. at 2032.
8. Id. at 7623.
9. Id. at 7646–47; (emphasis added).
10. Id. at 7647.

because they "are afraid that some secret commitments will be entered into and that the Congress will be by-passed, and that the Constitution will be ignored."[11]

The House passed the Fulbright Resolution, as introduced, 252 to 23.[12] The following day it voted again, after adding the language "through its constitutional processes," and this time the margin was 360 to 29.[13] The House action sharply challenged the Senate's presumed monopoly to define foreign policy for the legislative branch. The debate pointed out that both Houses had acted on the declaration of war for World War II, voted funds to sustain it, and conscripted American soldiers to fight the battles.[14] Recalling the Senate's role in rejecting the Treaty of Versailles, Congressman Mike Monroney (D-Okla.) said he was "unwilling to surrender to 33 Members of the Senate, one-third of that body, the life or death veto over the security of future generations of Americans."[15]

The Senate ignored the Fulbright Resolution, which had been introduced as a concurrent resolution (H. Con. Res. 25) and therefore needed concurrence by the Senate. Instead, the Senate considered a resolution (S. Res. 192) that required only its own action. Debate on this resolution, the Connally Resolution, stretched from October 25 through November 5. Similar to the House resolution, it included the phrase "through its constitutional processes" to prevent the President from joining the United Nations without explicit congressional support.[16] Congressional processes meant the "powers of Congress"—*both* Houses, not just the Senate.[17] A few Senators thought of congressional action solely through the treaty process, excluding the House,[18] but the majority recognized that international commitments (in this case joining the United Nations) could be made either by treaty or by a majority of each House voting on a bill or joint resolution.[19]

The final version of the Connally Resolution, approved 85 to 5, provides that the United States, "acting through its constitutional processes," joins in the establishment of an international authority with power to prevent aggression. The final paragraph states that any treaty made to effect

11. Id.
12. Id. at 7655.
13. Id. at 7728–29.
14. Id. at 7705 (Congressman Richards).
15. Id. at 7706.
16. Id. at 9187 (Senator Willis, first column).
17. Id. at 8662 (reading by the legislative clerk).
18. Id. at 9187 (Senator Willis, first column); id. at 9189 (Senator Brooks); id. at 9205 (Senator Wherry).
19. Id. at 9207 (Senator Hayden).

the purposes of the resolution shall be made only with the concurrence of two-thirds of the Senate.[20] Senator Robert Taft (R-Ohio) said that the requirement for Senate action was added because of the fear that the President "has shown some indications of a desire to do by executive agreement things which certainly in my opinion ought to be the subject of a treaty."[21]

Little was said during this lengthy Senate debate about congressional controls over the use of American troops in a UN action. Senator Claude Pepper (D-Fla.) opposed any delegation of Congress's war-declaring power to an international body but believed that it would be permissible for American troops to be used, without prior congressional approval, as a "police force" to combat aggression in small wars.[22] The loose notion of a "police action" would be later used by President Truman as a legal pretext for going to war in Korea without congressional approval. Truman was a member of the Senate at the time Pepper made that remark.

Senate action on the Connally Resolution occurred during a four-nation conference that endorsed an international peacekeeping organization. On October 30, 1943, the United States, the United Kingdom, the Soviet Union, and China issued the Moscow Declaration, which set forth a number of guiding principles. The declaration recognized "the necessity of establishing at the earliest practicable date a general international organization . . . for the maintenance of international peace and security."

Those same nations met a year later at Dumbarton Oaks, in Washington, D.C., to give further definition to the international organization. Legal specialists who monitored these meetings speculated on the procedures for going to war. Edwin Borchard later surmised: "Constitutionally, the plan seems to assume that the President, or his delegate, without consulting Congress, the war-making and declaring authority, can vote for the use of the American quota of armed forces, if that can be limited when the 'aggressor' resists."[23] Two weeks after the end of the conference at Dumbarton Oaks, President Roosevelt delivered an address in which he indicated the need for advance congressional approval:

> The Council of the United Nations must have the power to act quickly and decisively to keep the peace by force, if necessary. A policeman would not be a very effective policeman if, when he saw a

20. Id. at 9222.
21. Id. at 9101.
22. Id. at 8742–43.
23. Edwin Borchard, "The Dumbarton Oaks Conference," 39 Am. J. Int'l L. 97, 101 (1945).

felon break into a house, he had to go to the town hall and call a town meeting to issue a warrant before the felon could be arrested.

It is clear that, if the world organization is to have any reality at all, our representatives must be endowed in advance by the people themselves, by constitutional means through their representatives in the Congress, with authority to act.[24]

But Borchard learned that after Roosevelt's death, President Truman sent a cable from Potsdam stating that all agreements involving U.S. troop commitments to the United Nations would first have to be approved by both Houses of Congress.[25] Borchard, too, believed that the Constitution required approval by both Houses, not merely the Senate,[26] but another perspective appeared in a letter to the *New York Times*. Six specialists of international law analyzed the President's authority to contribute troops to the United Nations. They recognized the risks for congressional prerogatives: "It is doubtless true that Congress will feel a certain hesitancy in permitting the President, acting through the Security Council, to engage even a small policing force in international action because it will fear that this might commit the United States to further military action and thus might impair the discretion of Congress in respect to engagement in 'war.' " Yet they suggested that Presidents in the past had had broad discretion in the use of military force and had frequently acted without explicit congressional authority. The American constitutional system, they said, relied heavily on good-faith actions and sensitive political judgment by the President: "Congress has always been dependent upon the good faith of the President in calling upon it when the situation was so serious that a large-scale use of force may be necessary."[27]

The meetings at Dumbarton Oaks were followed by a conference in San Francisco in 1945, attended by fifty nations and lasting nine weeks. Unlike Wilson's futile strategy for the Versailles Treaty, half of the eight members of the U.S. delegation came from Congress: Senators Tom Connally (D-Tex.) and Arthur H. Vandenberg (R-Mich.) and Representatives Sol Bloom (D-N.Y.) and Charles A. Eaton (R-N.J.).[28] John Foster Dulles, later to

24. 11 Dep't of State Bull. 447, 448 (1945).

25. Edwin Borchard, "The Charter and the Constitution," 39 Am. J. Int'l L. 767, 767–68 (1945).

26. Id. at 770–71.

27. New York Times, November 5, 1944, 8E. Signers of the letter: John W. Davis, W. W. Grant, Philip C. Jessup, George Rublee, James T. Shotwell, and Quincy Wright.

28. "The Charter of the United Nations," hearings before the Senate Committee on Foreign Relations, 79th Cong., 1st Sess. 197 (1945).

be Secretary of State under President Eisenhower, told the Senate Foreign Relations Committee in 1945 that in the past he had had "some doubts as to the wisdom of Senators participating in the negotiation of treaties." After his experience at the San Francisco conference, he said, those doubts "were dispelled."[29]

Out of the San Francisco conference came the United Nations Charter, which was submitted to the Senate for approval. The United Nations consisted of a General Assembly representing all member states, an eleven-member Security Council (including China, France, the Soviet Union, the United Kingdom, and the United States as permanent members), a Secretariat, an International Court of Justice, and specialized councils. Chapter VII of the Charter dealt with UN responses to threats to peace, breaches of the peace, and acts of aggression. Procedures were established to permit the United Nations to employ military force to deal with such threats. All UN members would make available to the Security Council, "on its call and in accordance with a special agreement or agreements," armed forces and other assistance for the purpose of maintaining international peace and security. The agreements were to be concluded between the Security Council and member states and "shall be subject to ratification by the signatory states in accordance with their respective constitutional processes." Thus, the decision of who would grant that approval in the United States—Congress, the President, or the two branches acting jointly—was deliberately deferred. Each nation would determine its own "constitutional processes."

From July 9 to July 13, 1945, the Senate Foreign Relations Committee held hearings on the Charter. Leo Pasvolsky, a special assistant to the Secretary of State, was asked whether Congress would have ultimate control over the special agreements to use armed force. Pasvolsky replied: "That is a domestic question which I am afraid I cannot answer."[30] Senator Vandenberg volunteered that, in his opinion, the President would not need "the consent of Congress to every use of our armed forces."[31]

John Foster Dulles, an adviser to the U.S. delegation at San Francisco, testified that the procedure for special agreements would need the approval of the Senate and could not be done unilaterally by the President.[32] Dulles elaborated: "It is clearly my view, and it was the view of the entire United States delegation, that the agreement which will provide for the

29. Id. at 644.
30. "The Charter of the United Nations," hearings before the Senate Committee on Foreign Relations, 79th Cong., 1st Sess. 298 (1945).
31. Id. at 299.
32. Id. at 645–46.

United States military contingent will have to be negotiated and then submitted to the Senate for ratification in the same way as a treaty." Senator
Connally agreed with that interpretation.[33] When Senator Walter F.
George (D-Ga.) suggested that congressional approval could be by statute,
involving both Houses, Dulles disagreed: "The procedure will be by
treaty—agreements submitted to the Senate for ratification."[34] Senator
Eugene Millikin (R-Colo.) tried to distinguish between "policing powers"
(to be exercised exclusively by the President) and "real war problems"
(reserved for congressional action).[35] Dulles replied sympathetically: "If
we are talking about a little bit of force necessary to be used as a police
demonstration, that is the sort of thing that the President of the United
States has done without concurrence by Congress since this Nation was
founded."[36]

During floor debate, Senator Scott Lucas (D-Ill.) took sharp exception to
Dulles's contention that special agreements would come back to Congress
as treaties to be disposed of solely by the Senate. Such agreements, Lucas
said, required action by both Houses, and he cited constitutional passages
giving to the entire Congress powers to raise and support armies and to
make rules for the government and regulation of the land and naval
forces.[37] Action by both Houses is required to declare war and to appropriate funds for the military. A number of Senators agreed with Lucas in rejecting the proposition advanced by Dulles.[38]

As the debate continued Senator Vandenberg reached Dulles by phone
to clarify his position. Dulles explained that when the issue came up in
the hearings, he thought the question was between unilateral action by
the President (through executive agreements) or retaining congressional
control (which Dulles took to mean action on treaties). The central point
he wanted to make, Dulles said, was that "the use of force cannot be made
by exclusive Presidential authority through an executive agreement." He
was positive about that. On the other issue—whether Congress should
act by treaty or by joint resolution—he was less certain.[39]

At other points during the debate Senator Harlan Bushfield (R-S.Dak.)
said he had objected, "and I still object, to a delegation of power to one

33. Id. at 646.
34. Id. at 652.
35. Id. at 654.
36. Id. at 655.
37. 91 Cong. Rec. 8021 (1945).
38. Id. at 8021–24 (Senators McClellan, Hatch, Fulbright, Maybank, Overton, HIll, Ellen-
der, and George).
39. Id. at 8027–28.

man or to the Security Council, composed of 10 foreigners and 1 American, to declare war and to take American boys into war." Such a proposal "is in direct violation of the Constitution." Congress did not have the power, Bushfield said, "to make such a delegation even if we desired to do so."[40] Senator Burton Wheeler (D-Mont.) was also emphatic on that point: "If it is to be contended that if we enter into this treaty we take the power away from the Congress, and the President can send troops all over the world to fight battles anywhere, if it is to be said that that is to be the policy of this country, I say that the American people will never support any Senator or any Representative who advocates such a policy; and make no mistake about it."[41]

President Truman, aware of the Senate debate on which branch controlled the sending of armed forces to the United Nations, wired a note from Potsdam to Senator Kenneth McKellar on July 27, 1945, in which he pledged: "When any such agreement or agreements are negotiated it will be my purpose to ask the Congress for appropriate legislation to approve them."[42] In asking "Congress" for legislation, Senators understood that Congress "consists not alone of the Senate but of the two Houses."[43] With that understanding, the Senate granted its approval of the UN Charter by a vote of 89 to 2.[44]

Having approved the Charter, Congress now had to pass additional legislation to implement it and to determine the precise mechanisms for the use of force. The specific procedures, brought into conformity with "constitutional processes," are included in the UN Participation Act of 1945.

The UN Participation Act

Nothing in the passage of the Fulbright and Connally Resolutions or the history of the UN Charter supports the notion that Congress, by endorsing the structure of the United Nations as an international peacekeeping body, altered the Constitution by reading itself out of the war-making power. Congress did not—it could not—do that, a conclusion driven home sharply by the legislative history of the UN Participation Act.

Under the provisions of the UN Charter, in the event of any threat to the

40. Id. at 7156.
41. Id. at 7988.
42. Id. at 8185.
43. Id. (Senator Donnell).
44. Id. at 8190.

peace, breach of the peace, or act of aggression, the UN Security Council
may decide under Article 41 of the UN Charter to recommend "measures
not involving the use of armed force." If those measures prove inadequate, Article 43 provides that all UN members shall make available to the
Security Council—in accordance with special agreements—armed forces
and other assistance. These agreements would spell out the numbers and
types of forces, their degree of readiness and general location, and the nature of the facilities and assistance to be provided. It was anticipated that
each nation would ratify these agreements "in accordance with their respective constitutional processes."

The meaning of U.S. constitutional processes is defined by Section 6 of
the UN Participation Act of 1945. Without the slightest ambiguity, this
statute requires that the agreements "shall be subject to the approval of
the Congress by appropriate Act or joint resolution." Statutory language
could not be more clear. The President must seek congressional approval
in advance. Two qualifications are included in Section 6:

> The President shall not be deemed to require the authorization of the
> Congress to make available to the Security Council on its call in order
> to take action under Article 42 of said Charter and pursuant to such
> special agreement or agreements the armed forces, facilities, or assis-
> tance provided therein: *Provided*, That nothing herein contained
> shall be construed as an authorization to the President by the Con-
> gress to make available to the Security Council for such purpose
> armed forces, facilities, or assistance in addition to the forces, facili-
> ties, and assistance provided for in such special agreements or agree-
> ments.[45]

The first qualification states that once the President receives the approval
of Congress for a special agreement, he does not need subsequent approval from Congress to provide military assistance under Article 42 (under which the Security Council determines that peaceful means are inadequate and military action is necessary). Congressional approval is needed
for the special agreement, not subsequent implementations of that agreement. The second qualification clarifies that nothing in the UN Participation Act is to be construed as congressional approval of other agreements
attempted by the President.

Thus, the qualifications do not eliminate or weaken the need for congressional approval. Presidents could commit armed forces to the United

45. 59 Stat. 621, sec. 6 (1945).

Nations only after Congress gave its explicit consent. That point is crucial. The League of Nations Covenant foundered precisely on the issue of needing congressional approval before using armed force. The framers of the UN Charter knew of that history and very consciously included protections for congressional prerogatives.[46]

The legislative history of the UN Participation Act reinforces the need for advance congressional approval. In his appearance before the House Committee on Foreign Affairs, Under Secretary of State Dean Acheson explained that only after the President receives the approval of Congress is he "bound to furnish that contingent of troops to the Security Council; and the President is not authorized to furnish any more than you have approved of in that agreement."[47] When Congresswoman Edith Rogers (R-Mass.) remarked that Congress "can easily control the [Security] Council," Acheson agreed unequivocally: "It is entirely within the wisdom of Congress to approve or disapprove whatever special agreement the President negotiates."[48] Congressman John Kee (D-W.Va.) wondered whether the qualifications in Section 6 of the UN Participation Act permitted the President to provide military assistance to the Security Council without consulting or submitting the matter to Congress. Acheson firmly rejected that possibility. No special agreement, Acheson said, could have any "force or effect" until Congress approved it:

> This is an important question of Judge Kee, and may I state his question and my answer so that it will be quite clear here: The judge asks whether the language beginning on line 19 of page 5, which says the President shall not be deemed to require the authorization of Congress to make available to the Security Council on its call in order to take action under article 42 of the Charter, means that the President may provide these forces prior to the time when any special agreement has been approved by Congress.
>
> The answer to that question is "No," that the President may not do that, that such special agreements refer to the special agreement which shall be subject to the approval of the Congress, so that until the special agreement has been negotiated and approved by the Congress, it has no force and effect.[49]

46. Michael J. Glennon, "The Constitution and Chapter VII of the United States Charter," 85 Am. J. Int'l L. 74, 75–77 (1991).

47. "Participation by the United States in the United Nations Organization," hearings before the House Committee on Foreign Affairs, 79th Cong., 1st Sess. 23 (1945).

48. Id.

49. Id. at 25–26.

Other parts of the legislative history support this understanding. In reporting the UN Participation Act, the Senate Foreign Relations Committee anticipated a shared, coequal relationship between the President and Congress:

> Although the ratification of the Charter resulted in the vesting in the executive branch of the power and obligation to fulfill the commitments assumed by the United States thereunder, the Congress must be taken into close partnership and must be fully advised of all phases of our participation in this enterprise. The Congress will be asked annually to appropriate funds to support the United Nations budget and for the expenses of our representation. It will be called upon to approve arrangements for the supply of armed forces to the Security Council and thereafter to make appropriations for the maintenance of such forces.[50]

The Senate Foreign Relations Committee further noted that "all were agreed on the basic proposition that the military agreements could not be entered into solely by executive action."[51] Nevertheless, during floor debate, Senators Connally and Taft agreed that in "certain emergencies" the President and the Security Council might be able to act without first obtaining authority from Congress.[52] These comments are interesting, but they do not change the statutory requirement that special agreements be approved in advance by "appropriate Act or joint resolution." Moreover, Connally and Taft seemed to be laboring under concepts left over from the San Francisco conference and the Senate debate over the UN Charter. They were endorsing the President's ability to become engaged in "police actions" without any congressional involvement.

Connally's confusion is evident a few pages later where he agrees with Senator Kenneth Wherry (R-Neb.) that special agreements could be made by treaty.[53] That misinterpretation, originally pushed by John Foster Dulles and others, was explicitly corrected by the language in Section 6 of the UN Participation Act. Later, an amendment was offered in the Senate to authorize the President to negotiate a special agreement with the Security Council solely with the support of two-thirds of the Senate.[54] Senator Vandenberg opposed the amendment on these grounds:

50. S. Rept. No. 717, 79th Cong., 1st Sess. 5 (1945).
51. Id. at 8.
52. 91 Cong. Rec. 10965–66 (1945).
53. Id. at 10974.
54. Id. at 11296.

If we go to war, a majority of the House and Senate puts us into war. . . . The House has equal responsibility with the Senate in respect of raising armies and supporting and sustaining them. The House has primary jurisdiction over the taxation necessities involved in supporting and sustaining armies and navies, and in maintaining national defense.

. . . [The Senate Foreign Relations Committee] chose to place the ratification of that contract in the hands of both Houses of Congress, inasmuch as the total Congress of the United States must deal with all the consequences which are involved either if we have a war or if we succeeded in preventing one.[55]

Vandenberg's reasoning prevailed. The great majority of Senators, recognizing that the decision to go to war must be made by both Houses of Congress, defeated the amendment decisively, 57 to 14.[56]

The House of Representatives also designed the UN Participation Act to protect congressional prerogatives over war and peace. In reporting the bill, the House Foreign Affairs Committee drew attention to the vote in the Senate rejecting the idea that special agreements could be handled solely by the Senate through the treaty process. The committee "believes that it is eminently appropriate that the Congress as a whole pass upon these agreements under the constitutional powers of the Congress."[57] During floor debate, Congressman Sol Bloom (D-N.Y.), one of the delegates at the San Francisco conference, underscored that point: "The position of the Congress is fully protected by the requirement that the military agreement to preserve the peace must be passed upon by Congress before it becomes effective. Also, the obligation of the United States to make forces available to the Security Council does not become effective until the special agreement has been passed upon by Congress."[58]

The restrictions on the President's power under Section 6 to use armed force were clarified by amendments adopted in 1949, allowing the President on his own initiative to provide military forces to the United Nations for "cooperative action." However, presidential discretion to deploy these forces is subject to stringent conditions: they can serve only as observers and guards, can perform only in a noncombatant capacity, and cannot exceed 1,000 in number.[59] Moreover, in providing these troops to

55. Id. at 11301.
56. Id. at 11303.
57. H. Rept. No. 1383, 79th Cong., 1st Sess. 7 (1945).
58. 91 Cong. Rec. 12267 (1945).
59. 63 Stat. 735–36, sec. 5 (1949).

the United Nations the President shall assure that they not involve "the employment of armed forces contemplated by chapter VII of the United Nations Charter."[60] Clearly, there is no opportunity in the UN Participation Act or its amendments for unilateral military action by the President.

The Korean War

With these safeguards supposedly in place to protect congressional prerogatives, on June 26, 1950, President Truman announced to the American public that he had conferred with the Secretaries of State and Defense, their senior advisers, and the Joint Chiefs of Staff "about the situation in the Far East created by unprovoked aggression against the Republic of Korea."[61] He said that the UN Security Council had acted to order a withdrawal of the invading forces to positions north of the 38th parallel and that "in accordance with the resolution of the Security Council, the United States will vigorously support the effort of the Council to terminate this serious breach of the peace."[62] At that point, he made no commitment of U.S. military forces.

On the next day, however, President Truman announced that North Korea had failed to cease hostilities and to withdraw to the 38th parallel. He summarized the UN action in this manner: "The Security Council called upon all members of the United Nations to render every assistance to the United Nations in the execution of this resolution. In these circumstances I have ordered United States air and sea forces to give the [South] Korean Government troops cover and support."[63]

In addition, Truman said that "the occupation of Formosa by Communist forces would be a direct threat to the security of the Pacific area and to United States forces performing their lawful and necessary functions in that area."[64] Finally, he advised that all members of the United Nations "will consider carefully" the consequences of Korea's aggression "in defiance of the Charter of the United Nations" and that a "return to the rule of force in international affairs" would have far-reaching effects. The United States, he said, "will continue to uphold the rule of law."[65]

In fact, Truman violated the unambiguous statutory language and legis-

60. Id.
61. Public Papers of the Presidents, 1950, 491.
62. Id.
63. Id. at 492.
64. Id.
65. Id.

lative history of the UN Participation Act. How could he pretend to act militarily in Korea under the UN umbrella without any congressional approval? The short answer is that he ignored the special agreements that were the vehicle for assuring congressional approval in advance of any military action by the President. With the Soviet Union absent, the Security Council voted 9 to 0 to call upon North Korea to cease hostilities and to withdraw their forces. Two days later the Council requested military assistance from UN members to repel the attack, but by that time Truman had already ordered U.S. air and sea forces to assist South Korea.

Truman's legal authority was nonexistent for two reasons. First, it cannot be argued that the President's constitutional powers vary with the presence or absence of Soviet delegates to the Security Council. As Robert Bork noted in 1971, "the approval of the United Nations was obtained only because the Soviet Union happened to be boycotting the Security Council at the time, and the President's Constitutional powers can hardly be said to ebb and flow with the veto of the Soviet Union in the Security Council."[66]

Second, the Truman administration did not act pursuant to UN authority, even though it strained to make that case. On June 29, 1950, Secretary of State Acheson claimed that all U.S. actions taken in Korea "have been under the aegis of the United Nations."[67] Aegis is a fudge word, meaning shield or protection. Acheson was using the word to suggest that the United States was acting under the legal banner of the United Nations, which of course was not the case.

Acheson falsely claimed that Truman had done his "utmost to uphold the sanctity of the Charter of the United Nations and the rule of law," and that the administration was in "conformity with the resolutions of the Security Council of June 25 and 27, giving air and sea support to the troops of the Korean government."[68] Yet Truman committed U.S. forces before the Council called for military action. General Douglas MacArthur was immediately authorized to send supplies of ammunition to the South Korean defenders. On June 26, Truman ordered U.S. air and sea forces to give South Koreans cover and support.[69] After Acheson had summarized the military situation for some members of Congress at noon on June 27, President Truman exclaimed: "But Dean, you didn't even mention the

66. Robert H. Bork, "Comments on the Articles on the Legality of the United States Action in Cambodia," 65 Am. J. Int'l L. 79, 81 (1971).

67. 23 Dep't of State Bull. 43 (1950).

68. Id. at 46.

69. Public Papers of the Presidents, 1950, 529.

U.N.!"[70] Later that evening the Security Council passed the second resolution. In his memoirs, Acheson admitted that "some American action, said to be in support of the resolution of June 27, was in fact ordered, and possibly taken, prior to the resolution."[71] After he left the presidency, Truman was asked whether he had been prepared to use military force in Korea without UN backing. He replied, with customary bluntness: "No question about it."[72]

President Truman did not seek the approval of members of Congress for his military actions in Korea. As Acheson suggested, Truman might only wish to "tell them what had been decided."[73] Truman met with congressional leaders at 11:30 A.M. on June 27, after the administration's policy had been established and implementing orders issued.[74] He later met with congressional leaders to give them briefings on developments in Korea, but never asked for authority.[75] Some consideration was given to presenting a joint resolution to Congress to permit legislators to voice their approval, but the draft resolution never left the administration.[76]

On June 29, at a news conference, Truman was asked whether the country was at war. His response: "We are not at war."[77] Asked whether it would be more correct to call the conflict "a police action under the United Nations," he agreed: "That is exactly what it amounts to."[78] The United Nations exercised no real authority over the conduct of the war. Other than token support from a few nations, it was an American war. The Security Council requested that the United States designate the commander of the forces and authorized the "unified command at its discretion to use the United Nations flag."[79] Truman designated General MacArthur to serve as commander of this so-called unified command.[80] Measured by troops, money, casualties, and deaths, it remained an American war.

70. Glenn D. Paige, The Korean Decision 188 (1968).

71. Dean Acheson, Present at the Creation 408 (1969). See also Edwin C. Hoyt, "The United States Reaction to the Korean Attack: A Study of the Principles of the United Nations Charter as a Factor in American Policy-Making," 55 Am. J. Int'l L. 45, 53 (1961).

72. Merle Miller, Plain Speaking: An Oral Biography of Harry S. Truman 276n (1973).

73. FRUS, 1950. vol. 7, 182 (1976).

74. Id., 200–202.

75. Id., 257.

76. Id., 282–83, notes 1 and 2; 287–91.

77. Public Papers of the Presidents, 1951, 503.

78. Id. at 504. On July 13, at a news conference, he again called the Korean War a "police action." Id. at 522.

79. Id., at 520.

80. Id.

Federal courts had no difficulty in defining the hostilities in Korea as war. A federal district court noted in 1953: "We doubt very much if there is any question in the minds of the majority of the people of this country that the conflict now raging in Korea can be anything but war."[81] During Senate hearings in June 1951, Secretary of State Acheson conceded the obvious by admitting "in the usual sense of the word there is a war."[82]

Truman's violation of constitutional and statutory requirements may have resulted from a mistaken reading of history. In deciding whether North Korean aggression could go unanswered, he looked, in his own lifetime, to Japan's invasion of Manchuria and Germany's reoccupation of the Rhineland. He did not consider other historical parallels where force had been used, such as the American Civil War or nineteenth-century efforts in Germany for unification. Apparently it did not occur to him that the situation in Korea resembled the latter more than it did Manchuria and the Rhineland.[83]

Even if a case could be made that the emergency facing Truman in June 1950 required him to act promptly without first seeking and obtaining legislative authority, nothing prevented him from returning to Congress and asking for a supporting statute or retroactive authority. John Norton Moore has made this point: "As to the suddenness of Korea, and conflicts like Korea, I would argue that the President should have the authority to meet the attack as necessary but should immediately seek congressional authorization."[84] I would put it a little differently: In a genuine emergency, a President may act without congressional authority (and without express legal or constitutional authority), trusting that the circumstances are so urgent and compelling that Congress will endorse his actions and confer a legitimacy that only Congress, as the people's representatives, can provide.

Political Repercussions

Congress's reaction to Truman's usurpation of the war power was largely passive. Some members offered the weak justification that "history will

81. Weissman v. Metropolitan Life Ins. Co., 112 F.Supp. 420, 425 (S.D. Cal. 1953). See also Gagliormella v. Metropolitan Life Ins. Co., 122 F.Supp. 246 (D. Mass. 1954); Carius v. New York Life Insurance Co., 124 F.Supp. 388 (D. Ill. 1954); and A. Kenneth Pye, "The Legal Status of the Korean Hostilities," 45 Geo. L. J. 45 (1956).

82. "Military Situation in the Far East" (part 3), hearings before the Senate Committees on Armed Services and Foreign Relations, 82d Cong., 1st Sess. 2014 (1951).

83. Richard S. Kirkendall, Harry S Truman and the Imperial Presidency 11, 16 (1975).

84. John N. Moore, "The National Executive and the Use of the Armed Forces Abroad," 21 Naval War College Rev. 28, 32 (1969).

show that on more than 100 occasions in the life of this Republic the President as Commander in Chief has ordered the fleet or the troops to do certain things which involved the risk of war" without seeking congressional consent."[85] This list of alleged precedents for unilateral presidential action contains not a single military adventure that even comes close to the magnitude of the Korean War. As Edward S. Corwin noted, the list consists largely of "fights with pirates, landings of small naval contingents on barbarous or semi-barbarous coasts, the dispatch of small bodies of troops to chase bandits or cattle rustlers across the Mexican border, and the like."[86]

A few legislators insisted that Truman should have gone to Congress for authority first.[87] Congressman Vito Marcantonio (ALP-N.Y.) delivered this indictment: "When we agreed to the United Nations Charter we never agreed to supplant our Constitution with the United Nations Charter. The power to declare and make war is vested in the representatives of the people, in the Congress of the United States."[88] Senator Taft warned that if the President could intervene in Korea "without congressional approval, he can go to war in Malaya or Indonesia or Iran or South America." Taft conceded that U.S. entry into the United Nations created a new framework, "but I do not think it justifies the President's present action without approval by Congress." Taft referred to Section 6 of the UN Participation Act, noting that no special agreement had ever been negotiated by the Truman administration and submitted to Congress for its approval.[89]

Almost a year after the war began, a number of Senators participated in a lengthy debate that thoroughly shredded the administration's legal pretenses. Truman's commitment of troops to Korea violated the UN Charter, the UN Participation Act, and repeated assurances given to Congress by Acheson and other executive officials. Truman used military force before the second Security Council resolution. It was a war, not a police action, and it was an American, not a UN, operation. On all those points the record is abundantly clear.[90]

Just as the Vietnam War spelled defeat for the Democrats in 1968, so did the Korean War help put an end to twenty years of Democratic control of the White House. "Korea, not crooks or Communists, was the ma-

85. 96 Cong. Rec. 9229 (1950). Statement of Senator Scott Lucas (D-Ill.).
86. Edward S. Corwin, "The President's Power," New Republic, January 29, 1951, at 16.
87. 96 Cong. Rec. 9233 (1950). Statement of Senator Arthur V. Watkins (R-Utah). See also Arthur V. Watkins, "War by Executive Order," 4 West. Pol. Q. 539 (1951).
88. 96 Cong. Rec. 9268 (1951). Marcantonio was a member of the American Labor Party.
89. Id. at 9323.
90. 97 Cong. Rec. 5078–5103 (1951).

jor concern of the voters," writes Stephen Ambrose.[91] The high point of
the 1952 campaign came on October 24, less than two weeks before the
election, when Dwight D. Eisenhower announced that he would "go to
Korea" to end the war.[92] Two authors of a study on Eisenhower described
the crucial influence of the Korean War: "Dissatisfaction with the war destroyed Truman's popularity and had much to do with Eisenhower's emphatic victory in the election of 1952."[93]

Some leading academics rushed to Truman's support but failed to give
proper attention to constitutional principles. Henry Steele Commager, a
prominent historian, was one. Writing for the *New York Times* on January
14, 1951, Commager remarked that the objections to Truman's unilateral
actions "have no support in law or in history."[94] His own research into law
and history, on this point, was superficial and misinformed. Consider this
reasoning by Commager:

> . . . it is an elementary fact that must never be lost sight of that trea-
> ties are laws and carry with them the same obligation as laws. When
> the Congress passed the United Nations Participation Act it made the
> obligations of the Charter of the United Nations law, binding on the
> President. When the Senate ratified the North Atlantic Treaty it made
> the obligations of that treaty law, binding on the President.
>
> Both of these famous documents require action by the United
> States which must, in the nature of the case, be left to a large extent to
> the discretion of the Executive.[95]

Commager not only overstated the President's power under mutual defense treaties but ignored the statutory text and legislative history of the
UN Participation Act.

Arthur S. Schlesinger, Jr., was also an early defender of Truman's action
in Korea. In a letter to the *New York Times* on January 9, 1951, he disputed the statement by Senator Robert Taft that President Truman "had
no authority whatever to commit American troops to Korea without consulting Congress and without Congressional approval" and that by sending troops to Korea he "simply usurped authority, in violation of the laws

91. 1 Stephen E. Ambrose, Eisenhower: Soldier, General of the Army, President-Elect 569
(1983).

92. Id.

93. Chester J. Pach, Jr., and Elmo Richardson, The Presidency of Dwight D. Eisenhower
46 (1991).

94. Henry Steele Commager, "Presidential Power: The Issue Analyzed," New York
Times, January 14, 1951, p. 11.

95. Id. at 24

and the Constitution." Schlesinger said that Taft's statements "are demonstrably irresponsible." Harking back to Jefferson's use of ships to repel the Barbary pirates, Schlesinger claimed that American Presidents "have repeatedly committed American armed forces abroad without prior Congressional consultation or approval."[96]

Schlesinger neglected to point out that Jefferson told Congress he was "unauthorized by the Constitution, without the sanction of Congress, to go beyond the line of defense." It was the prerogative of Congress to authorize "measures of offense also."[97] Congress enacted ten statutes authorizing action by Presidents Jefferson and Madison in the Barbary wars. Schlesinger did not cite, nor could he, a similar presidential initiative of the magnitude of the Korean War. Years later he expressed regret that in calling Taft's statement "demonstrably irresponsible," he had responded with "a flourish of historical documentation and, alas, hyperbole."[98]

Edward S. Corwin took Commager and Schlesinger to task by labeling them the "high-flying prerogative men."[99] However, Corwin himself had been careless in earlier publications in describing the scope of presidential war power. Writing in 1949, he said that the original grant of authority to the President to "repel sudden attacks" had developed into an "undefined power—almost unchallenged from the first and occasionally sanctified judicially—to employ without Congressional authorization the armed forces in the protection of American rights and interests abroad whenever necessary."[100] He did note the significance of the UN Participation Act, which he said was based on the theory that American participation in the United Nations "is a matter for Congressional collaboration."[101]

In the late 1960s, with the nation mired in a bitter war in Vietnam, Commager and Schlesinger both publicly apologized for their earlier unreserved endorsements of presidential war power. By 1966 Schlesinger was counseling that "something must be done to assure the Congress a more authoritative and continuing voice in fundamental decisions in foreign policy."[102] In 1973 he stated that the "idea of prerogative was *not* part

---

96. Arthur Schlesinger, Jr., "Presidential Powers: Taft Statement on Troops Opposed, Actions of Past Presidents Cited," New York Times, January 9, 1951, at 28.

97. 1 Richardson 315.

98. Arthur M. Schlesinger, Jr., The Imperial Presidency 139 (1973).

99. Edward S. Corwin, "The President's Power," New Republic, January 29, 1951, at 15.

100. Edward S. Corwin, "Who Has the Power to Make War?," New York Times Magazine, July 31, 1949, at 14.

101. Id.

102. Arthur M. Schlesinger, Jr., and Alfred de Grazia, Congress and the Presidency 27–28 (1967).

of presidential powers as defined by the Constitution," although it "remained in the back of [the framers'] mind."[103] Commager told the Senate in 1967 that there should be a reconsideration of executive-legislative relations in the conduct of foreign relations,[104] and while testifying in 1971 he appealed for stronger legislative checks on presidential war powers.[105]

103. Schlesinger, The Imperial Presidency, at 9; (emphasis in original).
104. "Changing American Attitudes towards Foreign Policy," hearings before the Senate Committee on Foreign Relations, 90th Cong., 1st Sess. 21 (1967).
105. "War Powers Legislation," hearings before the Senate Committee on Foreign Relations, 92d Cong., 1st Sess. 7–74 (1971).

5

TAKING STOCK: 1951–1964

President Truman's commitment of U.S. troops to Korea in 1950 produced an initial trauma to executive-legislative relations, and an aftershock hit a year later when he announced the dispatch of U.S. forces to Europe without seeking congressional approval. Led by Senator Taft, the Senate spent three months in a "Great Debate" that focused on the role of Congress in curbing presidential war power. Part of the Senate's concern dealt with inflated executive interpretations of the President's power to send troops abroad pursuant to the North Atlantic Treaty (NATO) and other mutual security treaties.

In 1952, in the Steel Seizure Case, the Supreme Court held that Truman had acted without constitutional or statutory authority when he seized the nations's steel mills, which he had justified under his commander-in-chief powers to prosecute the war in Korea. The protracted war, with no end in sight, cost the Democrats the White House. After Eisenhower's election, he promoted cooperation between the two branches in decisions involving the use of American troops overseas. His policy, implemented through "area resolutions," came to a halt eight years later with the election of John F. Kennedy, who believed he could invoke military force without seeking congressional authority.

Mutual Security Treaties

In addition to invoking authority under the UN Charter, Presidents cite mutual security treaties as an additional source of authority for sending U.S. troops abroad. The problem of defining "constitutional processes" under Article 43 of the UN Charter arises also with language in mutual defense treaties. For example, the NATO treaty was signed in 1949 by the United States, Canada, and ten European countries. Article 5 provides that "an armed attack against one or more of them in Europe or North America shall be considered an attack against them all"[1] and further provides that, in the event of an attack, these nations may exercise the right of indi-

---

1. 63 Stat. 2244 (1949).

vidual or collective self-defense recognized by Article 51 of the UN Charter and assist the country or countries attacked by taking "such action as it deems necessary, including the use of armed force." Article 11 of the North Atlantic Treaty states that it shall be ratified "and its provisions carried out by the Parties in accordance with their respective constitutional processes."[2]

Similar procedures appear in the Rio Treaty, signed in 1947 by the United States and eighteen countries in Central America, South America, and the Caribbean (Nicaragua joined the pact a year later). These nations agreed to assist one another in the event of an attack, with an armed attack against one state considered "as an attack against all the American states."[3]

The formula of an attack on one nation constituting an attack on all nations was rejected in the mutual defense treaty signed between the United States and the Republic of Korea in 1953. The treaty declares the "common determination" of both countries to "defend themselves against external armed attack,"[4] and each party recognizes that "an armed attack in the Pacific area on either of the Parties in territories now under their respective administrative control . . . would be dangerous to its own peace and safety and declares that it would act to meet the common danger in accordance with its constitutional processes."[5]

The Southeast Asia Treaty (SEATO) was signed in 1954 by the United States, Australia, France, New Zealand, Pakistan, the Philippines, Thailand, and the United Kingdom. Each party recognized that armed aggression against one of the parties "would endanger its own peace and safety, and agreed that it will in that event act to meet the common danger in accordance with its constitutional processes."[6] This language was deliberately chosen to avoid the constitutional controversy provoked by the North Atlantic Treaty that "an attack upon one is an attack upon all."[7] As with NATO, the SEATO treaty "shall be ratified and its provisions carried out by the Parties in accordance with their respective constitutional processes."[8] Clearly, these defense treaties require definition and understanding of "constitutional processes."

Mutual defense treaties do not empower the President to use armed

2. Id. at 2246.
3. 62 Stat. 1700 (1947) (Art. 3).
4. 5 UST 2371.
5. Id. at 2372–73.
6. 6 UST 83 (1954) (Art. IV).
7. 101 Cong. Rec. 1051 (1951) (statement by Senator George).
8. 6 UST 84 (Art. IX.2).

force abroad without congressional consent. Treating an attack on one nation as an attack on all does not require an immediate response from any nation. As noted in the Rio Treaty, "no State shall be required to use armed force without its consent."⁹ During debate on this treaty, Senator Connally, chairman of the Foreign Relations Committee, noted: "It is left to the discretion and wish of each of the nations to adopt such measures as it may approve in carrying out the obligation to assist the victim of the attack."¹⁰

The notion that mutual security treaties do not provide for an automatic commitment to war is addressed in the legislative history. Secretary of State Dean Acheson explained to the Senate Foreign Relations Committee the basic premise in Article V of the NATO treaty that "an armed attack upon any party would so threaten the national security of the other parties as to be in effect an armed attack upon all." He said that the language "does not mean that the United States would automatically be at war if one of the other signatory nations were the victim of an armed attack. Under our Constitution, the Congress alone has the power to declare war."¹¹ He and Chairman Connally engaged in this exchange:

> THE CHAIRMAN . . . it is up to each country to determine for itself, is it not, what action it deems necessary to restore the security of the Atlantic Pact area?
> Secretary ACHESON. There is no question about that, Senator. That is true.¹²

Acheson later entered into the same understanding with Senator Vandenberg, who asked whether there was anything in the treaty "which will lead automatically to a declaration of war on our part." Acheson replied: "No, sir." Vandenberg pressed the issue: "The answer, of course, is unequivocally 'No.'" Acheson shot back: "Unequivocally 'No.'"¹³ When Acheson testified in 1951 before two Senate committees he acknowledged that the NATO treaty does not compel any nation "to take steps

9. 62 Stat. 1703 (Art. 20).
10. 93 Cong. Rec. 11124 (1947).
11. "North Atlantic Treaty" (part 1), hearings before the Senate Committees on Foreign Relations, 81st Cong. 1st Sess. 11 (1949).
12. Id. at 21.
13. Id. at 25.

contrary to its convictions, and none is obligated to ignore its national interests."[14]

When military force is used pursuant to a mutual defense treaty, it should be unleashed only after following constitutional processes, and that includes Congress (both Houses). The NATO treaty did not give the President any power beyond that provided in the UN Charter. In reporting the North Atlantic Treaty, the Senate Foreign Relations Committee was careful to point out that the provisions of the defense pact "are expressly subordinated to the purposes, principles, and provisions of the United Nations Charter."[15]

By providing that the NATO treaty be carried out according to constitutional processes, the Senate Foreign Relations Committee "intended to ensure that the Executive Branch of the Government should come back to the Congress when decisions were required in which the Congress has a constitutional responsibility."[16] As noted in one study of the NATO treaty, it "does not transfer to the President the Congressional power to make war."[17]

Mutual security treaties do not—they cannot—alter the constitutional allocation of the war power. It would be impermissible for the Senate and the President to use the treaty process to deny the House of Representatives its Article I powers in determining whether the nation should commit itself to war.[18] Senator Walter George said this about SEATO: "The treaty does not call for automatic action; it calls for consultation. If any course of action shall be agreed upon or decided upon, then that course of action must have the approval of Congress, because the constitutional process is provided for."[19]

Congress clarified that point when it enacted the War Powers Resolution of 1973. Section 8(a) provides that authority to introduce U.S. forces into hostilities shall not be inferred "from any treaty heretofore or hereafter ratified unless such treaty is implemented by legislation specifically authorizing" the introduction of American troops.[20] As noted by the Senate

14. "Assignment of Ground Forces of the United States to Duty in the European Area," hearings before the Senate Committee on Foreign Relations and Armed Services, 82d Cong., 1st Sess. 85 (1951).

15. S. Exec. Rept. No. 8, 81st Cong., 1st Sess. 8 (1949).

16. Richard H. Heindel et al., "The North Atlantic Treaty in the United States Senate," 43 Am. J. Int'l L. 633, 649 (1949).

17. Heindel, "The North Atlantic Treaty in the United States Senate," at 650.

18. Michael J. Glennon, "United States Mutual Security Treaties: The Commitment Myth," 24 Colum. J. Transnat'l L. 509 (1986).

19. 101 Cong. Rec. 1051 (1955).

20. 87 Stat. 558 (1973).

Foreign Relations Committee, the purpose of this language is to "ensure that both Houses of Congress must be affirmatively involved in any decision of the United States to engage in hostilities pursuant to a treaty."[21]

One part of the legislative history of the North Atlantic Treaty suggests that Congress considered, but rejected, an amendment that would have required explicit, advance congressional approval before the President could use armed force. Senator Arthur Watkins offered this reservation to the treaty:

> The United States understands and construes article V of the treaty as follows:
> That the United States assumes no obligation to restore and maintain the security of the North Atlantic area or to assist any other party or parties in said area, by armed force, or to employ the military, air, or naval forces of the United States under article V of any article of the treaty, for any purpose, unless in any particular case the Congress, which under the Constitution, has the sole power to declare war or authorize the employment of the military, air, or naval forces of the United States, shall by act or joint resolution so provide.[22]

Watkins's reservation was rejected, eighty-four Senators voting against and only eleven Senators in favor.[23] However, rejection of the Watkins reservation does not imply that the President has unilateral authority to use armed force without congressional approval. Senate votes do not change the meaning of the Constitution and nullify the prerogatives of the House of Representatives. In legislative history, a negative does not produce a positive. For example, Watkins also offered this reservation, which gained only eight votes with eighty-seven Senators opposed:

> The United States further understands and construes article 5 to the effect that in any particular case or event of armed attack on any other party or parties to the treaty, the Congress of the United States is not expressly, impliedly, or morally obligated or committed to declare war or authorize the employment of the military, air, or naval forces of the United States against the nation or nations making said attack, or to assist with its armed forces the nation or nations attacked, but shall have complete freedom in considering the circum-

21. S. Rept. No. 220, 93d Cong., 1st Sess. 26 (1973).
22. 95 Cong. Rec. 9806, 9898 (1949).
23. Id. at 9916.

stances of each case to act or refuse to act as the Congress in its discretion shall determine.[24]

Defeat of this second reservation does not imply that the United States has an express or moral obligation to use military force in the event of an attack on a member of NATO. The legislative history is entirely to the contrary. Despite the rejection of Watkins's second reservation, each nation decides for itself whether to intervene militarily.

The "Great Debate" in 1951

In 1951 President Truman announced that he would send ground forces to Europe. Asked at a press conference on January 4 whether he believed that he needed congressional approval before sending troops abroad, he replied: "No, I do not."[25] A week later, at another news conference, he was asked to respond to the comment by Senator Connally that the executive branch, in the future, would consult with Congress on troop commitments to Europe. Truman read from a prepared statement:

> Under the President's constitutional powers as Commander in Chief of the Armed Forces he has the authority to send troops anywhere in the world. That power has been recognized repeatedly by the Congress and the courts.
> This Government will continue to live up to its obligations under the United Nations, and its other treaty obligations, and we will continue to send troops wherever it is necessary to uphold these obligations.[26]

Truman said that Acheson had made it "perfectly plain" to the Senate Foreign Relations Committee that the North Atlantic Treaty did not require that troops be sent, and that each country itself would make up its own mind as to what action to take.[27] He omitted Acheson's reassurance that troop commitments would be made consistent with constitutional processes and that only Congress could declare war. To the extent that Truman would consult with Congress on troop commitments abroad, he identified only the Senate Committees on Foreign Relations and Armed

24. Id. at 9901; Senate vote at 9916.
25. Public Papers of the Presidents, 1951, 4 (question 18).
26. Id. at 19.
27. Id.

Services, apparently taking the view that these troop commitments would be pursuant to treaty obligations and therefore would exclude the House.[28] He was very explicit on the limited role of these committees: "I don't ask their permission, I just consult them."[29] Although he excluded the House from these deliberations, he later conceded that "it is necessary for the Congress to appropriate the money for the Government to be carried on."[30]

When Acheson appeared before the Senate Committee on Foreign Relations and Armed Services on February 16, he found the topic of congressional versus executive power plainly annoying. Having assured Congress on numerous occasions that its constitutional prerogatives would be respected, he would now assert, on an impatient if not petulant note:

> It seems to me that perhaps a little more is involved here, and that we are in a position in the world today where the argument as to who has the power to do this, that, or the other thing, is not exactly what is called for from America in this very critical hour, and if we could all agree on the fact that something should be done, we will perform a much greater role in the world, than by quarreling about who ought to do it.[31]

These haughty lectures from the Truman administration helped precipitate a major confrontation with Congress. In an extremely powerful floor statement, Senator Taft delivered a 10,000-word speech urging legislators to defend their prerogatives and arguing that constructive criticism from Congress on foreign policy is essential to the safety of the nation. His speech repudiated the idea that criticism of the administration's foreign policy "is an attack on the unity of the Nation, that it gives aid and comfort to the enemy, and that it sabotages any idea of a bipartisan foreign policy for the national benefit."[32] That mind-set, he said, rested on a dangerous fallacy that threatened the existence of the nation. Members of Congress, and particularly Senators, had "a constitutional obligation to reexamine constantly and discuss the foreign policy of the United States." The trend toward secrecy on the part of recent administrations, com-

28. Id. at 20.

29. Id.

30. Id. at 21.

31. "Assignment of Ground Forces of the United States to Duty in the European Area," hearings before the Senate Committees on Foreign Relations and Armed Services, 82d Cong., 1st Sess. 93 (1951).

32. 97 Cong. Rec. 55 (1951).

bined with the failure of Presidents to consult Congress and seek its advice, deprived members of Congress "of the substance of the powers conferred on them by the Constitution."[33] Taft feared that Truman, having embarked on a war in Korea without congressional authority, was about to do the same in Europe.[34] "Mr. Republican," the leading conservative of his time, concluded with these remarks: "And finally the policy we adopt must be approved by Congress and the people after full and free discussion. The commitment of a land army to Europe is a program never approved by Congress, into which we should not drift. The policy of secret executive agreements has brought us to danger and disaster. It threatens the liberties of our people."[35]

For three months in 1951 the Senate debated the scope and limits of presidential power. The principal resolution, S. Res. 99, supported the sending of additional divisions to Europe only on the condition that future commitments would be approved by Congress. As a Senate resolution, the measure was not legally binding, but it gave Senators an opportunity to debate in substantial detail the boundaries of congressional and presidential powers.

Taft believed that Congress had the power to prevent the President from sending troops anywhere in the world if doing so might involve the nation in war. He felt it was "incumbent upon the Congress to assert clearly its own constitutional powers unless it desires to lose them." In what could be read as a precursor to the War Powers Resolution of 1973, Taft urged Congress to assert its powers in the form of a joint resolution (requiring action by both Houses and submission to the President for his signature or veto).[36] Senator Wherry took Taft at his word and offered an amendment to replace the pending Senate resolution with a joint resolution, to make it legally binding. Wherry's amendment was ruled out of order.[37] Senator John Bricker (R-Ohio) attempted to recommit the Senate resolution and have it reported back as a joint resolution, but that tactic failed, 31 to 56.[38]

Senators wanted to express their sentiments in a resolution without having to worry about obtaining the concurrence of the House and the President. As a nonbinding resolution, the step was more modest than public opinion, as polls showed that Americans preferred stronger legisla-

33. Id.
34. Id. at 59.
35. Id. at 61.
36. Id. at 2987.
37. Id. at 3065.
38. Id. at 3199.

tive measures. A Gallup poll revealed that the public, by a margin of 64 percent to 28 percent, believed that Presidents should not be allowed to send U.S. troops overseas unless Congress first granted its approval.[39]

S. Res. 99 served many purposes. To Senator Edward Thye (R-Minn.), it highlighted the need to have "a closer relationship between the executive and legislative branches of our Government with reference to such questions as the assignment of troops abroad. Congress is close to the people and has a definite responsibility."[40] Senator John McClellan (D-Ark.) offered an amendment requiring congressional approval of future plans to send troops abroad. Although the amendment was initially rejected 44 to 45, it was later accepted,[41] 49 to 44. A weak amendment by Senator Herbert Lehman (D-N.Y.), merely calling for the "fullest collaboration" between Congress and the President on future troop actions, was decisively beaten, 35 to 55.[42]

The Senate passed the resolution by a vote of 69 to 21. It approved Truman's sending of four divisions to Europe but stated that "in the interests of sound constitutional processes, and of national unity and understanding, congressional approval should be obtained of any policy requiring the assignment of American troops abroad when such assignment is in implementation of article 3 of the North Atlantic Treaty." No ground troops in addition to the four divisions should be sent "without further congressional approval."[43]

Earlier in the session, Representative Frederick Coudert (R-N.Y.) introduced legislation to require the authorization of Congress before military forces could be sent abroad.[44] After the Senate had completed action on its resolution, Coudert proposed that no part of the appropriations in the defense appropriations bill could be used for the cost of sending or maintaining additional ground troops in Europe. His amendment failed, 84 to 131.[45]

The 1951 debate provoked both Houses of Congress to rethink the congressional role in foreign affairs and the war power. A report for the House Foreign Affairs Committee in 1951 correctly spotlighted the significance of the Korean War: "The action of the United States in Korea is in one sense unprecedented. For the first time the United States has commit-

39. Id. at 3015.
40. Id. at 3041.
41. Id. at 3082–83, 3095–96.
42. Id. at 3104.
43. Id. at 3283 (para. 6).
44. Id. at 34 (H.J. Res. 9).
45. Id. at 9746.

ted large military forces in a foreign country in response to the action of an international organization. United States forces were committed in Korea by Presidential action."[46]

A House study in 1956 on the President's powers as Commander in Chief drew attention to the fact that the period since the 1930s signaled something fundamentally new and troubling in executive-legislative relations. The study concluded that "in no other period of 20 years of American history have so many different Presidents been called on to exercise this constitutional power [of Commander in Chief] in so many different kinds of situations, each one of major importance."[47]

The Steel Seizure Case

After two years of a costly and apparently unwinnable war, public opposition steadily drained support from the administration, and in the midst of these difficulties Truman faced a nationwide strike of steelworkers. He reacted in 1952 by issuing Executive Order 10340, directing the Secretary of Commerce to take possession of and operate the plants and facilities of eighty-seven major steel companies. As justification for averting a work stoppage, the order referred to Truman's proclamation of December 16, 1950, declaring the existence of a nationwide emergency and the dispatch of American soldiers to Korea. The order called steel "indispensable" for producing weapons and war materials.[48]

Although Truman based the order on authority under "the Constitution and laws of the United States, and as President of the United States and Commander-in-Chief of the armed forces of the United States," the Justice Department later argued in court that Truman had acted solely on inherent executive power without any statutory support. Assistant Attorney General Homer Baldridge told David A. Pine, a federal district judge, that courts were powerless to control the exercise of presidential power when directed toward emergency conditions.[49] At a news conference on April 17, Truman was asked if he could seize the steel mills under his inherent powers, could he "also seize the newspapers and/or the radio stations?"

46. "Background Information on the Use of United States Armed Forces in Foreign Countries," printed for the use of the House Committee on Foreign Affairs, 82d Cong., 1st Sess. 1 (Committee Print 1951).

47. H. Doc. No. 443, 84th Cong., 2d Sess. viii (1956).

48. 17 Fed. Reg. 3139 (1952).

49. "U.S. Argues President Is Above Courts," New York Times, April 25, 1952, at 1.

Truman answered: "Under similar circumstances the President of the United States has to act for whatever is for the best of the country."[50]

A few days later, recognizing that this theory of virtually limitless presidential power was offensive to the country, Truman wrote a letter to the Senate stating that Congress could, "if it wishes, reject the course of action I have followed in this matter."[51] At a news conference on April 24, he said that there had been "a lot of hooey" about presidential power to seize the press and the radio.[52] In a further gesture to defuse the controversy, Truman wrote a letter to a private citizen on April 27, stating that presidential powers are derived from the Constitution and are limited by provisions in the Constitution, "particularly those that protect the rights of individuals."[53]

Those gestures were not enough to undo the damage done in district court. On April 29, Judge Pine wrote a blistering opinion rejecting the Justice Department's analysis of inherent presidential power. In holding Truman's seizure of the steel mills to be unconstitutional, he acknowledged that a nationwide strike could do extensive damage to the country but believed that a strike "would be less injurious to the public than the injury which would flow from a timorous judicial recognition that there is some basis for this claim to unlimited and unrestrained Executive power, which would be implicit in a failure to grant the injunction."[54]

On June 2 the Supreme Court, split 6 to 3, sustained Judge Pine's decision. Each of the five concurring Justices wrote separate opinions, advancing different views of the President's emergency power. Only Justices Hugo Black and William Douglas insisted on specific constitutional or statutory authority to support presidential seizure of private property. The other four concurring Justices (Felix Frankfurter, Robert Jackson, Harold Burton, and Tom Clark) did not try to delimit the President's authority to act in future emergencies.

Jackson's concurrence is the most interesting. He identified three categories of presidential power ranging from actions based on express or implied congressional authorization (putting executive authority at its maximum) to executive measures that were incompatible with congressional policy (reducing presidential power to its lowest ebb). In between lay a "zone of twilight" in which the President and Congress shared authority. Jackson said that congressional inertia, indifference, or quiescence might

50. Public Papers of the Presidents, 1952, 273.
51. Id. at 284.
52. Id. at 290.
53. Id. at 301.
54. Youngstown Sheet & Tube Co. v. Sawyer, 103 F.Supp. 569, 577 (D.D.C. 1952).

enable, if not invite, independent presidential action.[55] Jackson concluded by saying that he had no illusion that any decision by a court "can keep power in the hands of Congress if it is not wise and timely in meeting its problems." Although the power to legislate for emergencies belongs in the hands of Congress, "only Congress itself can prevent power from slipping through its fingers."[56] His concurring opinion remains the most perceptive advice to Congress: the political dynamics of presidential power is such that Congress must invoke the institutional tools at its command rather than expect assistance from the federal judiciary. (The deficiencies of Jackson's opinion are explored more closely in Chapter 9.)

Eisenhower's Philosophy

After these sharp collisions between President Truman and Congress, the Eisenhower administration avoided unilateral moves in dispatching troops abroad. Although Eisenhower believed that Truman's decision to intervene in Korea was "wise and necessary,"[57] he came to realize that it was a serious mistake, politically and constitutionally, to commit the nation to war in Korea without congressional approval. Eisenhower thought that national commitments would be stronger if entered into jointly by both branches and therefore asked Congress for specific authority to deal with national security crises. He stressed the importance of *collective* action by Congress and the President: "I deem it necessary to seek the cooperation of the Congress. Only with that cooperation can we give the reassurance needed to deter aggression."[58]

Herbert Brownell, who served as Eisenhower's Attorney General and confidante, described Eisenhower's sensitivity to separation of powers:

> [His] view of the president's place within a constitutional system of government allowed him to understand the rightful roles that the various institutions and political actors occupy in our political system so that he did not overextend the scope of presidential interest across the whole gamut of governmental activities. Moreover, it fostered an understanding of the need to establish a sense of comity with those individuals in the other branches with whom a president must necessarily deal. This is an aspect of presidential leadership quite different

55. Youngstown Co. v. Sawyer, 343 U.S. 579, 637 (1952).
56. Id. at 654.
57. Dwight D. Eisenhower, Mandate for Change 82 (1963).
58. Public Papers of the Presidents, 1957, 11.

from the imperial presidency some of his successors would come to embrace.[59]

When international emergencies arose, Eisenhower wanted the backing of Congress. He did not want to "expose himself to the kind of criticism that Taft and other Republicans had leveled against Truman for entering the Korean War without consulting Congress."[60] In 1954, when he was under pressure to intervene in Indochina to save beleaguered French troops, he refused to act unilaterally. He told reporters in a news conference: "There is going to be no involvement of America in war unless it is a result of the constitutional process that is placed upon Congress to declare it. Now, let us have that clear; and that is the answer."[61] Eisenhower told Secretary of State John Foster Dulles that in "the absence of some kind of arrangement getting support of Congress," it "would be completely unconstitutional & indefensible" to give any assistance to the French.[62] Eisenhower's attitude about covert operations was different (see Chapter 8 for his authorization of such actions in Iran, Guatemala, and Cuba without seeking congressional support or authority).

Area Resolutions

Eisenhower's theory of government and international relations invited congressional enactment of area resolutions that authorized presidential action. He believed that the Korean War resulted in part from the Communists' belief that "under no circumstances would the United States move to the assistance of the Korean Republic."[63] To forestall such misconceptions in his administration, he wanted other nations to know that Congress and the President were united in their foreign policy.

Conditions in the Formosa Straits threatened to deteriorate into a military confrontation between the United States and China. In a memorandum in 1954, Secretary of State Dulles noted that "it is doubtful that the issue can be exploited without Congressional approval."[64] One issue was whether President Eisenhower could order an attack on airfields in China. He said that "to do that you would have to get Congressional au-

59. Herbert Brownell with John P. Burke, Advising Ike: The Memoirs of Attorney General Herbert Brownell 289 (1993).
60. 2 Stephen E. Ambrose, Eisenhower the President 232 (1984).
61. Public Papers of the Presidents, 1954, 306.
62. FRUS, 1952–1954, vol. 13, part 1, 1242.
63. Eisenhower, Mandate for Change, 467.
64. FRUS, 1952–1954, vol. 14, part 1, 611.

thorization, since it would be war. If Congressional authorization were not obtained there would be logical grounds for impeachment. Whatever we do must be in a Constitutional manner."[65] Dulles remarked that "if we act without Congress now we will not have anyone in the United States with us."[66]

In 1955, in response to a dangerous turn of events in the Formosa Straits, Eisenhower appealed to Congress for joint action. Communist China had begun shelling the island of Quemoy. It also mounted air attacks against other islands north of Formosa and seized the island of Ichiang. Eisenhower believed that the situation was one "for appropriate action of the United Nations," but unlike Truman he did not go to the United Nations and exclude Congress. Quite the opposite. Instead of waiting for the United Nations to act, he urged Congress "to participate now, by specific resolution, in measures designed to improve the prospects for peace." The resolution would contemplate the use of U.S. armed forces "if necessary to assure the security of Formosa and the Pescadores."[67] While identifying his prerogatives as Commander in Chief, Eisenhower preferred to act jointly with Congress:

Authority for some of the actions which might be required would be inherent in the authority of the Commander-in-Chief. Until Congress can act I would not hesitate, so far as my Constitutional powers extend, to take whatever emergency action might be forced upon us in order to protect the rights and security of the United States.

However, a suitable Congressional resolution would clearly and publicly establish the authority of the President as Commander-in-Chief to employ the armed forces of this nation promptly and effectively for the purposes indicated if in his judgment it became necessary. It would make clear the unified and serious intentions of our Government, our Congress, and our people.[68]

Eisenhower noted that he did not expect the United States to enlarge "its defensive obligations" beyond Formosa and the Pescadores.[69] How the world of presidential war power had changed since the framers: U.S. *defensive* obligations in the offshore islands of China! But it was settled wisdom in the Eisenhower administration that the western barrier to

65. Id. at 618.
66. Id. at 620.
67. Public Papers of the Presidents, 1955, 209.
68. Id. at 209–10.
69. Id. at 209.

Communist aggression, consisting of Japan, Formosa, and the Philippines, had to be maintained.

During joint hearings before the Senate Committees on Foreign Relations and Armed Services, Secretary of State John Foster Dulles presented the administration's case. He was reminded of Eisenhower's remark that he would not hesitate to act under his own constitutional powers if necessary while awaiting congressional action. Dulles told the committees: "There is at least doubt as to whether or not the President could, without congressional authorization, take the kind of action which I am talking about."[70] Sherman Adams, Eisenhower's chief of staff, later recalled that Eisenhower was determined "not to resort to any kind of military action without the approval of Congress."[71]

Congress responded quickly to Eisenhower's request. On the same day that he addressed Congress, the House Foreign Affairs Committee held a hearing in executive session and reported the resolution unanimously without amendment. With regard to constitutional issues, the committee offered this assessment: "Its conclusion was that the resolution in this form, while making it clear that the people of the United States stand behind the President, does not enter the field of controversy as to the respective limitations of power in the executive and the legislative branches. Acting together, there can be no doubt that all the constitutional powers necessary to meet the situation are present."[72] This position recalls Justice Jackson's concurrence in *Youngstown Co. v. Sawyer* (1952), stating that presidential power is "at its maximum" when the President acts on the basis of his constitutional power plus those that Congress delegates to him.[73] The Formosa Resolution passed the House a day later, 410 to 3.[74]

The Senate Foreign Relations Committee also held hearings in executive session and reported the resolution without amendment. The committee vote was 27 to 2 with one Senator absent.[75] After rejecting several floor amendments, the Senate passed the resolution by a margin of 85 to 3, and the resolution became law a day later.[76]

Officials in the Eisenhower administration considered using nuclear weapons against China in the dispute over Formosa. Secretary Dulles sug-

70. "Senate Joint Resolution 28—The Formosa Resolution," joint hearings before the Senate Committees on Foreign Relations and Armed Services, 84th Cong., 1st Sess. 87 (1955). Executive sessions of the Senate Foreign Relations Committee (historical series), made public April 1978.
71. Sherman Adams, First-Hand Report 109 (1962).
72. H. Rept. No. 4, 84th Cong., 1st Sess. 4 (1955).
73. 343 U.S. at 635–36.
74. 101 Cong. Rec. 680–81 (1955).
75. S. Rept. No. 13, 84th Cong., 1st Sess. 7 (1955).
76. 101 Cong. Rec. 994–95 (1955); 69 Stat. 7 (1955).

gested that small nuclear weapons could be directed against military targets rather than larger bombs against cities.[77] Smaller nuclear weapons, he said, could be utilized with precision without radioactive fall-out problems.[78] At a news conference, President Eisenhower agreed that tactical, small atomic weapons could be used: "Now in any combat where these things can be used on strictly military targets and for strictly military purposes, I see no reason why they shouldn't be used just exactly as you would use a bullet or anything else."[79] The idea of unleashing tactical atomic weapons "sent a shudder through almost every Ambassador" in Washington, D.C. The "overwhelming reaction from press and pulpit was loudly opposed to intervention."[80] The Formosa crisis eventually passed without warfare between the United States and China.

Eisenhower asked for another area resolution in 1957. In an address delivered in person before a joint session, he asked Congress to pass a joint resolution authorizing him to employ armed forces in the Middle East. After alerting Congress to Soviet ambitions in the Middle East, he said that thoughts "naturally turn to the United Nations as a protector of small nations."[81] But he reminded the legislators that Russia had recently used its veto in the Security Council to block UN actions concerning Russia's intervention in Hungary, implying that Russia would also veto any constructive UN response to the situation in the Middle East.

Under these conditions, Eisenhower emphasized the importance of executive-legislative coordination: "I deem it necessary to seek the cooperation of the Congress. Only with that cooperation can we give the reassurance needed to deter aggression."[82] Effective action meant that "basic United States policy should now find expression in joint action by the Congress and the Executive."[83] If military action became necessary he promised "hour-by-hour" contact with Congress if it were in session. If recessed or adjourned, "and if the situation had grave implications, he would "of course, at once" call Congress into special session.[84]

In his memoirs, Eisenhower explained the choice between invoking executive prerogatives or seeking congressional support. On New Year's Day in 1957, he met with Secretary of State Dulles and congressional

77. New York Times, March 16, 1955, 1.
78. Id., 2.
79. Public Papers of the Presidents, 1955, 332.
80. James Reston, "Quemoy-Matsu Trend," New York Times, April 7, 1955, 13.
81. Public Papers of the Presidents, 1957, 10.
82. Id. at 11.
83. Id. at 12.
84. Id. at 15.

leaders of both parties. House Majority Leader John McCormack (D-Mass.) asked Eisenhower whether he, as Commander in Chief, already possessed authority to carry out actions in the Middle East without congressional action. Eisenhower replied that

> greater effect could be had from a consensus of Executive and Legislative opinion, and I spoke earnestly of the desire of the Middle East countries to have reassurance now that the United States would stand ready to help. . . . Near the end of this meeting I reminded the legislators that the Constitution assumes that our two branches of government should get along together.[85]

Congress was not as compliant as it had been in 1955 with the Formosa Resolution. This time legislators objected to giving Eisenhower a blank check. Congressional debate consumed several months and resulted in several restrictions on the delegated authority. For example, the authority in the Formosa Resolution expired whenever the President determined "that the peace and security of the area is reasonably assured by international conditions created by action of the United Nations or otherwise, and shall so report to the Congress."[86] The 1957 statute kept this provision but also permitted Congress to terminate the authority by passing a concurrent resolution, which requires action by both Houses but is not presented to the President for his signature or veto.[87] As the House Foreign Affairs Committee explained, a concurrent resolution permitted Congress to terminate the President's authority by a simple majority vote of each House, instead of acting by a bill or joint resolution subject to a presidential veto.[88]

Even with that change the Middle East Resolution encountered major congressional opposition. The House Foreign Affairs Committee held hearings morning and afternoon over a period of two weeks and held four executive sessions."[89] After two full days of debate the House passed the resolution by a vote of 355 to 61.[90] Two Senate committees, Foreign Relations and Armed Services, met jointly for almost a month, holding public hearings and meeting in executive session.[91]

---

85. Dwight D. Eisenhower, Waging Peace 179 (1965).
86. 69 Stat. 7 (1955).
87. 71 Stat. 6, sec. 6 (1957).
88. H. Rept. No. 2, 85th Cong., 1st Sess. 13 (1957).
89. Id. at 2.
90. 103 Cong. Rec. 1323–24 (1957).
91. S. Rept. No. 70, 85th Cong., 1st Sess. 2–3 (1957) (report of the Senate Committees on Foreign Relations and Armed Services).

Several amendments were adopted on the Senate floor while others were rejected. Senator Wayne Morse (D-Oreg.) offered an amendment that built on Eisenhower's promise to meet "hour-by-hour" with Congress and call it in special session if adjourned: "Prior to the employment of armed forces the President shall give notice to Congress. If, in the judgment of the President, an emergency arises in which such notice to Congress is not possible, he shall, upon the employment of armed forces, forthwith inform Congress and submit his action for its approval or disapproval."[92]

The administration opposed the amendment, stating that "it would appear to raise serious question as to the President's power to use the Armed Forces under the resolution, and would impair the effectiveness of the resolution."[93] The Morse amendment failed on a vote of 28 to 64.[94] Senator Carl Curtis (R-Nebr.) proposed a third way to terminate the President's authority under the resolution, letting it expire on a fixed date—February 1, 1961—unless terminated earlier by the President or by Congress. The administration considered the amendment "highly undesirable" because a fixed date would imply that U.S. interests in the region would end on that date and therefore encourage potential aggressors to take advantage of the expiration.[95] The Curtis amendment was rejected 30 to 58.[96] The entire resolution then passed on a vote of 72 to 19,[97] and the House agreed to the Senate amendments, 350 to 60.[98]

On the day that the two Houses finally agreed to the resolution, Eisenhower was asked at a press conference whether he, as Commander in Chief, could send troops wherever he wanted without seeking the approval of Congress. Instead of stressing his independent and inherent powers he pointed to the practical importance of interbranch collaboration:

Q. . . . Mr. President, in the resolution as passed by the Senate, apparently to be approved today by the House, the original concept suggested in your version of authorizing you to use the Armed Forces was stricken out, and we understand you have approved the substitute voted by the Senate.

92. 103 Cong. Rec. 3120 (1957).
93. Id. at 3121.
94. Id.
95. Id. at 3123.
96. Id. at 3126.
97. Id. at 3129.
98. Id. at 3265–66.

Does this mean, sir, that you accept the constitutional interpretation that you have always had, as Commander-in-Chief, the right to
send the Armed Forces into action in such a situation in the national
interest without that specific authorization?

THE PRESIDENT. Well, I don't think . . . that I have to go into the constitutional argument again. I would point out that I haven't spent my
life in the study of constitutional law.

I do think the legislative history of this resolution shows that the
Senate approves—the Congress approves of what we are trying to do
in the area, and that is the important thing.[99]

Upon signing the legislation, Eisenhower followed through on his commitment to interbranch cooperation. He selected James P. Richards,
former chairman of the House Foreign Affairs Committee, to head a special mission to the Middle East countries to explain the purpose of the resolution and to report back to Eisenhower on the most effective ways of
carrying out the purposes of the legislation.[100]

However, when Eisenhower actually sent troops to Lebanon in 1958,
he referred only indirectly to the Middle East Resolution by telling Congress that U.S. forces were being deployed "to assist the Government of
Lebanon in the preservation of Lebanon's territorial integrity and independence, which have been deemed vital to United States national interests and world peace."[101] (The Middle East Resolution recognized that the
United States "regards as vital to the national interest and world peace the
preservation of the independence and integrity of the nations of the Middle East."[102]) Eisenhower referred to two other factors: the responsibility
to protect and safeguard about 2,500 American citizens in Lebanon and
the right of all nations (under the UN Charter) to "work together and to
seek help when necessary to preserve their independence" through collective self-defense.[103] He said that he had taken advice from leaders of
Congress[104] and that the sending of U.S. forces to Lebanon was not an "act
of war."[105]

Eisenhower's general position on the war power was extremely perceptive. He knew that lawyers and policy advisers in the executive branch

99. Public Papers of the Presidents, 1957, 177–78.
100. Id. at 187.
101. Public Papers of the Presidents, 1958, 550–51, 556.
102. 71 Stat. 5, sec. 2 (1957).
103. Public Papers of the Presidents, 1958, 552.
104. Id. at 553.
105. Id. at 549.

could always try to assert a multitude of incidents to justify unilateral presidential action. It was his seasoned judgment, however, that a commitment by the United States would have much greater impact on allies and enemies alike because it would represent the collective judgment of the President and Congress. Single-handed actions taken by a President, without the support of Congress and the people, can threaten national prestige and undermine the presidency. Eisenhower's position was sound then. It is sound now.

Kennedy Reasserts Executive Power

Eisenhower's experiment with interbranch cooperation was short-lived. Unlike Eisenhower, President John F. Kennedy was prepared to act during the Cuban missile crisis solely on his own constitutional authority. At a news conference on September 13, 1962, he warned of a Communist buildup (with Soviet assistance) in Cuba. A series of "offensive missile sites," he said, were in preparation, the purpose of which "can be none other than to provide a nuclear strike capability against the Western Hemisphere."[106] However, he did not request a joint resolution. Under his power as Commander in Chief he said: "I have full authority now to take such action" militarily against Cuba.[107] During the news conference he gave this revealing response:

> Q. Mr. President, you said in your opening statement that you now had full authority to act in the Cuban affair. In view of this, do you think there's any virtue in the Senate or the Congress passing the resolution saying you have that authority?
> THE PRESIDENT. No. I think the Members of Congress would, speaking as they do with a particular responsibility—I think it would be useful, if they desired to do so, for them to express their view. And as I've seen the resolutions which have been discussed—a resolution which I think Senator [Mike] Mansfield [D-Mont.] introduced and which Chairman [Carl] Vinson [D-Ga.] introduced in the House—and I would think that—I'd be very glad to have those resolutions passed if that should be the desire of the Congress.[108]

Kennedy imposed a quarantine on all offensive military equipment being shipped to Cuba. Any ship containing cargoes of offensive weapons

106. Public Papers of the Presidents, 1962, 806.
107. Id. at 674.
108. Id. at 679.

would be turned back. He announced that it would be his policy to re-
gard any nuclear missile launched from Cuba against any nation in the
Western Hemisphere "as an attack by the Soviet Union on the United
States, requiring a full retaliatory response upon the Soviet Union."[109]

On October 3, Congress passed the Cuba Resolution, stating that the
United States is "determined to prevent by whatever means may be necessary, including the use of arms, the Marxist-Leninist regime in Cuba from
extending, by force or the threat of force, its aggressive or subversive activities to any part of this hemisphere."[110] The resolution also stated the
determination of the United States to prevent in Cuba "the creation or use
of an externally supported military capability endangering the security of
the United States." The resolution did not, however, authorize presidential action. It merely expressed the sentiments of Congress. Since no authority was delegated, there was no provision for termination by concurrent resolution.

The Senate passed the resolution 86 to 1.[111] Senators deferred broadly
to the President's supposed authority in foreign affairs and the war power.
Senator George Smathers (D-Fla.) remarked: "We all recognize that the final decision is left to the President of the United States by the Constitution."[112] Precisely when and how the Constitution had been amended he
neglected to say. Senator Bourke Hickenlooper (R-Iowa) offered another
sweeping assertion: "Basically the Executive has the responsibility for
and is in charge of foreign policy operations."[113] He explained that the
joint resolution sidestepped any effort to deal with the constitutional issue. The resolution "eliminated the question of whether or not the President or Congress shall declare war."[114] That point, one would think, had
been settled in 1788 with ratification of the Constitution.

The two committee reports, by the Senate Committee on Foreign Relations and the House Committee on Foreign Affairs, were brief and perfunctory.[115] House floor debate was similarly sluggish in defending congressional prerogatives. The resolution passed the House with only token
opposition, 384 to 7.[116]

109. Id. at 808.
110. 76 Stat. 697 (1962).
111. 108 Cong. Rec. 20058 (1962).
112. Id. at 20026.
113. Id. at 20029.
114. Id. at 20030.
115. S. Rept. No. 2111, 87th Cong., 2d Sess. (1962); H. Rept. No. 2441, 87th Cong., 2d
Sess. (1962).
116. 108 Cong. Rec. 20910–11 (1962).

Kennedy acted on October 23 to interdict offensive weapons being delivered to Cuba, basing his action on "the authority entrusted to me by the Constitution as endorsed by the resolution of the Congress."[117] The Organ of Consultation of the American Republics met on that same day to recommend that member states take all measures, individually and collectively, including the use of armed force, to prevent Cuba from receiving threatening weapons from China and Russia. The language in Kennedy's proclamation read: "NOW, THEREFORE, I, JOHN F. KENNEDY, President of the United States of America, acting under and by virtue of the authority conferred upon me by the Constitution and statutes of the United States, in accordance with the aforementioned resolutions of the United States Congress and of the Organ of Consultation of the American Republics."[118]

Little thought was given to the prerogatives of Congress. A proposal to call Congress back to Washington and ask for a declaration of war was quickly discarded. Dean Acheson, part of the administration's team that explored various options, was true to form. This was no time, he counseled, to worry about legal formalities.[119] The Soviet Union removed the missiles, but the prospect of nuclear war led one analyst to estimate that never before "had there been such a high probability that so many lives would end suddenly," risking the deaths of 100 million Americans, more than 100 million Russians, and millions of Europeans.[120]

Next came the fateful Southeast Asia Resolution of 1964, better known as the Tonkin Gulf Resolution. Enacted in the middle of a presidential election year, this massive grant of authority to President Lyndon B. Johnson was a key step in the escalation of the Vietnam War, a conflict that eventually drove Johnson from office and prepared the way for the War Powers Resolution of 1973.

117. Public Papers of the Presidents, 1962, 807.
118. Id. at 810.
119. Elie Abel, The Missiles of October: The Story of the Cuban Missile Crisis 84 (1969).
120. Graham T. Allison, Essence of Decision: Explaining the Cuban Missile Crisis 1 (1971).

6

VIETNAM AND THE WAR POWERS RESOLUTION

By the time Lyndon Johnson entered the White House, three American Presidents had taken decisive steps to involve the nation in Vietnam. Truman and Eisenhower provided substantial economic and military assistance to aid the French in Indochina. Under Truman, the United States paid for between one-third and one-half the cost,[1] and American aid climbed to about 75 percent during the Eisenhower years. President Eisenhower made the first commitment of soldiers, sending 200 military personnel to assist the French.[2]

In 1954 Eisenhower told his Secretary of State, John Foster Dulles, to ask Congress to pass a resolution giving the President authority to use American air and sea power in Southeast Asia. Members of Congress balked at the thought of another Korea and insisted that any involvement by the United States would have to include the support of the British and other allies. Faced with those requirements, Dulles decided against submitting the resolution to Congress.[3] The French wanted the United States to intervene with bombing missions, including two or three atomic bombs, but Eisenhower ruled out the use of atomic weapons. He also said that any air strike, without congressional support, would be "completely unconstitutional and indefensible."[4] Eisenhower continued to insist that if the United States ever intervened it would have to be in the company of allies, including Great Britain.

After the French surrendered at Dienbienphu in 1954, Vietnam was divided between the northern part, including Hanoi, and the southern part. President Kennedy continued sending American advisers and providing U.S. weapons to South Vietnam. The number of American military advisers rose from 700 to 16,000. Kennedy initiated the Strategic Hamlet Program in an unsuccessful attempt to build support among the peasants, involved military advisers in combat roles, and supported South

---

1. 2 Memoirs by Harry S. Truman, Years of Trial and Hope 337, 339, 519 (1956).
2. 2 Stephen Ambrose, Eisenhower: The President 175–76 (1984).
3. Id. at 178.
4. Id. at 179. See also Chalmers M. Roberts, "The Day We Didn't Go to War," The Reporter, September 14, 1954, at 31–35.

Vietnamese raids against North Vietnam.[5] Armed helicopters, piloted by Americans, were used against the North Vietnamese.[6]

In August 1964, after President Johnson reported attacks against U.S. vessels in the Gulf of Tonkin, Congress hurriedly passed legislation to authorize the use of armed force. Several years later, with U.S. soldiers mired in a land war in Southeast Asia and confronting huge casualties, Congress began the slow process of reevaluating its role in twentieth-century wars. Even for conflicts on the vast scale of Korea and Vietnam, a declaration of war now seemed inappropriate. Without that check, how could Congress limit the President's ability to plunge the nation into war? Out of a long national debate emerged the War Powers Resolution of 1973.

Gulf of Tonkin Resolution

On August 3, 1964, President Lyndon B. Johnson ordered the Navy to take retaliatory actions against the North Vietnamese for their attacks in the Gulf of Tonkin.[7] He acted following an attack on the U.S. destroyer *Maddox* by Communist PT boats. An August 4 radio and television report to the American public provided further details on the incident and described a second attack, this one against two American destroyers. There were no U.S. losses at sea, and American strikes sunk at least two North Vietnamese boats. Air attacks were carried out against gunboats and supporting facilities in North Vietnam, with two U.S. aircraft lost in those missions.

Calling the North Vietnamese attacks an "outrage," Johnson said that the U.S. response would be "limited and fitting."[8] At joint hearings conducted by the Senate Committee on Armed Services and Foreign Relations, Secretary of Defense Robert McNamara testified that the U.S. objective was "to move our forces as rapidly out of Vietnam as that Government can maintain its independence and as rapidly as the North Vietnamese stop their attempts to subvert it."[9]

Johnson met with the leaders of both parties in Congress and asked for a resolution making clear "[our] determination to take all necessary mea-

5. Gary R. Hess, "Commitment in the Age of Counterinsurgency: Kennedy's Vietnam Options and Decisions, 1961–1963," in David L. Anderson, ed., Shadow on the White House: Presidents and the Vietnam War, 1945–1975, 67–68 (1993).

6. Stanley Karnow, Vietnam: A History 275 (1991).

7. Public Papers of the Presidents, 1964, II, 926.

8. Id. at 927.

9. "Southeast Asia Resolution," joint hearings before the Senate Committees on Foreign Relations and Armed Services, 88th Cong., 2d Sess. 25 (1964).

sures in support of freedom and in defense of peace in southeast Asia."[10] Johnson noted that his opponent for the presidency in 1964, Senator Barry Goldwater (R-Ariz.), was "glad to say that he has expressed his support of the statement that I am making to you tonight."[11] A special message to Congress on August 5 formalized Johnson's request for the joint resolution. In asking Congress to join in affirming the national determination that all attacks by North Vietnam will be met, Johnson said that the United States "intends no rashness, and seeks no wider war."[12] He referred, as models, to previous area resolutions for Formosa, the Middle East, and Cuba.

Although it appeared that the resolution was submitted in response to the incidents in the Tonkin Gulf, it had been conceived as early as February and put in draft form by late May.[13] A draft dated May 25, 1964, included dollar limits ("The President is hereby authorized to use for assistance under this joint resolution not to exceed $————"),[14] but the Tonkin Gulf Resolution submitted to Congress was a blank check.

Congress spent little time debating the resolution. Senate debate started on August 6 and concluded the next day, with an endorsement of the resolution by a vote of 88 to 2. The House passed the measure on August 7 without a single dissenting vote, 416 to 0. The Tonkin Gulf Resolution approved and supported the determination of the President, as Commander in Chief, to take "all necessary measures to repel any armed attack against the forces of the United States and to prevent further aggression." The statute further declared that the United States was prepared, "as the President determines, to take all necessary steps, including the use of armed force," to assist any member or protocol state (South Vietnam, Cambodia, and Laos) of SEATO requesting assistance in defense of its freedom. The resolution could expire by two methods: presidential determination or when terminated earlier by concurrent resolution of Congress.[15]

Neither House bothered to conduct independent investigations to verify Johnson's account. Senator Mike Mansfield (D-Mont.) believed that Johnson had acted "in the hope of restraining the dogs of war."[16] Senator J. William Fulbright (D-Ark.), in words he would later regret, said that the

10. Public Papers of the Presidents, II, 927.
11. Id. at 928.
12. Id. at 931.
13. Karnow, Vietnam, at 373, 376.
14. The Pentagon Papers, as published by New York Times 287 (1971 paper ed.).
15. 78 Stat. 384 (1964).
16. 110 Cong. Rec. 18399 (1964).

facts of the Tonkin Gulf incident "are clear."[17] One of the two opponents in the Senate, Wayne Morse (D-Oreg.), displayed an uncanny gift for prophecy: "Unpopular as it is, I am perfectly willing to make the statement for history that if we follow a course of action that bogs down thousands of American boys in Asia, the administration responsible for it will be rejected and repudiated by the American people. It should be."[18]

In signing the Tonkin Gulf Resolution, Johnson explained that the military response to North Vietnam "was mine—and mine alone" as Commander in Chief. But as President he said there remained another responsibility: "the responsibility of submitting our course to the representatives of the people, for them to verify it or veto it."[19]

Subsequent investigations of the Tonkin Gulf incidents cast a heavy shadow over the account presented by President Johnson and administration officials. Secretary McNamara testified on August 6, 1964, that the *Maddox* was engaged in a "routine patrol in International waters."[20] In fact, those patrols had helped provide support for South Vietnamese attacks on North Vietnam. In February 1964, Johnson had accelerated attacks on North Vietnam by using South Vietnamese commandos backed by U.S. warships.[21]

The first attack, on August 2, was too minor to justify asking Congress for a resolution authorizing military action. The second alleged attack, on August 4, may never have happened. Conflicting accounts have been given. The ship's radar showed blips that might have indicated gunfire from North Vietnamese boats, but the evidence is inconclusive. The commander of the *Maddox* sent this cable on August 4: "Review of action makes many recorded contacts and torpedoes fired appear doubtful. Freak weather effects and over-eager sonarman may have accounted for many reports. No actual visual sightings by *Maddox*. Suggest complete evaluation before any further action."[22] Most, if not all, of the sonar reports identifying torpedoes were probably reflections from the *Maddox* as it made its evasive weaving turns.[23]

17. Id.

18. Id. at 18427.

19. Public Papers of the Presidents, 1964, II, 946.

20. "Southeast Asia Resolution," joint hearing before the Senate Committees on Foreign Affairs and Armed Services, 88th Cong., 2d Sess. 7 (1964).

21. William Conrad Gibbons, The U.S. Government and the Vietnam War: Executive and Legislative Roles and Relationships, Part II: 1961–1964, 228–35 (1986).

22. "The Gulf of Tonkin, The 1964 Incidents," hearing before the Senate Foreign Relations Committee, 90th Cong., 2d Sess. 54 (1968).

23. Joseph C. Goulden, Truth Is the First Casualty: The Gulf of Tonkin Affairs—Illusion and Reality (1969); Gibbons, The U.S. Government and the Vietnam War, at 291–92.

President Johnson used the incidents in the Tonkin Gulf, and the authority derived from the Tonkin Gulf Resolution, to widen the war. A few weeks before the election, however, he told an audience in Ohio that "we are not about to send American boys 9 or 10,000 miles away from home to do what Asian boys ought to be doing for themselves."[24] In that speech he estimated that there were about 18,000 American soldiers in Vietnam.

Once elected, he prepared the groundwork for massive intervention. Large bombing runs began in February 1965. By May the troop strength had grown to 42,000, and on July 28 he increased U.S. combat forces from 75,000 to 125,000, promising additional forces if needed.[25] U.S. involvement continued to deepen, eventually putting 500,000 American troops in Vietnam. Officials in the Johnson administration believed that increased application of military power would lead to North Vietnam's breaking point, but appalling casualties on both sides produced a bloody stalemate, spawned a powerful antiwar movement at home, and led to Johnson's announcement in 1968 that he would not run again for President.

Richard Nixon, elected in 1968 to end the war in Vietnam, actually widened it to include Cambodia and Laos. His "incursion" into Cambodia in 1970 triggered nationwide protests and provoked Congress to enact restrictive amendments in 1971 to forbid the introduction of U.S. ground combat troops or advisers into Cambodia.[26] By denying funds for all combat activities in Southeast Asia in 1973, Congress finally brought the war to an end.

Free World Forces

At the beginning of the Vietnam War, President Johnson made it easy for members of Congress to register their support or opposition. Instead of funding the war through an omnibus defense appropriations bill, which might have been difficult for legislators to vote against, he requested appropriations in a supplemental bill crafted exclusively for Southeast Asia. His message to Congress was clear: "For each Member of Congress who supports this request is voting to continue our effort to try to halt com-

---

24. Public Papers of the Presidents, 1963–64, II, 1391.
25. Public Papers of the Presidents, 1965, II, 795.
26. 84 Stat. 1943, sec. 7(a) (1971).

munist aggression."[27] Congress supported this supplemental bill by votes of 408 to 7 in the House and 88 to 3 in the Senate.[28]

Later, in an effort to build public support for the war, Johnson resorted to deception and stealth. For example, in September 1966 he expressed his "deep admiration as well as that of the American people for the action recently taken by the Philippines to send a civic action group of 2,000 men to assist the Vietnamese in resisting aggression and rebuilding their country."[29] Other announcements from the White House created the false impression that not only the Philippines but also Thailand, South Korea, and other members of what the administration called the "Free World Forces" had shown a willingness to sacrifice blood and resources in the stand against communism.

Hearings by Senator Stuart Symington (D-Mo.) in 1969 and 1970 discovered a number of secret agreements between the Johnson administration and the Free World Forces. The hearings revealed that the United States had offered sizable subsidies to those countries. For their modest assistance the Philippines received from the United States river patrol craft, engineer equipment, a special overseas allowance for their soldiers sent to Vietnam, and additional equipment to strengthen Philippine forces at home. It cost the United States $38.8 million to send one Filipino construction battalion to Vietnam.[30] Senator Fulbright remarked that it was his own feeling that "all we did was go over and hire their soldiers in order to support our then administration's view that so many people were in sympathy with our war in Vietnam."[31] Although the Philippine government denied that U.S. contributions represented a subsidy or a fee in return for sending the construction battalion, an investigation by the General Accounting Office (GAO) confirmed that quid pro quo assistance had indeed been given to the Philippines.[32]

The Symington subcommittee uncovered an agreement that the Johnson administration had made with the Royal Thai government in 1967 to cover any costs associated with the sending of Thai soldiers to Vietnam. An interim GAO report estimated that the U.S. government had invested "possibly more than $260 million in equipment, allowances, subsistence, construc-

27. Public Papers of the Presidents, 1965, I, 484.

28. 111 Cong. Rec. 9540–41, 9772 (1965); 74 Stat. 109 (1965).

29. Public Papers of the Presidents, 1966, II, 1029.

30. "United States Security Agreements and Commitments Abroad: The Republic of the Philippines" (part 1), hearings before the Senate Foreign Relations Committee, 91st Cong., 1st Sess. 255, 358 (1969).

31. Id. at 261.

32. New York Times, November 20, 1969, 13; 116 Cong. Rec. 9259–60 (1970).

tion, military sales concessions, and other support to the Thais for their contribution under the Free World Military Assistance program to Vietnam."[33] Other estimates put the total cost closer to $1 billion to obtain the deployment of a Thai division to fight in South Vietnam.[34] The Foreign Ministry of Thailand denied what evidence amply proved: the United States had offered payments to induce Thailand to send armed forces to Vietnam.[35]

U.S. subsidies were also used to support the sending of South Korean forces to Vietnam. American largesse included equipment to modernize Korean forces at home, equipment and additional costs to cover the deployment of Korean forces in Vietnam (including the payment of overseas allowances), loans from the Agency of International Development, and increased ammunition and communications facilities in Korea. For the period from fiscal 1965 to fiscal 1970, Korea's presence in Vietnam cost the United States an estimated $927.5 million.[36]

The legal basis for assistance to Free World Forces in Vietnam derived from legislation passed in 1966. Funds were made available to support Vietnamese "and other free world forces in Vietnam, and related costs . . . on such terms and conditions as the Secretary of Defense may determine."[37] Assistance was broadened in 1967 to include local forces in Laos and Thailand.[38] Reports on such expenditures were submitted only to the Armed Services and Appropriations Committees of both Houses. The general language of the statutes did not reveal the types of financial arrangements the Administration might enter into or with what country. Staff members who had access to the report told me that they did not know the nature and dimension of financing the Free World Forces until hearings were held by the Symington subcommittee.

National Commitments Resolution of 1969

Unilateral executive commitments, both financial and military, caused Senator Fulbright to reverse his position on presidential war power. In

33. 116 Cong. Rec. 40521 (1970); "United States Security Agreements and Commitments Abroad: Kingdom of Thailand" (part 3), hearings before the Senate Foreign Relations Committee, 91st Cong., 1st Sess. 624–25, 657 (1969).

34. New York Times, December 1, 1969, p. 1, col. 8.

35. New York Times, December 16, 1969, p. 10, col. 1.

36. "United States Security Agreements and Commitments Abroad: Republic of Korea" (part 6), hearings before the Senate Foreign Relations Committee, 91st Cong., 2d Sess. 1529–45 (1970).

37. 80 Stat. 37, sec. 401 (1966); 80 Stat. 82, sec. 102 (1966).

38. 81 Stat. 53, sec. 301 (196); 81 Stat. 248, sec. 639 (1967).

1961 he had written that "for the existing requirements of American foreign policy we have hobbled the President by too niggardly a grant of power."[39] Although it might be "distasteful and dangerous to vest the executive with powers unchecked and unbalanced," he questioned whether "we have any choice but to do so."[40] Having served as the point man in the Senate for the Tonkin Gulf Resolution, Fulbright was stunned in 1965 when President Johnson intervened in the Dominican Republic. In a lengthy speech, Fulbright dissected and repudiated the intervention, accusing the Johnson administration of relying on an exaggerated fear of communism.[41] That speech put an end to the Johnson-Fulbright alliance and freed Fulbright to challenge the policy in Vietnam.[42] By 1967 Fulbright could see "great merit in the checks and balances of our 18th century Constitution."[43]

The Senate passed a resolution in 1969 challenging the right of the President to commit the nation without congressional action. In an important sense, the resolution marked a return to Eisenhower's philosophy of interbranch cooperation and a recognition that Congress had been derelict in defending its constitutional powers. In reporting the resolution, the Senate Foreign Relations Committee noted the expansion of presidential power and said that if blame is to be apportioned "a fair share belongs to the Congress" because of its acquiescence and passivity.[44] This acquiescence by Congress "is probably the most important single fact accounting for the speed and virtual completeness of the transfer" of the war power from the legislative branch to the President.[45]

The committee report offered an interesting analysis to explain this acquiescence. Partly it was the unfamiliarity of the United States with its new role as a world power after 1900. Legislative decisions were made in an atmosphere of urgency, both real and contrived, and members of Congress might have been "overawed by the cult of executive expertise." Moreover, the Senate's rejection of the Covenant of the League of Nations might have created in Congress "a kind of penance for its prewar isolationism, and that penance has sometimes taken the form of overly hasty

39. J. William Fulbright, "American Foreign Policy in the 20th Century Under an 18th-Century Constitution," 47 Corn. L. Q. 1, 2 (1961).

40. Id. at 7.

41. 111 Cong. Rec. 23858–59 (1965).

42. Rowland Evans and Robert Novak, Lyndon B. Johnson: The Exercise of Power 529 (1966).

43. "U.S. Commitments to Foreign Powers," hearings before the Senate Foreign Relations Committee, 90th Cong., 1st Sess. 3 (1967).

44. S. Rept. No. 129, 91st Cong., 1st Sess. 8 (1969).

45. Id. at 15.

acquiescence in proposals for the acceptance of one form or another of international responsibility."[46]

Turning to the Tonkin Gulf Resolution, the report claimed that there was a discrepancy between the language of the resolution and what Congress intended. Although the statutory language appears to endorse a full-scale war in Southeast Asia, should the President determine that was necessary, few members of Congress expected a war of that magnitude. Many thought they were helping to prevent a large-scale conflict by taking a firm stand against aggression. Whatever the motivation, the delegation of such authority to the President was careless and irresponsible:

> In adopting a resolution with such sweeping language, however, Congress committed the error of making a *personal* judgment as to how President Johnson would implement the resolution when it had a responsibility to make an *institutional* judgment, first, as to what *any* President would do with so great an acknowledgment of power, and, second, as to whether, under the Constitution, Congress had a right to grant or concede the authority in question.[47]

The National Commitments Resolution, passed by a vote of 70 to 16, defined a national commitment as the use of U.S. armed forces on foreign territory or a promise to assist a foreign country by using U.S. armed forces or financial resources "either immediately or upon the happening of certain events." The resolution provides that "it is the sense of the Senate that a national commitment by the United States results only from affirmative action taken by the executive and legislative branches of the United States government by means of a treaty, statute, or concurrent resolution of both Houses of Congress specifically providing for such commitment."[48] Passed in the form of a Senate resolution, it had no legal effect. However, it signaled an important expression of constitutional principles by a bipartisan Senate. The Democrats supported it 43 to 3; the Republicans voted in favor 17 to 13.

This new attitude was revealed in 1970, following President Nixon's intervention in Cambodia. Secretary of State William Rogers explained to the Senate Foreign Relations Committee: "I think it is true that when we ask for military assistance and economic assistance for Cambodia we do

46. Id. at 16.
47. Id. at 23; (emphasis in original).
48. 115 Cong. Rec. 17245 (1969).

certainly take on some obligation for some continuity."[49] Congress enacted language to limit that commitment: "Military and economic assistance provided by the United States to Cambodia and authorized or appropriated pursuant to this or any other Act shall not be construed as a commitment by the United States to Cambodia for its defense."[50]

Disputes in the Courts

After intervening in Cambodia in 1970, President Nixon told the nation that the "only remaining American activity in Cambodia after July 1 [1970] will be air missions to interdict the movement of enemy troops and material where I find that is necessary to protect the lives and security of our men in South Vietnam."[51] Congress responded with other statutory restrictions. Section 601 of the military authorization bill in 1971 declared it the policy of the United States to terminate "at the earliest practicable date" all military operations in Southeast Asia and to provide for the "prompt and orderly withdrawal of all United States military forces at a date certain," subject to the release of all American prisoners of war. The statutory language placed upon the President the responsibility for establishing a final date for the withdrawal of all U.S. military forces.[52]

In signing the bill, Nixon said that Section 601 "does not represent the policies of this Administration" and was "without binding force or effect."[53] A federal district judge chided Nixon for his language, noting that when the bill embodying Section 601 was signed by the President "it established 'the policy of the United States' to the exclusion of any different executive or administration policy, and had binding force and effect on every officer of the Government. No executive statement denying efficacy to the legislation could have either validity or effect." The judge regarded Nixon's statement as "very unfortunate."[54]

Disagreement continued on the issue of whether appropriation bills are instruments for setting congressional policy. Officials in the Johnson administration argued that Congress had authorized the Vietnam War by appropriating funds for that purpose. Initially, federal judges accepted ap-

---

49. "Supplemental Foreign Assistance Authorization, 1970," hearings before the Senate Committee on Foreign Relations, 91st Cong., 2d Sess. 27 (1970).
50. 84 Stat. 1943, sec. 7(b) (1971).
51. Public Papers of the Presidents, 1970, 478.
52. 85 Stat. 430, sec. 601 (1971).
53. Public Papers of the Presidents, 1971, 1114.
54. DaCosta v. Nixon, 55 F.R.D. 145, 146 (E.D. N.Y. 1972).

propriations statutes as sufficient authority and rejected any claim to the contrary. Said one judge: "That some members of Congress talked like doves before voting with the hawks is an inadequate basis for a charge that the President was violating the Constitution in doing what Congress by its words had told him he might do."[55]

Experts from the academic community challenged that reasoning, advising the judiciary that appropriations bills do not encompass major declarations of policy. They cited House and Senate rules that are designed to prevent substantive legislation from being included in appropriations bills.[56] However, other court decisions endorsed the theory that Congress could indirectly assent to war by appropriating the necessary funds.[57] Some of those judges later found this theory unpersuasive. Federal appellate Judge Charles E. Wyzanski commented in a 1973 decision:

> This court cannot be unmindful of what every schoolboy knows: that in voting to appropriate money or to draft men a Congressman is not necessarily approving of the continuation of a war no matter how specifically the appropriation or draft act refers to that war. A Congressman wholly opposed to the war's commencement and continuation might vote for the military appropriations and for the draft measures because he was unwilling to abandon without support men already fighting. An honorable, decent, compassionate act of aiding those already in peril is no proof of consent to the actions that placed and continued them in that dangerous posture. We should not construe votes cast in pity and piety as though they were votes freely given to express consent.[58]

Similarly, federal appellate Judge Arlan Adams argued that it would be impossible to decide whether Congress, through its appropriations, meant to authorize the military activities in Vietnam: "To explore these issues would require the interrogation of members of Congress regarding what they intended by their votes, and then synthesization of the various

55. Berk v. Laird, 317 F.Supp. 715, 724 (E.D. N.Y. 1970), aff'd sub nom. Orlando v. Laird, 443 F.2d 1039 (2d Cir. 1971), cert. denied, 404 U.S. 869 (1971).

56. Id. at 718, 721 (testimony of Professors Richard F. Fenno, Jr., and Don Wallace, Jr.).

57. Orlando v. Laird, 317 F.Supp. 1013, 1018–19 (E.D. N.Y. 1970); Orlando v. Laird, 443 F.2d 1039, 1042 (2d Cir. 1971); Berk v. Laird, 429 F.2d 302, 305 (2d Cir. 1970); and DaCosta v. Laird, 448 F.2d 1368, 1369 (2d Cir. 1971).

58. Mitchell v. Laird, 476 F.2d 533, 538 (D.C. Cir. 1973). This decision was later withdrawn by court order.

answers. To do otherwise would call for a gross speculation in a delicate matter pertaining to foreign relations."[59]

The basis for continued U.S. military action seemed to have disappeared with the signing of a cease-fire agreement in Paris on January 27, 1973, and the withdrawal of all American troops from Vietnam by March 28, 1973. Nevertheless, the Nixon administration persisted with a massive bombing operation in Cambodia. The State Department submitted an analysis of the President's authority to continue U.S. air combat operations in Cambodia. Part of the justification rested on the "cooperation" of Congress in bringing about the cease-fire agreement: "This cooperation has been shown through consultations and through the authorization and appropriation process." The statement noted that Congress had rejected proposals by some members to cut off appropriations for necessary military expenditures and foreign assistance.[60]

On March 21, 1973, President Nixon asked Congress to increase from $750 million to $1.25 billion the Pentagon's authority to transfer funds from one appropriation account to another. John McClellan (D-Ark.), chairman of the Senate Appropriations Committee, asked whether it was correct to say that even if Congress denied the requested additional amount of $500 million in transfer authority, "the Cambodian proceedings and operations will go on anyway, that the administration feels it has the authority to continue these operations and incur the cost involved irrespective of whether the Congress grants this transfer authority." Defense Secretary Elliot Richardson answered: "Yes, that is correct."[61]

The House Appropriations Committee reduced the transfer authority to $430 million. Eight Democratic members of the committee joined in a separate statement expressing strong opposition to the committee's position. They felt it amounted to a "Congressional blank check approving combat activities of the Defense Department which have already taken place and giving Congressional approval to any future combat activities which may be deemed necessary to preserve our flexibility." The grant of transfer authority reminded them of the Gulf of Tonkin Resolution and the erosion of congressional influence in decisions affecting Southeast Asia. To approve the transfer request would start the "entire sordid chain of events in motion once again."[62]

---

59. Atlee v. Laird, 347 F.Supp. 689, 706 (E.D. Pa. 1972) (three-judge court), aff'd, Atlee v. Richardson, 411 U.S. 911 (1973).

60. 68 Dep't of State Bull. 655 (1973).

61. "Second Supplemental Appropriations for Fiscal Year 1973" (part 2), hearings before the Senate Committee on Appropriations, 93d Cong., 1st Sess. 1987 (1973).

62. H. Rept. No. 164, 93d Cong., 1st Sess. 22–23, 122 (1973).

The appropriations bill reached the House floor on May 10. An amendment by Joseph Addabbo (D-N.Y.) to delete the additional transfer authority carried 219 to 188, thus overturning the recommendation of the House Appropriations Committee. In addition, the House adopted an amendment by Clarence Long (D-Md.) to prohibit the use of any funds in the supplemental bill to support directly or indirectly U.S. combat activities in, over, or from off the shores of Cambodia. That amendment passed 224 to 172.[63]

The Senate Appropriations Committee voted to recommend only $170 million in increased transfer authority, prohibiting any transfers for the purpose of supporting combat activities in Cambodia and Laos.[64] Stronger measures would be needed, however. Even if denied transfer authority or access to funds in the supplemental appropriations bill, executive officials could finance the bombing with funds that had been appropriated in prior years. To close that door, the Senate Appropriations Committee adopted a more comprehensive amendment (the Eagleton amendment) to forbid the use of *any* funds to support U.S. combat activities in Cambodia or Laos—a restriction that covered funds contained in the supplemental bill as well as all funds made available by previous appropriations.

The two Houses reached a compromise on the amount of additional transfer authority: $75 million, provided that none of the funds could be used to support U.S. combat activities in Cambodia or Laos. The House also accepted the stronger Eagleton amendment. Nixon vetoed the bill on June 27, claiming that the Cambodia rider would "cripple or destroy the chances for an effective negotiated settlement in Cambodia and the withdrawal of all North Vietnamese troops." He also warned that the bill contained a number of appropriations that were essential for the continuation of governmental operations. Within a day, he said, nine agencies would have exhausted their authority to pay the salaries and expenses of their employees.[65]

A stalemate loomed as the dispute moved to its climax. An attempt to override the veto in the House of Representatives failed by a vote of 241 to 173, short of the necessary two-thirds.[66] A revised supplemental bill was drafted to delay the effect of the Eagleton amendment until August 15, allowing the President to bomb Cambodia for another forty-five days. Nixon signed that bill, which retained the substance of the Long amend-

63. 119 Cong. Rec. 15317, 15323 (1973).
64. S. Rept. No. 160, 93d Cong., 1st Sess. 21 (1973).
65. Public Papers of the Presidents, 1973, 621–22.
66. 119 Cong. Rec. 21778 (1973).

ment by prohibiting the use of any funds in the bill for combat activities in Southeast Asia. The additional $75 million in transfer authority was stricken from the bill.[67]

The August 15 compromise affected litigation that had been progressing in the federal courts. Congressman Robert Drinan (D-Mass.) and three other members of the House asked that the 1973 bombing of Cambodia be declared a violation of domestic and international law. Judge Joseph Tauro, a federal judge in Massachusetts, ruled that only in situations when a conflict between the executive and legislative branches appeared to be incapable of resolution should the courts intervene. Adoption of the August 15 compromise, he said, "demonstrates clearly and objectively that the branches were not in resolute conflict." Had Congress indicated an unwillingness to compromise, "we would have a clear issue of conflict before us that would have required judicial determination."[68]

Congresswoman Elizabeth Holtzman (D-N.Y.) filed a separate suit to have the courts determine that the President could not engage in combat operations in Cambodia and elsewhere in Southeast Asia in the absence of congressional authorization. Judge Orrin Judd, a federal judge in New York, held that Congress had not authorized the bombing of Cambodia. Its inability to override the veto and its subsequent adoption of the August 15 deadline could not be taken as an affirmative grant of authority: "It cannot be the rule that the President needs a vote of only one-third plus one of either House in order to conduct a war, but this would be the consequence of holding that Congress must override a Presidential veto in order to terminate hostilities which it has not authorized."[69] Judd enjoined President Nixon from engaging in combat operations in Cambodia but postponed the injunction for forty-eight hours to permit the administration to apply for a stay.

When the Second Circuit ordered a stay of the injunction until August 13, Holtzman appealed to the Supreme Court. Justice Marshall, assigned to oversee the proceedings of the Second Circuit, denied the Holtzman motion to vacate the stay. Marshall noted that once the August 15 date was reached, "the contours of this dispute will then be irrevocably altered. Hence, it is difficult to justify a stay for the purpose of preserving the status quo, since no action by this Court can freeze the issues in their present form."[70]

---

67. 87 Stat. 129, sec. 307 (1973).
68. Drinan v. Nixon, 364 F.Supp. 854, 860, 861 (D. Mass. 1973).
69. Holtzman v. Schlesinger, 361 F.Supp. 553, 565 (E.D. N.Y. 1973).
70. Holtzman v. Schlesinger, 414 U.S. 1304, 1310 (1973). On August 4 Justice Douglas vacated the stay, 414 U.S. 1316, but later that same day Justice Marshall reinstated the stay and announced that other members of the Court were unanimous in overruling the Douglas order, 414 U.S. 1321.

The Judd order was reversed on August 8 by the Second Circuit, which treated the dispute as basically a political question to be resolved by the executive and legislative branches. However, the Second Circuit did note that the August 15 date constituted congressional approval of the bombing in Cambodia.[71]

The War Powers Resolution

After decades of intense debate, Congress passed legislation in 1973 to limit presidential war power. The statute calls for "collective judgment" by Congress and the President before U.S. troops are sent into combat, especially for long-term military engagements. Although not the congressional intent, the War Powers Resolution has had the effect of allowing the President to make war unilaterally for up to ninety days. Congressional approval was supposedly required after that period, but that part of the resolution has not worked out as planned either. The statute also requires the President to report to Congress and encourages the President to consult with legislators before taking action.

Given the political atmosphere at the time of War Powers Resolution, it is tempting to view it solely as a response to the Vietnam War. The legislative history is filled with partisan attacks on Lyndon Johnson and Richard Nixon, but the resolution represents something greater than a mixture of partisan and personal politics. It is the product of almost four decades of bipartisan effort to recapture legislative authority that had drifted to the President. The resolution is better described as a slow, evolutionary culmination of institutional struggles and constitutional debate than as a narrow preoccupation with the Vietnam War.

Action by the House of Representatives in 1970 on the War Powers Resolution conceded a measure of war power to the President. Passed by a vote of 289 to 39, the resolution recognized that the President "in certain extraordinary and emergency circumstances has the authority to defend the United States and its citizens without specific prior authorization by the Congress." Instead of trying to define the precise conditions under which Presidents may act, the House opted for procedural safeguards. The President would be required, "whenever feasible," to consult with Congress before sending American forces into armed conflict. He was also to report the circumstances necessitating the action; the constitutional, legislative, and treaty provisions authorizing the action, together

71. Holtzman v. Schlesinger, 484 F.2d 1307, 1313–14 (2d Cir. 1973).

with his reasons for not seeking specific prior congressional authorization; and the estimated scope of activities.[72] The House passed the same resolution a year later,[73] but the Senate did not act on either measure.

Both Houses later passed the War Powers Resolution that went beyond mere reporting requirements. The House of Representatives, adhering to its earlier practices, did not try to define or codify presidential war powers. It directed the President "in every possible instance" to consult with Congress before sending forces into hostilities or situations in which hostilities might be imminent. If unable to do so, he was to report to Congress within seventy-two hours, setting forth the circumstances and details of his action. Unless Congress declared war within 120 days or specifically authorized the use of force, the President had to terminate the commitment and remove the troops. Congress could also direct disengagement at any time during the 120-day period by passing a concurrent resolution.[74]

The Senate thought it could identify the precise conditions under which Presidents could act unilaterally. Armed force could be used in three situations: (1) to repel an armed attack upon the United States, its territories and possessions, retaliate in the event of such an attack, and forestall the direct and imminent threat of such an attack; (2) to repel an armed attack against U.S. armed forces located outside the United States, its territories and possessions, and forestall the direct and imminent threat of such an attack; and (3) to rescue endangered American citizens and nationals in foreign countries or at sea. The first situation (except for the final clause) agrees with the understanding reached at the Philadelphia convention. The other situations reflect the changes in presidential power that developed later, including the broad concept of defensive war and actions taken to protect American lives and property.

The Senate bill required the President to cease military action unless Congress, within thirty days, specifically authorized him to continue. A separate provision allowed the President to sustain military operations beyond the thirty-day period if he determined that "unavoidable military necessity respecting the safety" of the armed forces required their continued use for purposes of "bringing about a prompt disengagement."[75] This attempt to codify presidential war powers carried a number of risks. Because of ambiguities in the language, legislation might broaden presiden-

---

72. 116 Cong. Rec. 37398–408 (1970).
73. 117 Cong. Rec. 28870–78 (1971).
74. 119 Cong. Rec. 24653–708 (1973).
75. Id. at 25051–120.

tial power instead of restricting it. Executive officials could give broad interpretations of such terms as "necessary and appropriate retaliatory actions," "imminent threat," and "endangered citizens."

After meeting in conference the two Houses developed a bill that included a mix of House and Senate provisions. President Nixon vetoed that bill because he believed it encroached upon the President's constitutional responsibilities as Commander in Chief. He also thought it was impractical and dangerous to try to fix in a statute the procedures by which the President and Congress would share the war power. He told Congress that the "only way in which the constitutional powers of a branch of the Government can be altered is by amending the Constitution—and any attempt to make such alterations by legislation alone is clearly without force."[76]

Both Houses overrode the veto. The House narrowly got the two-thirds (284 to 135); the Senate vote (75 to 18) was more decisive. Some of the congressional support for the War Powers Resolution was based more on partisan motivations than on constitutional analysis. Fifteen members of the House voted against the House bill and the conference version, arguing that it gave the President too much power. They should have sustained the veto to prevent the bill from becoming law, yet they voted to override.[77] In part they may have feared that a vote to sustain might have indirectly endorsed the views advanced by Nixon in his veto message. A failure to enact the bill could have been interpreted as support for the constitutional claims of Johnson and Nixon.

Other legislators used the override vote as part of the effort to impeach Nixon. One of those who voted against the House resolution and conference version, yet switched to override the veto, was Congresswoman Bella Abzug (D-N.Y.). She predicted that the override "could be a turning point in the struggle to control an administration that has run amuck. It could accelerate the demand for the impeachment of the President."[78] Another factor unrelated to the substance of the War Powers Resolution was the desire of Democrats to override Nixon, who had vetoed bills successfully eight straight times during the 93d Congress, with the two Houses unable to override. Some legislators saw the War Powers Resolution as a way to test congressional power.[79]

The vote on the War Powers Resolution was clouded by the Watergate

76. Public Papers of the Presidents, 1973, 893.

77. Representatives Abzug, Drinan, Duncan, Flynt, Harsha, Hechler (W.Va.), Holtzman, Hungate, Landrum, Lott, Maraziti, Milford, Natcher, Stubblefield, and Whitten.

78. 119 Cong. Rec. 36221 (1973).

79. Thomas F. Eagleton, War and Presidential Power 213–20 (1974).

scandal. The "Saturday Night Massacre," which sent Special Prosecutor Archibald Cox, Attorney General Elliot Richardson, and Deputy Attorney General William Ruckelshaus out of the government, occurred just four days before Nixon's veto of the War Powers Resolution. Ten days before the Saturday Night Massacre, Spiro Agnew had resigned as Vice President in the face of criminal charges. Much of the sober and balanced analysis that had preceded Nixon's veto was easily overshadowed by these sensational events.

Strengths and Weaknesses

The heart of the War Powers Resolution is Section 2(a), which states that the purpose of the resolution is "to ensure the collective judgment" of both branches when U.S. forces are introduced into hostilities. Surely that principle fits foursquare with the text of the Constitution and the intent of the framers. Two other sections—on consultation and reporting—are consistent with constitutional principles. The President is to consult with Congress "in every possible instance," leaving considerable discretion to the President but placing the emphasis on interbranch collaboration. The legislative history makes it clear that consultation goes beyond simply being informed that the President has made a decision. Consultation means that "a decision is pending on a problem and that Members of Congress are being asked by the President for their advice and opinions and, in appropriate circumstances, their approval of action contemplated."[80] After introducing forces into hostilities, the President is required to report to Congress within forty-eight hours.

The War Powers Resolution contemplated two means of legislative control: a supposed deadline of sixty to ninety days on presidential initiatives to use force and the use of a concurrent resolution to require him to remove troops engaged in hostilities. Neither control has been effective. The effort to combine elements of House and Senate bills resulted in a statute that is internally inconsistent.

For example, Section 2(c) attempts to define the President's constitutional powers as Commander in Chief to introduce U.S. forces into hostilities "or into situations where imminent involvement in hostilities is clearly indicated by the circumstances." The President may introduce troops *only* pursuant to (1) a declaration of war, (2) specific statutory authorization, or (3) "a national emergency created by attack upon the

80. H. Rept. No. 287, 93d Cong., 1st Sess. 6–7 (1973).

United States, its territories, or its armed forces."[81] Those three conditions are fairly much in accord with the Constitution and the framers' intent.

However, Section 4, governing reports to Congress, is not consistent with Section 2(c). Presidents may report under a broad range of circumstances unrelated to attacks on the United States, its territories, or its armed forces. Presidents may report when U.S. troops are introduced

(1) into hostilities or into situations where imminent involvement in hostilities is clearly indicated by the circumstances;

(2) into the territory, airspace or waters of a foreign nation, while equipped for combat, except for deployments which relate solely to supply, replacement, repair, or training of such forces; or

(3) in numbers which substantially enlarge United States Armed Forces equipped for combat already located in a foreign nation.[82]

This language appears to sanction presidential use of military force in situations wholly unrelated to attacks against U.S. territory and troops. Under this broader reading, the President may dispatch troops to intervene in Grenada, invade Panama or Haiti, or assist in Somalia and Bosnia.

Congressional control is further weakened by awkward language that fails to start the sixty-to-ninety-day clock. According to the War Powers Resolution, if the President introduces troops into hostilities he is to remove them unless Congress approves within sixty days. The President may extend the deadline by an additional thirty days if he determines that such an extension is necessary to protect and remove the troops. The problem with this procedure is that the clock does not start ticking for the sixty-to-ninety-day limit unless the President reports under a very specific section: Section 4(a)(1). For fairly obvious reasons, Presidents do not submit reports under that section. Instead, they report more generally. For example, when President Reagan reported to Congress on his air strikes against Libya in 1986, he reported "consistent with the War Powers Resolution."[83] The clock never started.

Only twice has Section 4(a)(1) been used. President Ford reported under Section 4(a)(1) to describe the capture of the U.S. merchant ship *Mayaguez* by Cambodian forces. However, by the time his report reached Congress, the military operation was already over. Reporting under Section 4(a)(1) did not restrict his actions. The second time Section 4(a)(1) was used was in 1983 when Congress passed the Lebanon Resolution. En-

81. 87 Stat. 555, sec. 2(c) (1973).
82. Id. at 555–56.
83. Public Papers of the Presidents, 1986, I, 478.

acted on October 12, 1983, the statute declared that Section 4(a)(1) had been activated on August 29, 1983. There were two weaknesses to this approach. It took a statute to start the clock, rather than a presidential report. Moreover, Congress authorized President Reagan to keep troops in Lebanon not for three months but for up to *eighteen* months.[84] He removed most of the U.S. Marines in February 1984.

The second form of congressional control—passage of a concurrent resolution—has been challenged on constitutional grounds. The legal adviser to the State Department told a House committee in 1975 that if the President has the power to put U.S. troops into combat, "that power could not be taken away by concurrent resolution because the power is constitutional in nature."[85] That position appeared to be strengthened by the Supreme Court in *INS* v. *Chadha* (1983), which held that Congress can control executive actions only by presenting a bill or joint resolution to the President for signature or veto.[86] Concurrent resolutions pass the House and the Senate but are not submitted to the President. (In Chapter 9, I argue in favor of the constitutionality of the concurrent resolution.)

Although the War Powers Resolution has not worked precisely as intended, especially the two key congressional controls, the general effect has been consistent with expectations in 1973. Even if the clock does not tick on the sixty-to-ninety-day deadline, executive officials *behave* as though it does. Military operations in Grenada and Panama were conducted as though the sixty-day limit was enforceable—if not legally, then politically. A former high-ranking member of the Joint Chiefs of Staff during the Reagan years revealed that as the sixty-day deadline drew near, administrative officials believed "it would not be politically wise" to challenge Congress on this particular issue.[87] For longer and more dangerous operations, such as in the Middle East in 1983 and in Iraq in 1991, Presidents have come to Congress to seek authorization. Specific experiences with the War Powers Resolution are covered in Chapter 7, and Chapter 9 analyzes a number of possible amendments to the resolution.

84. 97 Stat. 805 (1983).

85. "War Powers: A Test of Compliance," hearings before the House Committee on International Relations, 94th Cong., 1st Sess. 91 (1975).

86. 462 U.S. 919 (1983).

87. Christopher B. Howard, "The Role of the House Armed Services and Foreign Affairs Committees in Force Employment Policymaking: 97th–100th Congresses" (M. Phil. thesis, Oxford University, 1993), chap. 3, 55.

7

MILITARY INITIATIVES FROM FORD TO CLINTON

From Ford through Clinton, Presidents have used military force on numerous occasions by citing their power as Commander in Chief. Although they have challenged the constitutionality of the War Powers Resolution, the record since 1973 has been fairly uniform. Presidents have acted unilaterally when using force for short-term operations in areas of the world that are relatively isolated, with little chance of the conflict spreading. For military operations in regions that pose extreme danger of involving other nations, such as in the Middle East, they have sought congressional approval in advance (without fully admitting that they needed it).

The pattern of reports under the War Powers Resolution indicates an increased reliance on U.S. military forces. Presidents Ford and Carter reported only five uses of armed forces, and three of the occasions under Ford involved military efforts to evacuate American citizens and foreign nationals from Southeast Asia. Ignoring those three operations, in the six and a half years of Ford's and Carter's terms of office there were only two presidential initiatives to use armed forces: the rescue effort of the *Mayaguez* crew in 1975 and the attempt to rescue American hostages in Iran in 1980.

Military activity accelerated during the Reagan, Bush, and Clinton administrations. President Reagan submitted fourteen reports under the War Powers Resolution, President Bush six, and in his first year President Clinton issued five. Several of these reports covered major military operations: the dispatch of U.S. Marines to Lebanon in 1982, the invasion of Grenada in 1983, air strikes against Libya in 1986, military actions in the Persian Gulf in 1987 and 1988, the invasion of Panama in 1989, war against Iraq in 1991, military operations in Somalia in 1993, the launching of missiles against Baghdad in 1993, and air strikes in Bosnia.[1]

---

1. A thorough list of military activities since 1973 is provided by Ellen C. Collier, "The War Powers Resolution: Twenty Years of Experience," Congressional Research Service Rept. No. 94-42F (Jan. 11, 1994).

Evacuations from Southeast Asia

Early drafts of the War Powers Resolution discussed the President's responsibility to protect the lives and property of Americans. A bill introduced by Senator Jacob Javits (R-N.Y.) in 1971 would have permitted the President to use armed force "to protect the lives and property, as may be required, of United States nationals abroad." Javits later deleted the words "and property" for fear that they might be interpreted in nineteenth-century fashion to protect American businesses in other countries.[2] The rest of his language disappeared in the House-Senate negotiations leading to final passage of the War Powers Resolution.

This lack of explicit statutory authority, combined with other statutory restrictions on the use of force in Southeast Asia, produced a difficult decision for President Ford in 1975. He asked Congress to clarify the statutory restrictions to permit him to evacuate American citizens and foreign nationals from South Vietnam and Cambodia. Congress was given nine days to produce the desired legislation.[3] Instead of trying to act while a presidential timer ticked away, party leaders in Congress could have issued a statement saying that the President had sufficient authority for the evacuations provided he used a minimum of force and did not spread the conflict. Ford had already announced that the War Powers Resolution, as he interpreted it, gave the President "certain limited authority to protect American lives. And to that extent, I will use that law."[4] Why then ask Congress for clarifying authority with such a short deadline? The legal issue was complicated by the need to rescue foreign nationals as well, but it was politically unreasonable and unrealistic to expect Congress to complete legislation on such an explosive issue in nine days.

Members agonized for weeks, searching for language that would give Ford the authority he needed for the evacuations without possibly inviting military reinvolvement in Southeast Asia. Given the limitations of language and the history of bad-faith relations between the branches, it was unlikely that the legislative process would be successful. Legislators were whipsawed by conflicting emotions. On the one hand they wanted to relate all military operations to the procedures established in the War Powers Resolution; on the other, they were apprehensive that any legislation, no matter how meticulously drawn, would become anachronous

---

2. "War Powers Resolution," hearings before the Senate Committee on Foreign Relations, 92d Cong., 1st Sess. 35–36, 95–96, 128 (1971).

3. Public Papers of the Presidents, 1975, II, 464.

4. Id. at 414–15.

and ambiguous because of the rapidly changing conditions in Southeast Asia.

While Congress anguished over the wording of the legislation, Ford went ahead with the evacuations from Cambodia and South Vietnam. In each case he based his action on the President's "executive power" under the Constitution and his authority as Commander in Chief.[5] He took action before Congress could deliver the "clarifying authority," but even after the evacuations were over some members of Congress insisted that the legislation should still be passed. They reasoned that the President had conducted the evacuations within the limitations of the legislation under consideration (although Ford cited only constitutional sources in his reports) and therefore Congress should enact the legislation and legalize the President's action. Other legislators believed that the bill was moot because the evacuations were completed. Passage of the legislation, they feared, would merely lift the restrictions that barred any reintroduction of troops into Southeast Asia. The House, capping three weeks of legislative frenzy, voted down the conference report—an ignominious finale to an ill-conceived legislative exercise.[6]

Following the evacuations from Southeast Asia, Senator Thomas F. Eagleton (D-Mo.) introduced legislation explicitly recognizing the President's right to protect American lives (but not property) and stipulating various conditions to limit this presidential power. The citizens to be rescued would have to be involuntarily held with the express or tacit consent of the foreign government; there would have to be a direct and imminent threat to their lives; the foreign government either could not or would not protect the individuals; and the evacuations would have to take place as expeditiously as possible and with a minimum of force.[7] Congress took no action on this legislation.

The *Mayaguez* Capture

In May 1975, the U.S. merchant ship *Mayaguez*, traveling from Hong Kong to Sattahip, Thailand, was seized by Cambodians. Two days later the United States recovered the vessel and its crew after President Ford had ordered air strikes against Cambodia and introduced U.S. Marine ground

5. H. Doc. Nos. 105 and 124, 94th Cong., 1st Sess. (1975).

6. 121 Cong. Rec. 12752–64 (1975). For a GAO decision holding that the evacuation of Vietnamese nationals was necessarily incident to the rescue of Americans, see 55 Comp. Gen. 1081 (1976).

7. 121 Cong. Rec. 15579–82 (1975).

forces. Ford reported to Congress in accordance with Section 4(a)(1) of the War Powers Resolution, thereby triggering the sixty-day clock, but only after the operation was over. Thus, invoking 4(a)(1) had no practical effect. He said that the operation was ordered and conducted "pursuant to the President's constitutional Executive power and his authority as Commander-in-Chief of the United States Armed Forces."[8] Ford acted in light of North Korea's capture of the USS *Pueblo* in 1968, when the American crew was held captive for more than a year.

Although months would pass by before members of Congress had an adequate picture of what had taken place, on the very day of the recovery they rushed forward with glowing words of praise. A spirit of jingoism filled the air, and the episode became a "proud new chapter in our history." Legislators expressed pride in their country and in their President, exclaiming with youthful enthusiasm that it was "great to be an American."[9]

A few members reserved judgment, which was sensible, because no one knew exactly what had happened or why. A legislator could have announced: "I am happy that the crew is back. Unfortunately, many lives were lost in the rescue effort. It is still too early, and the facts too incomplete, for us to make a judgment." Most members, however, felt compelled to outdo each other with words of commendation and jubilation.

As details of the incident trickled in, Ford's action looked less and less appealing. Approximately forty-one Americans had lost their lives trying to rescue thirty-nine crewmen. The administration spent little effort probing diplomatic avenues before resorting to force, and the quality of military intelligence was not reassuring. U.S. Marines suffered heavy casualties during the assault on Koh Tang Island under the erroneous impression that the crewmen were detained there. As noted in one study, "18 of the 41 Marines who died . . . were killed raiding the wrong place."[10] A punitive spirit seemed to infuse the operations. The United States bombed the Cambodian mainland *after* the crew had been released. A 15,000-pound bomb—the largest conventional bomb in America's arsenal—was dropped on a Cambodian island that measured just a few square miles.[11]

8. Public Papers of the Presidents, 1975, I, 670.

9. See especially the Congressional Record of May 15, 1975.

10. Charles F. Bennett, "The Mayaguez Re-examined: Misperception in an Information Shortage," 1 Fletcher Forum 15, 16 (1976).

11. "Seizure of the Mayaguez" (parts I and II), hearings before the House Committee on International Relations, 94th Cong., 1st Sess. (1975); 121 Cong. Rec. 18312–13 (1975) (statement by Senator Javits); Jordan J. Paust, "The Seizure and Recovery of the Mayaguez," 85 Yale L. J. 774 (1976).

Administration officials insisted that this use of force contained valuable lessons regarding America's determination to meet its international commitments.[12] How that solitary event could help guide future emergencies is difficult to envision. Anthony Lewis of the *New York Times* said that for "all the bluster and righteous talk of principle, it is impossible to imagine the United States behaving that way toward anyone other than a weak, ruined country of little yellow people who have frustrated us."[13] An editorial in the *Washington Post* noted with alarm that the use of force by the greatest power in the world against a small country could serve as such a tonic in the nation's capital: "That anyone could find the Mayaguez affair a valid or meaningful guide to the requirements of post-Vietnam foreign policy at other times and places defies common sense."[14]

It is remarkable that one month after the costly disengagement from Southeast Asia, after the United States had finally broken free from a lengthy and violent war that had racked the country, there could be such a celebration of force. What happened to the "deliberative process" of Congress? The vaunted independent legislative capability? The promise of closer scrutiny of executive actions? Unless members take the time personally to analyze a President's decision, Congress cannot expect a co-equal status or a share in "collective judgment." Instead, legislators will become prematurely associated with a war policy they may later find unworthy of support.[15]

A federal district judge received a case in which former crewmen of the *Mayaguez* brought an action seeking damages for personal injuries suffered during the rescue effort. They claimed that U.S. agencies had knowledge of previous hostile acts by Cambodia and failed to give proper warning to the *Mayaguez*. They also argued that the military operation was executed in a negligent fashion. After stating that the "responsibility for the use of military forces is clearly committed to the President by the Constitution" and citing *Durand* v. *Hollins* (1860) as good law on the President's authority to implement military decisions without having to undergo judicial scrutiny, the judge held that Ford's action was immune from judicial review under the political question doctrine.[16]

12. "Seizure of the Mayaguez" (part 1), hearings before the House Committee on International Relations, 94th Cong., 1st Sess. 61–130 (1975).

13. The New York Times, May 19, 1975, at 29.

14. Washington Post, May 16, 1975, at A26.

15. Robert Zutz, "The Recapture of the S. S. Mayaguez: Failure of the Consultation Clause of the War Powers Resolution," 8 N.Y.U. J. Int'l L. & Pol. 457 (1976).

16. Rappenecker v. United States, 509 F.Supp. 1024, 1029, 1030 (N.D. Cal. 1980).

Desert One Rescue Effort

In November 1979, Iranian militants seized the U.S. embassy in Tehran and took more than fifty American citizens as hostage. They were held captive for the next 444 days, throughout the remainder of the Carter administration. Unable to obtain the release of the hostages by diplomatic efforts, Carter ordered a military raid that involved sending eight American helicopters to Iran to a remote staging area called Desert One. The helicopters were supposed to join up with six C-130 cargo planes carrying ninety commandos, leading to a military raid into Tehran. However, two of the helicopters malfunctioned and never reached Desert One. When a third developed a serious hydraulic problem, Carter canceled the operation. In leaving the site, a helicopter and a cargo plane collided, killing eight Americans and injuring several others. The surviving personnel were placed aboard the remaining cargo planes, leaving the abandoned helicopters at the staging site.

When President Carter reported to Congress on the use of military force in this rescue attempt, he reported "consistent" with the War Powers Resolution and relied on the President's authority as Chief Executive and Commander in Chief.[17] Secretary of State Cyrus Vance, who believed that several remaining political and diplomatic options should be considered before resorting to military force, was angry that the administration had decided on the rescue mission while he was out of town for a weekend.[18] Vance resigned in protest.

Vance believed that Carter should have notified the Democratic and Republican leaders in Congress about the planned raid, but Carter decided to consult with legislators only after the rescue operation had reached the point of no return.[19] On the evening prior to the operation, Carter met with Senate Majority Leader Robert C. Byrd (D-W.Va.) to discuss the possibility of military action in Iran and told Byrd that before he took any of the military actions mentioned in the press (mining, blockade, and so forth) he would consult first with Congress. Carter said that Byrd made a "sharp distinction" between consulting with Congress on military plans and informing Congress "at the last minute" about covert operations. Carter had planned to let Byrd know about the impending rescue attempt at the end of the conversation but chose to delay that briefing until the following evening after the U.S. team was actually in place and ready to

17. Public Papers of the Presidents, 1980–81, I, 779.
18. Cyrus Vance, Hard Choices 409 (1983).
19. Jimmy Carter, Keeping Faith 511 (1982).

enter Tehran. After Byrd left the White House, Carter wondered if it would have been better to confide in him: "His advice would have been valuable to me then—and also twenty-four hours later."[20]

Lebanon

Military initiatives by President Reagan in 1982 revealed severe weaknesses in the War Powers Resolution. Although hostilities were not merely "imminent" in Lebanon but had actually broken out, Reagan sent in troops without reporting under Section 4(a)(1). Consistent with Ford and Carter, he deployed troops pursuant to the President's "constitutional authority with respect to the conduct of foreign relations and as Commander-in-Chief of the United States Armed Forces."[21] Because Reagan refused to trigger the clock under the War Powers Resolution, Congress passed legislation in the fall of 1983, providing that the requirements of Section 4(a)(1) became operative on August 29, 1983.[22] However, instead of confining Reagan to sixty or ninety days, Congress authorized military action for eighteen months.[23]

Members supported this massive delegation partly on the assumption that Reagan, by signing the bill, would concede the legitimacy of the procedures established by the War Powers Resolution. Several of his public statements indicated the need and desirability of joint executive-legislative action. Writing to Congress on September 27, 1983, before enactment of the resolution triggering Section 4(a)(1), Reagan said it was his intention to "seek Congressional authorization" if it became necessary to substantially expand the number or role of U.S. armed forces in Lebanon.[24] After House action on the resolution, he announced that a "spirit of cooperation between members of the two parties, and between the executive and the legislative branches of our Government, has been the traditional hallmark of a successful foreign policy."[25] A day later he praised the Senate for passing the resolution, observing that the votes by the two Houses send a signal that "we speak with one voice."[26]

However, in signing the resolution he took exception to many of its

20. Id. at 514.
21. Public Papers of the Presidents, 1982, II, 1238.
22. 97 Stat. 805, sec. 2(b) (1983).
23. Id. at 807, sec. 6.
24. Public Papers of the Presidents, 1983, II, 1368.
25. Id. at 1384.
26. Id. at 1389.

provisions. With regard to the clock beginning on August 29, 1983, he noted that "the initiation of isolated or infrequent acts of violence against the United States Armed Forces does not necessarily constitute actual or imminent involvement in hostilities, even if casualties to those forces result."[27] As to the eighteen-month deadline, he thought it unwise and unconstitutional for Congress to establish precise periods for presidential use of force. He made it clear that he felt no constitutional obligation to seek congressional authorization after the expiration of the eighteen-month period if, in his view, further use of military action was necessary.[28] The possible confrontation over the deadline never materialized because the Lebanese operation was so lacking in congressional and public support that Reagan withdrew U.S. Marines in the spring of 1984.

Invasion of Grenada

On October 25, 1983, President Reagan announced that he had ordered U.S. troops to Grenada as part of a multilateral effort. A coup had resulted in the killing of Prime Minister Maurice Bishop, three cabinet members, two labor leaders, and other citizens. Participating in this invasion were contingents from Antigua, Barbados, Dominica, Jamaica, St. Lucia, and St. Vincent. These countries, with the exception of Barbados and Jamaica, were members of the Organization of Eastern Caribbean States (OECS), which voted unanimously for the military intervention. Reagan gave three justifications for the invasion: (1) the protection of lives, including up to a thousand Americans, (2) to forestall "further chaos," and (3) to assist in the restoration of "conditions of law and order and of governmental institutions" to the island of Grenada.[29]

President Reagan reported to Congress, "consistent with the War Powers Resolution," on the deployment of U.S. forces to Grenada. A total of 1,900 U.S. Army and Marine Corps personnel landed in Grenada, supported by elements of the U.S. Navy and Air Force. Member states of the OECS provided approximately 300 personnel. Reagan stated that he deployed U.S. forces pursuant to his constitutional authority "with respect to the conduct of foreign relations and as Commander-in-Chief of the United States Armed Forces."[30] In a later address he said that Grenada "was a Soviet-Cuban colony, being readied as a major military bastion to

27. Id. at 1444.
28. Id. at 1444–45.
29. Id. at 1505–06.
30. Id. at 1513.

export terror and undermine democracy."[31] There is little question, however, that intervention in Grenada permitted Reagan to shift attention away from mounting problems in Lebanon. On October 23, two days before his action in Grenada, a terrorist in Beirut drove a truck loaded with explosives into the U.S. Marine barracks, killing 241 American soldiers.[32]

Although Presidents regularly object to the constitutionality of the War Powers Resolution, the Reagan administration seemed to accept the sixty-day limit. The House of Representatives passed legislation stating that the requirements of Section 4(a)(1) of the War Powers Resolution became operative on October 25, 1983. This legislation, passed by a vote of 403 to 23, required the Reagan administration to conclude military operations within sixty days, with an additional thirty days for removal of troops if needed.[33] The Senate was about to pass the same type of legislation.[34]

With this legislative activity under way, the administration announced that it planned to withdraw all combat troops from Grenada by December 23. Because of this timetable, the administration said there was no need for Congress to complete action on the bill triggering Section 4(a)(1). Larry Speakes, White House press secretary, announced that the administration did not anticipate "any additional hostilities, and combat troops will be out, as Department of Defense said, before the 60-day period expires."[35]

Eleven members of Congress went to court, claiming that President Reagan had violated the Constitution. A district judge held that it would be unwise for courts to intrude into this dispute until Congress, as an entire body, had used all of the institutional remedies available to it. Suits by individual legislators, representing a fraction of the institution, would not be favored.[36] Upon appeal, it was held that the issue was moot because the invasion had been terminated.[37]

Air Strikes Against Libya

On March 24, 1986, the Reagan administration announced that U.S. naval aircraft and ships in the Gulf of Sidra had been the subject of attack by six

---

31. Id. at 1521.

32. Denise M. Bostdorff, "The Presidency and Promoted Crisis: Reagan, Grenada, and Issue Management," 21 Pres. Studies Q. 737 (1991).

33. 129 Cong. Rec. 29994–99, 30285 (1983).

34. Id. at 30600.

35. The New York Times, November 17, 1983, at 3.

36. Conyers v. Reagan, 578 F.Supp. 323 (D.D.C. 1984).

37. Conyers v. Reagan, 765 F.2d 1124 (D.C. Cir. 1985).

surface-to-air missiles launched by Libyan forces. U.S. forces fired back, sinking three Libyan patrol boats and damaging another. There were no American casualties or loss of aircraft or ships.[38] President Reagan reported to Congress that he had taken the actions pursuant to his authority as Commander in Chief.[39] He defended the air strikes as an act of "self-defense" and a preemptive strike designed to "deter acts of terrorism by Libya."[40]

On April 14, Reagan ordered a series of air strikes against targets in Libya: command and control systems, intelligence, communications, logistics, and training facilities. Air strikes were also directed against targets that jeopardized U.S. forces engaged in this mission. A White House announcement explained that the strikes were in retaliation for the bombing of the LaBelle, a West Berlin disco, that resulted in the death of a U.S. soldier and injury to about fifty American servicemen. The administration attributed the bombing to Libyan terrorists.[41] In an address to the nation, President Reagan stated that whenever U.S. citizens are "abused or attacked anywhere in the world on the direct orders of a hostile regime, we will respond so long as I'm in the Oval Office. Self-defense is not only our right, it is our duty. It is the purpose behind the mission undertaken tonight, a mission fully consistent with Article 51 of the United Nations Charter."[42]

In his report to Congress on the air strikes, President Reagan gave a brief description of the raids and repeated the claim that the action was taken as self-defense under Article 51 of the UN Charter. He also said that the strikes were designed to deter acts of terrorism by Libya. The measures were undertaken "pursuant to my authority under the Constitution, including my authority as Commander in Chief of United States Armed Forces."[43]

Reagan received the approval of Prime Minister Margaret Thatcher, who permitted American planes to take off from British soil to make the attack.[44] However, he did not consult with Congress or seek the permission of any of its members, and congressional leaders were called to the White House only as U.S. bombers were approaching Libya.[45] Congressman

38. Public Papers of the Presidents, 1986, 394, 395.
39. Id. at 407.
40. Id. at 478.
41. Id. at 468.
42. Id. at 469.
43. Id. at 478.
44. Cong. Q. Weekly Rept., April 19, 1986, at 882.
45. Id. at 1023.

Dante B. Fascell, chairman of the House Committee on Foreign Affairs, objected to this circumvention of the War Powers Resolution. Given the relations between the United States and Libya, the presence of American warships in the Gulf of Sidra involved imminent hostilities and should have produced a Section 4(a)(l) report from President Reagan.[46]

Escort Operations in the Persian Gulf

On May 17, 1987, the USS *Stark* was hit by an Iraqi missile in the Persian Gulf, and thirty-seven American sailors were killed in the accidental attack. In response, the Reagan administration adopted the policy of "reflagging" Kuwaiti oil tankers (registering them under the U.S. flag) to provide safe naval escort in the Gulf. The U.S. fleet gradually increased to include warships, minesweepers, and small patrol boats. Despite the presence of hostilities in the Gulf and the potential for further military conflicts, President Reagan did not report to Congress. The USS *Bridgeton* was seriously damaged by a mine on July 24 and the U.S.-chartered *Texaco-Caribbean* hit a mine on August 10. Still Reagan did not report.

Not until U.S. naval forces on September 21 fired at an Iranian Navy ship that was laying mines did Reagan begin reporting to Congress under the War Powers Resolution. He justified the military actions as an exercise of the right of self-defense under Article 51 of the UN Charter, citing his "constitutional authority with respect to the conduct of foreign affairs and as Commander-in-Chief."[47] Congress considered passing an authorizing resolution, as it had for Lebanon in 1983, but no final action was taken.

Congressman Mike Lowry (D-Wash.) and 112 other members of Congress filed suit in federal court asking the court to declare that a presidential report under Section 4(a)(1) was required as a result of the U.S. escort operations beginning on July 22 and the September 21 attack on the Iranian ship. The court dismissed the suit as nonjusticiable. Prudential considerations and the political question doctrine convinced the court that the issue had to be returned to the elected branches. The determination of what constitutes "hostilities" was a question for the executive and legislative branches, not for the courts. Only in the event of a "true confrontation" between the branches marked by the passage of legislation to en-

---

46. "War Powers, Libya, and State-Sponsored Terrorism," hearings before the House Committee on Foreign Affairs, 99th Cong., 2d Sess. 2 (1986).

47. Public Papers of the Presidents, 1987, II, 1074.

force the War Powers Resolution would the courts have jurisdiction to hear and decide such a case.[48]

Panama

In December 1989, with Congress out of session, President Bush ordered 11,000 troops into Panama to join up with 13,000 American troops already in the Canal Zone. Bush cited a number of reasons for intervening with Operation Just Cause. He said that General Manuel Noriega's threats and attacks upon Americans in Panama created "an imminent danger" to the 35,000 American citizens there and that, as President, he had "no higher obligation than to safeguard the lives of American citizens." He also felt an obligation "to bring General Noriega to justice in the United States." Other justifications cited by Bush included defending democracy in Panama, combating drug trafficking, and protecting the integrity of the Panama Canal treaty.[49]

Through this military intervention the United States was able to restore to office President Guillermo Endara and Vice Presidents Ricardo Arias Calderon and Guillermo Ford, who had been elected in May 1989 but removed from power by Noriega. In his report to Congress, Bush cited the right of self-defense under Article 51 of the UN Charter (protecting American lives), fulfilling U.S. responsibilities under the Panama Canal treaties, and his authority with respect to foreign relations and as Commander in Chief.[50]

Noriega surrendered on January 3, 1990, and was taken to the United States to be tried on various criminal charges. Beginning on that date, U.S. combat troops started leaving Panama.[51] In an address to a joint session of Congress on January 31, Bush announced that the American troops sent in to Panama would be out by the end of February.[52] Whether consciously or not, the administration appeared to be restricting itself to the sixty-to-ninety-day clock of the War Powers Resolution.

On February 7, the House of Representatives passed a resolution stating that Bush had acted "decisively and appropriately in ordering United

---

48. Lowry v. Reagan, 676 F.Supp. 333 (D.D.C. 1987); on appeal, the D.C. Circuit dismissed the case on grounds that it was moot and presented a nonjusticiable political question.

49. Public Papers of the Presidents, 1989, II, 1722–23.

50. Id. at 1734.

51. Public Papers of the Presidents, 1990, I, 8.

52. Id. at 130.

States forces to intervene in Panama after making substantial efforts to resolve the crisis in Panama by political, economic, and diplomatic means in order to avoid resorting to military action." While praising Bush with this language, the House also sought to prevent the Panama invasion from becoming a precedent for U.S. intervention elsewhere, especially in regions that had been subject to such interventions in the past (Central America, Mexico, and the Caribbean). To make that point the resolution stated: "Whereas the United States' action in Panama was a response to a unique set of circumstances, and does not undermine the commitment of the government of the United States to the principle of non-intervention in the internal affairs of other countries."[53]

The resolution passed the House 389 to 26 but was not acted upon by the Senate. During House debate, Congressman Robert Kastenmeier (D-Wis.) took "great exception to that provision of the resolution which gratuitously commends President Bush for ordering the invasion of Panama, an independent and sovereign nation, an action which, in my view, does violate international law and which has been condemned by 20 or 21 Latin American countries."[54]

Those observations by Kastenmeier anticipated some of the legal criticisms that later appeared in professional journals. The isolated incidents in Panama involving American citizens did not justify the use of military force for "self-defense." The 13,000 American troops already stationed in the Canal Zone were a sufficient force to protect U.S. citizens. If the United States has the right to invade whenever American citizens are threatened or mistreated in another country, it would have cause for intervening in dozens of other sovereign countries.[55] But such actions are prohibited by the Organization of American States (OAS) Charter, which the United States and Panama signed. Article 20 provides that the territory of a nation is inviolable and it "may not be the object, even temporarily, of military occupation or of other measures of force taken by another State, directly or indirectly, on any grounds whatever." The OAS condemned the invasion of Panama by a vote of 20 to 1.

With regard to the claim that U.S. action was necessary to protect the Panama Canal, the operation of the canal was not jeopardized until U.S. troops intervened. Panama "had not breached its duty to permit the free

53. 136 Cong. Rec. 1507 (1990).
54. Id. at 1511.
55. John Quigley, "The Legality of the United States Invasion of Panama," 15 Yale J. Int'l L. 276, 281–97 (1990).

transit of ships through the Canal; and even if it had, the Canal treaties do not give the United States a right to intervene militarily against Panama."[56]

Another justification offered by President Bush—intervening in Panama to protect democracy—has rather obvious problems. The United States would not accept that rationale if Nazi Germany or the Soviet Union used it to invade nearby countries under the pretext of protecting democracy. The UN Charter does not sanction invading another country to safeguard its political processes. If such a premise were adopted, the United States would be busy intervening in other countries to bring their governments up to what it considered to be minimum democratic standards. Louis Henkin has correctly noted: "There are many illegitimate, undemocratically elected and undemocratically maintained governments . . . whose territories the United States has not invaded and which the U.S. government indeed has continued to treat as friends."[57]

Abraham D. Sofaer, who served as legal adviser to the State Department during the time of the invasion of Panama, acknowledged that the United States "does not accept the notion that a state is entitled to use force to overthrow the dictator of another state."[58] However, he made the case for "humanitarian intervention," especially when the population of the invaded country "broadly approved of the action."[59] Ambassador Luigi R. Einaudi, in his address to the OAS on December 22, 1989, made a similar distinction: "I am not here this morning to claim a right on behalf of the United States to enforce the will of history by intervening in favor of democracy where we are not welcomed."[60] This is tenuous ground. As Louis Henkin has noted, the fact that the Panamanian people might have "welcomed" the American invasion is legally irrelevant. In 1938, citizens of Austria supposedly gave Hitler's troops a "tumultuous welcome."[61]

The final justification cited by Bush—intervening to combat drug trafficking—collapses with the merest scrutiny. In his appearance before the UN Security Council on December 20, 1989, Ambassador Thomas R. Pickering tried to analogize drug operations in Panama with military attacks on the United States:

56. Id. at 299.

57. Louis Henkin, "The Invasion of Panama Under International Law: A Gross Violation," 29 Columb. J. Transnat'l L. 293, 298 (1991).

58. Abraham D. Sofaer, "The Legality of the United States Action in Panama," 29 Colum. J. Transnat'l L. 281, 288 (1991).

59. Id.

60. United States Department of State, Bureau of Public Affairs, "Panama: A Just Cause," Current Policy No. 1240, at 3.

61. Henkin, "The Invasion of Panama Under International Law: A Gross Violation," at 300 n.30.

Countries that provide safe haven and support for the international drug trafficking cartels menace the peace and security just as surely as if they were using their own conventional military forces to attack our societies. The truth is, and every one of us knows it, General Noriega turned Panama into a haven for drug traffickers and a center for money laundering and transshipment of cocaine. General Noriega could not be permitted falsely to wrap himself in the flag of Panamanian sovereignty while the drug cartels with which he is allied intervene throughout this hemisphere. That is aggression. It is aggression against us all, and now it is being brought to an end.[62]

Acceptance of that reason would be a green light for American military intervention in Mexico, Colombia, Turkey, and other nations that contribute to the flow of drugs to the United States. Obviously that is not U.S. policy. Simply to pursue the logic is to reject it.

The Gulf War

After Saddam Hussein invaded Kuwait on August 2, 1990, President Bush began deploying U.S. forces to Saudi Arabia and the Middle East. At that point the operation was purely defensive, to deter further Iraqi aggression, but Bush's decision in November to double the size of U.S. forces gave him the capacity to wage offensive war. The constitutional issue was clear-cut: May the President take the nation from a defensive posture to an offensive operation without congressional approval?

The Bush administration made no effort to seek authority from Congress. Instead, it directed its energy into obtaining support from other nations and encouraging the UN Security Council to authorize the use of force, which it did on November 29. The UN resolution did not *require* the United States to use force; it merely "authorized" member states to take all necessary means to enforce Security Council resolutions. Actions by the United States after that point were entirely permissive and to be guided by constitutional processes.

After the Security Council vote on November 29, Professor Thomas M. Franck of the New York University Law School wrote an article for the *New York Times* in which he argued that a congressional declaration of

---

62. United States Department of State, Bureau of Public Affairs, "Panama: A Just Cause," Current Policy No. 1240, at 2.

war "is inapplicable to U.N. police actions."[63] Franck claimed that the UN Charter "does not leave room for each state, once the Council has acted, to defer compliance until it has authority from its own legislature," but the legislative histories of the UN Charter and the UN Participation Act do not support Franck's position. Although a declaration of war by Congress is not required for UN actions, clearly Congress was expected to approve the use of military commitments to the United Nations. It did not surrender its constitutional power. Franck is further in error by suggesting that the contemplated action against Iraq was a "U.N. police action." It was, instead, a military action dominated by the United States with the assistance of a number of allies.[64]

Franck's willingness to remove Congress from the decision to go to war is remarkable. In an article published in 1991, he conceded that the purpose of the war-declaring clause "was to ensure that this fateful decision did not rest with a single person." Does that mean that Congress therefore has a role? Not to Franck. "The new system vests that responsibility in the Security Council, a body where the most divergent interests and perspectives of humanity are represented and where five of fifteen members have a veto power. This Council is far less likely to be stampeded by combat fever than is Congress."[65] In short, although the framers expected Congress to share the war power with the President, contemporary conditions permit that power to be shared between the Security Council and the President. We cannot, for contemporary convenience, exclude Congress from its constitutional responsibility.

Secretary of Defense Dick Cheney testified before the Senate Armed Services Committee on December 3, 1990, that President Bush did not require "any additional authorization from the Congress" before attacking Iraq.[66] Reacting to Cheney's claim, the House Democratic Caucus on the following day adopted a resolution stating that the President must first seek authorization from Congress unless American lives were in danger. The resolution passed by the vote of 177 to 37.[67]

The Justice Department argued in court that President Bush could or-

63. Thomas M. Franck, "Declare War? Congress Can't," New York Times, December 11, 1990, at A27.

64. See the letter to New York Times, December 29, 1990, at 22, by John M. Hillebrecht, and also Michael J. Glennon, "The Constitution and Chapter VII of the United Nations Charter," 85 Am. J. Int'l L. 74 (1991).

65. Thomas M. Franck and Faiza Patel, "UN Police Action in Lieu of War: 'The Old Order Changeth,' " 85 Am. J. Int'l L. 74 (1991).

66. "Crisis in the Persian Gulf Region: U.S. Policy Options and Implications," hearings before the Senate Committee on Armed Services, 101st Cong., 2d Sess. 701 (1990).

67. Congressional Quarterly Almanac, 1990, at 742.

der offensive actions in Iraq without seeking advance authority from Congress, The case was brought by fifty-four members of Congress, who challenged the constitutional authority of the President to initiate war in the Persian Gulf. Although the court held that the case was not ripe for judicial determination, at the same time it rejected many of the sweeping interpretations advanced by the administration for independent presidential war powers. The Justice Department maintained that definitions of the war power were left to the elected branches, not the judiciary. Courts were excluded from such judgments, according to the Justice Department. Judge Harold H. Greene rejected that argument, noting that if the President

> had the sole power to determine that any particular offensive military operation, no matter how vast, does not constitute war-making but only an offensive military attack, the congressional power to declare war will be at the mercy of a semantic decision by the Executive. Such an "interpretation" would evade the plain language of the Constitution, and it cannot stand.[68]

Judge Greene disagreed with other propositions advanced by the administration. The Justice Department insisted that the judiciary had no place in deciding such questions because it would have to "inject itself into foreign affairs, a subject which the Constitution commits to the political branches."[69] That argument, Greene, said, "must fail."[70] Other passages in his opinion repudiated the administration's position on the war power. Either because of the court's decision or other factors, on January 8, 1991, President Bush asked Congress to pass legislation supporting his policy in the Persian Gulf. He was asked by reporters the next day whether he needed a resolution from Congress. He replied: "I don't think I need it. . . . I feel that I have the authority to fully implement the United Nations resolutions."[71] The legal crisis was avoided on January 12 when Congress authorized President Bush to take offensive actions against Iraq. In signing the legislation two days later,[72] he indicated that he could have acted without congressional authority:

> As I made clear to congressional leaders at the outset, my request for congressional support did not, and my signing this resolution does

68. Dellums v. Bush, 752 F.Supp. 1141, 1145 (D.D.C. 1990).
69. Id. at 1146.
70. Id.
71. 27 Weekly Comp. Pres. Doc. 25 (1991).
72. 105 Stat. 3 (1991).

not, constitute any change in the long-standing positions of the executive branch on either the President's constitutional authority to use the Armed Forces to defend vital U.S. interests or the constitutionality of the War Powers Resolution.[73]

After the war was over, Bush offered his views on presidential power in a speech given at Princeton University. Of his power to take the country to war without congressional authority he said: "Though I felt after studying the question that I had the inherent power to commit our forces to battle after the U.N. resolution, I solicited congressional support before committing our forces to the Gulf War."[74] His attitude toward Congress is reflected in a more mean-spirited way in a speech given in Texas during the 1992 campaign. Bush said that some people asked why he couldn't bring the same kind of purpose and success to domestic policy as he did to the war in Iraq. His answer: "I didn't have to get permission from some old goat in the United States Congress to kick Saddam Hussein out of Kuwait. That's the reason."[75]

Bush's signing statement and his speeches at Princeton and in Texas do not alter the fact that the resolution passed by Congress specifically authorized him to act. In a war of the magnitude contemplated in the Persian Gulf, President Bush needed *authority* (not merely "support") from Congress. The resolutions adopted by the Security Council were insufficient authorization. The UN Charter does not take from Congress the constitutional responsibilities and duties vested in the representative branch. Under no interpretation could the Charter do that. As the people's branch, Congress must debate and authorize all major military, political, and financial commitments, including the decision to go to war. Those determinations may not be left to judgments reached merely between the Security Council and the President.

Launching Missiles Against Baghdad

On June 26, 1993, President Bill Clinton ordered air strikes against Iraq. In an address to the nation, he reviewed the attempted assassination of former President Bush during a visit to Kuwait. Sixteen suspects, including two Iraqi nationals, had been arrested. Although the trial of those suspects was still under way in Kuwait, the CIA concluded that there was

---

73. 27 Weekly Comp. Pres. Doc. 48 (1991).
74. Public Papers of the Presidents, 1991, 497.
75. Public Papers of the Presidents, 1992–93, 995.

"compelling evidence that there was, in fact, a plot to assassinate former President Bush and that this plot, which included the use of a powerful bomb made in Iraq, was directed and pursued by the Iraqi intelligence service."[76] Clinton called the attempted assassination of Bush "an attack against our country and against all Americans."[77] In a message to Congress, he said that the attack was ordered "in the exercise of our inherent right of self-defense as recognized in Article 51 of the UN Charter and pursuant to my constitutional authority with respect to the conduct of foreign relations and as Commander in Chief."[78]

Clinton did not consult with members of Congress before ordering the launching of twenty-three Tomahawk cruise missiles against the Iraqi intelligence service's principal command-and-control facility in Baghdad. The facility was badly damaged, but three of the missiles destroyed homes in the surrounding neighborhood, killing eight people and wounding at least twelve others. News analyses suggested that the White House appreciated that the use of force would help rebuild Clinton's image into that of a strong and decisive leader. After Clinton's ragged start as President, members of Congress and the public had questioned his ability to lead the nation. A White House aide noted that the cruise missile attack would "serve notice to one and all that Americans are prepared first of all to exercise leadership and to remain engaged and to act with military force as appropriate."[79]

President Clinton said that the attack on Baghdad "was essential to protect our sovereignty, to send a message to those who engage in state-sponsored terrorism, to deter further violence against our people, and to affirm the expectation of civilized behavior among nations."[80] That argument is not credible. As two attorneys of constitutional law noted, "calling the U.S. bombing of Iraq an act of self-defense for an assassination plot that had been averted two months previously is quite a stretch."[81] If the United States had evidence of terrorist activity by Syria, it would not launch cruise missiles against its intelligence facilities located in cities. Iraq was attacked because, like Cambodia, Grenada, and Libya, it fell into the cate-

76. 29 Weekly Comp. Pres. Doc. 1181.

77. Id.

78. Id. at 1183.

79. Ruth Marcus and Daniel Williams, "Show of Strength Offers Benefits for Clinton," Washington Post, June 28, 1993, at A1.

80. 29 Weekly Comp. Pres. Doc. 1181.

81. Michael Ratner and Jules Lobel, "Bombing Baghdad: Illegal Reprisal or Self-Defense?" Legal Times, July 5, 1993, at 24.

gory of a weak and isolated nation vulnerable to the use of American military force.

Combat Operations in Somalia

Shortly before leaving office, President Bush dispatched U.S. troops to Somalia as part of a multination relief effort. A quarter of a million people had died in the Somalia famine. Without prompt humanitarian assistance, another million could have starved to death. Bush explained to the nation that the mission had a limited objective: "To open the supply routes, to get the food moving, and to prepare the way for a U.N. peacekeeping force to keep it moving. This operation is not open-ended. We will not stay one day longer than is absolutely necessary."[82] There were no plans "to dictate political outcomes."[83] In a letter to congressional leaders he said that there was no intention for U.S. armed forces in Somalia to become "involved in hostilities."[84]

The humanitarian effort turned bloody in June 1993 when twenty-three Pakistani peacekeepers were killed. After UN military officials blamed their deaths on a Somali political figure, Mohamed Farah Aideed, U.S. warplanes launched a retaliatory attack, hitting a radio station and four weapons-storage sites. What began as a nonpolitical effort to help starving Somalis now turned into a personal operation against Aideed. President Clinton explained that armed force was needed

> to undermine the capacity of Aideed to wreak military havoc in Mogadishu. He murdered 23 U.N. peacekeepers. And I would remind you that before the United States and the United Nations showed up, he was responsible for the deaths of countless Somalis from starvation, from disease, and from killing.
>
> The military back of Aideed has been broken. A warrant has been issued for his arrest. . . .[85]

In August 1993, four U.S. soldiers were killed when a land mine blasted apart their Humvee vehicle in Mogadishu. The killings were again attributed to Aideed, who remained at large. Earlier conflicts had killed four other American soldiers. Because of the transformed nature of the effort

82. 28 Weekly Comp. Pres. Doc. 2330–31 (1992).
83. Id. at 2331.
84. Id. at 2339.
85. 29 Weekly Comp. Pres. Doc. 1101 (1993).

in Somalia, the Pentagon began awarding American soldiers "hostile fire pay" for service in Somalia and authorized U.S. Army troops to wear a combat patch on their uniforms. Moreover, officials in the Clinton administration began to talk of "nation building": rebuilding political structures in Somalia to form a stable order.

By September 1993, members of Congress were drafting legislation that would require Clinton to remove American troops within a fixed period of time unless Congress enacted legislation authorizing that they remain. Congressman Lee Hamilton (D-Ind.), chairman of the House Foreign Affairs Committee, objected to the new mission of U.S. troops in Somalia: "I do not believe that the United States should be engaged in nation building in Somalia. That is the task of the United Nations."[86] U.S. casualties continued to mount. Under pressure from Congress, Clinton announced on October 7 that all American troops would be out of Somalia no later than March 31, 1994, except for a few hundred support personnel in noncombat roles.[87] He repeated the March 31 pledge a week later in a message to Congress, at which time he said the U.S. military mission "is not now, nor was it ever one of 'nation building.' "[88]

President Clinton and Congress forged a compromise arrangement. The defense appropriations bill provided that no funds for the operations of U.S. armed forces in Somalia could be used for expenses after March 31, 1994, although that date could be extended "if so requested by the President and authorized by the Congress." The legislation further provided that funds could be used after the March 31 date to protect American diplomatic facilities and American citizens. Moreover, to assure that American forces would not be under UN control, the measure provided that U.S. combat forces in Somalia "shall be under the command and control of United States commanders under the ultimate direction of the President of the United States."[89]

Troops to Haiti

In October 1993, President Clinton sent about 600 U.S. soldiers to Haiti to assist in restoring the deposed government of President Jean-Bertrand Aristide. The troops were largely military engineers, sent to work on roads, bridges, and water supplies, but the operation was part of a UN-

86. 139 Cong. Rec. H7090 (daily ed. September 28, 1993).
87. 29 Weekly Comp. Pres. Doc. 2024.
88. Id. at 2066.
89. 107 Stat. 1475–77, sec. 8151 (1993).

brokered agreement to force Haiti's military rulers to resign by October 15. When the ships arrived, a group of armed civilians prevented the troops from landing. On October 15, President Clinton implied that he might have to use military force against Haiti, ticking off the telltale signs of an impending U.S. intervention: a thousand American citizens lived in Haiti, Americans helped to operate the embassy, and the United States had "an interest in promoting democracy in this hemisphere."[90]

To enforce economic sanctions imposed by the UN Security Council, Clinton ordered six destroyers to patrol the waters off Haiti and reported this fact to Congress under the War Powers Resolution. He also ordered an infantry company to be on standby at the Guantanamo Naval Base in Cuba. Madeleine K. Albright, U.S. Ambassador to the United Nations, said that the administration had "not ruled out" a unilateral use of force in Haiti. Lieutenant General Raoul Cedras, the Haitian Army commander, made clear that there was "no threat against any American on Haitian soil."[91] Congress debated placing a limit on Clinton's power to send troops to Haiti, unless specifically authorized by statute, but in the end settled for nonbinding language making it the "sense of Congress" that funds appropriated should not be expended for U.S. military operations in Haiti unless authorized in advance by Congress. There were two exceptions for advance authorization: when necessary to protect or evacuate U.S. citizens from a situation of "imminent danger" and when "vital to the national security interests of the United States" and there "is not sufficient time" to seek and receive congressional authorization.[92]

In May 1994, Clinton said that with regard to Haiti "we cannot afford to discount the prospect of a military option."[93] In expressing a desire to work peacefully with nations in the Caribbean and Latin America, he announced that the United States "never will interfere in the affairs of another country to try to seek to thwart the popular will there. This is a different case."[94] Later that month, the House of Representatives debated several amendments designed to limit Clinton's military options in Haiti. The amendment that passed, 223 to 201, declared it to be the sense of Congress "that the United States should not undertake any military action directed against the mainland of Haiti unless the President first certifies to Congress that clear and present danger to citizens of the United States or

90. 29 Weekly Comp. Pres. Doc. 2082 (1993).
91. Washington Post, October 18, 1993, at A16.
92. 107 Stat. 1474, sec. 8147 (1993).
93. 30 Weekly Comp. Pres. Doc. 967 (1994).
94. Id.

United States interests requires such action."[95] Even that amendment, weak as it is, was voted down two weeks later on a separate vote.[96]

Congress continued to express uncertainty about its authority to constrain Clinton. On June 29, 1994, the Senate rejected an amendment stating that funds could not be used for any U.S. military operation in Haiti unless authorized in advance by Congress. However, that limitation would not apply if the President reported to Congress that deployment of armed forces to Haiti "is justified by United States national security interests."[97] What appears to be a prohibition on the use of funds could be lifted simply by a presidential statement that U.S. force is necessary for national security interests. In effect, the amendment contemplated delegating legislative prerogatives and duties to the President. That procedure was later adopted by the Senate, on a vote of 93 to 4, after making the amendment a nonbinding "sense of Congress."[98]

By late July, there were strong rumors that the UN Security Council was about to pass a resolution authorizing an invasion of Haiti. Dante Caputo, the UN's special envoy to Haiti, wrote a "confidential" memo to UN Secretary General Boutros Boutros-Ghali describing political calculations within the Clinton White House. This memo, placed in the *Congressional Record*, states that Clinton's advisers believed that an invasion of Haiti would be politically desirable because it would highlight for the American public "the President's decision making capability and the firmness of leadership in international political matters."[99]

On July 31, the UN Security Council adopted a resolution "inviting" all states, particularly those in the region of Haiti, to use "all necessary means" to remove the military leadership in that island. On this occasion the Senate spoke promptly and with a clear voice, passing a "sense of the Senate" amendment that the Security Council resolution "does not constitute authorization for the deployment of United States Armed Forces in Haiti under the Constitution of the United States or pursuant to the War Powers Resolution (Public Law 93-148)." This amendment passed by a vote of 100 to 0.[100] At a news conference on August 3, President Clinton once again denied that he needed authority from Congress to invade

95. 140 Cong. Rec. H3938, H3945 (daily ed. May 24, 1994).
96. Id. at H4253 (daily ed. June 9, 1994).
97. Id. at S7902-32 (daily ed. June 29, 1994).
98. Id. at S7932-37.
99. Id. at H6433 (daily ed. July 28, 1994).
100. Id. at S10415-33 (daily ed. August 3, 1994).

Haiti: "Like my predecessors of both parties, I have not agreed that I was constitutionally mandated" to obtain the support of Congress.[101]

In a nationwide televised address on September 15, President Clinton told the American public that he was prepared to use military force to invade Haiti, referring to the UN resolution of July 31 and his willingness to lead a multinational force "to carry out the will of the United Nations."[102] An invasion became unnecessary when former President Jimmy Carter negotiated an agreement in which the military leaders in Haiti agreed to step down to permit the return of Aristide. U.S. troops were sent in to occupy Haiti and provide stability. It was also reported that President Clinton had signed a secret contingency plan that authorizes the CIA to engage in political activities for the purpose of countering the opponents of Aristide.[103]

House and Senate debates were strongly critical of Clinton's insistence that he could act militarily against Haiti without legislative authority. Both Houses passed legislation stating that "the President should have sought and welcomed Congressional approval before deploying United States Forces to Haiti."[104] Even legislators who voted against this legislation agreed that Clinton should have gotten approval from Congress.[105]

Air Strikes in Bosnia

In addition to using military force against Iraq and Somalia and considering the introduction of U.S. troops into Haiti, President Clinton periodically threatened to order air strikes in Bosnia. Age-old rivalries between Serbs, Croats, and Muslims precipitated a huge number of deaths from fighting and famine in former Yugoslavia. In concert with the United Nations and NATO, the United States participated in humanitarian airlifts into Sarajevo and helped enforce a "no-fly zone" (a ban on unauthorized flights over Bosnia-Herzegovina). The U.S. forces initially assigned in-

101. 30 Weekly Comp. Pres. Doc. 1616 (1994).

102. Id. at 1780.

103. New York Times, September 28, 1994, A8.

104. 140 Cong. Rec. S14346 (daily ed. October 6, 1994), passing S. J. Res. 229; 140 Cong. Rec. H11111-12, H11122 (daily ed. October 6, 1994), passing H. J. Res. 416. A day later the House, by unanimous consent, agreed to S. J. Res. 229; 140 Cong. Rec. H 11297 (daily ed. October 7, 1994).

105. For example, of the eight Senators who voted against S. J. Res. 229, at least four agreed that Clinton should have first obtained approval from Congress: Senator Baucus (140 Cong. Rec. S14343), Senator Bradley (140 Cong. Rec. S14340), Senator Byrd (140 Cong. Rec. S14321), and Senator Feingold (140 Cong. Rec. S14313-14, S14316).

cluded thirteen F-15 and twelve F-18A fighter aircraft, equipped for combat and ready to fire in self-defense. Clinton reported to Congress on these flights.[106]

In other statements, Clinton sketched out some general policies: the United States would act not alone but only as part of a multilateral force; he would not consider the introduction of American ground forces; and the United States would not become involved as a partisan for one side.[107] Although in these statements Clinton indicated that he would consult closely with Congress and seek its "support," he did not state that prior authorization from Congress would be required before ordering air strikes. He did say, at one point, that for air strikes "Congress would have to agree."[108] Later he stated that he would "welcome and encourage congressional authorization of any military involvement in Bosnia."[109]

Congress considered various restrictions on military initiatives by Clinton in Bosnia. One amendment, never enacted, would have prevented the deployment of additional U.S. forces to Bosnia and Herzegovina unless Congress gave advance approval.[110] In response to pending amendments to restrict presidential actions in Bosnia and Haiti, Clinton objected that they would infringe on his constitutional authority to make foreign policy and deploy troops. He promised to "strenuously oppose such attempts to encroach on the President's foreign policy powers."[111] When asked whether he would veto legislation requiring him to obtain congressional consent before using troops in Haiti and Bosnia, he replied:

All I can tell you is that I think I have a big responsibility to try to appropriately consult with members of Congress in both parties— whenever we are in the process of making a decision which might lead to the use of force. I believe that. But I think that, clearly, the Constitution leaves the President, for good and sufficient reasons, the ultimate decisionmaking authority.

. . . the President should be very circumspect and very careful in committing the welfare and the lives of even our All-Volunteer Army. We need to have a clear American interest there, and there needs to be clearly-defined conditions of involvement, and the burden is on the President to provide those. But still the President must make the

106. 29 Weekly Comp. Pres. Doc. 586 (1993).
107. Id. at 652, 654, 659–60, 828, 1237–38.
108. Id. at 1711.
109. Id. at 2123.
110. 139 Cong. Rec. S12334 (daily ed. September 23, 1993).
111. 29 Weekly Comp. Pres. Doc. 2097 (1993).

ultimate decision, and I think it's a mistake to cut those decisions off in advance.[112]

In a message to Congress a day later, Clinton expressed his "grave concern" about a number of amendments designed to restrict the use of American troops in Haiti, Bosnia, and UN peacekeeping operations. He was "fundamentally opposed" to amendments that "improperly limit my ability to perform my constitutional duties as Commander-in-Chief, which may well have unconstitutional provisions." Adversaries and allies, he said, must know with certainty that the United States can respond decisively "to protect the lives of Americans and to address crises that challenge American interests." Amendments regarding "command and control" of U.S. forces "would insert Congress into the detailed execution of military contingency planning in an unprecedented manner."[113] Clinton's objections were misplaced. Congress has full constitutional authority to place limits on the deployment of American soldiers even when such restrictions affect "command and control." Such statutory restrictions are not unprecedented. Indeed, they are consistent with constitutional principles.

After substantial debate on various amendments, Congress and the administration compromised on sense-of-Congress (nonbinding) observations about the placement of U.S. troops under foreign commanders and the conditions for such engagements.[114] Congress also stated its sense that funds appropriated for defense should not be available for deploying U.S. forces to participate in the implementation of a peace settlement in Bosnia-Herzegovina "unless previously authorized by the Congress."[115]

In 1994, Clinton continued to threaten air strikes to bomb Serbian militias in Bosnia. Such actions would be taken in response to UN Security Council resolutions, operating through NATO's military command. As Clinton explained: "The authority under which air strikes can proceed, NATO acting out of area pursuant to U.N. authority, requires the common agreement of our NATO allies."[116] In late February, U.S. jets shot down four Serbian bombers over Bosnia. Clinton reported to Congress: "U.S. Armed Forces participate in these operations pursuant to my constitutional authority to conduct U.S. foreign relations and as Commander in

112. Id. at 2101–02.
113. Id. at 2104.
114. 107 Stat. 1478–80, sec. 9001 (1993). See also 107 Stat. 1839–40, sec. 1511 (1993).
115. 107 Stat. 1474, sec. 8146 (1993).
116. 30 Weekly Comp. Pres. Doc. 219–20 (February 6, 1994).

Chief."[117] This was the first time in the history of NATO that its forces had been engaged in combat. In April 1994, U.S. planes bombed Bosnian Serb forces involved in laying a siege around the Muslim-held city of Gorazde. UN officials requested the air strikes ostensibly to protect twelve international peacekeepers deployed in the city.[118] In August 1994, U.S. jets again hit Serbian positions.[119]

Using military force under NATO auspices raises the perennial issue of the meaning of "constitutional processes." To claim that the President, acting in concert with NATO allies, has the power to order military strikes without advance congressional authority would mean that the President and the Senate, through the treaty process, can obliterate the constitutional power of the House of Representatives to decide whether to take the nation to war. That position, no matter how often asserted, is untenable.

In May 1994, the Clinton administration released an unclassified summary of its policy for reforming multilateral peace operations. Conditions are established to decide on U.S. participation in peace operations, "with the most stringent applying to U.S. participation in missions that may involve combat."[120] The policy directive states that the President "will never relinquish command of U.S. forces," although the President may place American forces under the operational control of a foreign commander when it serves American security interests.[121] Seven proposals are put forth to increase the flow of information and consultation between the executive and legislative branches, including "periodic consultations with bipartisan Congressional leaders on foreign policy engagements that might involve U.S. forces, including possible deployments of U.S. military units in UN peace operations."[122] The summary report also supports legislation to amend the War Powers Resolution to introduce a consultative mechanism with a small core of congressional leaders and to eliminate the sixty-day withdrawal provision.[123] (See Appendiz G.)

As a means of diminishing, or extinguishing, the constitutional role of Congress in matters of going to war, it would be difficult to top this posi-

117. Id. at 406.
118. "U.S. Jets Strike Serb Forces Near Bosnian Town," Washington Post, April 11, 1994, A1; "U.S. Planes Blast Serb Forces Again," Washington Post, April 12, 1994, at A1.
119. "U.S. Jets Hit Serbs After Raid on Arms," Washington Post, August 6, 1994, A1.
120. "The Clinton Administration's Policy on Reforming Multilateral Peace Operations," Department of State Publication 10161, Bureau of International Organization Affairs, May 1994, 1.
121. Id. at 2.
122. Id. at 14.
123. Id. at 15.

tion paper. The President, in concert with the UN Security Council and such regional alliances as NATO, claims sufficient constitutional authority to use military force without ever seeking, or obtaining, approval from Congress. A regular series of meetings and briefings with key congressional leaders are sufficient gestures to meet the constitutional test, according to the Clinton administration. Will Congress accept this subordinate, second-class role? Will the American people be satisfied with these procedures? Whatever happened to the expectation of the framers that Congress, as the people's representative, would have to approve in advance any use of U.S. forces against foreign government?

8

COVERT OPERATIONS

From modest beginnings, covert activities of the federal government proliferated after World War II. At first an exception to the rule, they became more frequent and disturbing, more aggressive abroad and intrusive at home. Minor incidents of spying over the first three-quarters of American history were later eclipsed by attempted assassinations of foreign leaders and interventions (political and military) into the internal affairs of other countries. Tactics included sabotage, propaganda, support for opposition groups, destruction of economic facilities, mining of harbors, and conducting guerrilla operations. Private citizens, American and foreign, were recruited for these operations. After World War II, Congress authorized secret funding for the intelligence agencies, making it easier to conceal abuses.

Congressional oversight of covert operations, largely desultory in earlier years, gradually led in the 1970s to the creation of separate intelligence committees in the House and the Senate and the enactment of specific restrictions and procedures. The purpose: to make the President personally accountable for covert actions (previous Presidents hid behind the doctrine of "plausible deniability") and to provide for regular reporting to Congress. Legislative control remains inadequate and episodic, as witnessed by the Iran-Contra debacle during the Reagan years.

Seeds of Secrecy

Two constitutional provisions offer some potential for covert actions. One is the authority to grant letters of marque and reprisal, permitting the use of private individuals to commit military action against foreign governments. This constitutional power to substitute private parties for regular military forces was lodged solely in Congress, but in later years the executive branch turned to private citizens to conduct "paramilitary" operations. The other constitutional provision giving some support to covert actions is the Statement and Account Clause, which requires Congress to make a regular accounting of public funds to the people "from time to time." Those four words invite an element of secret funding. Neither passage resulted in serious covert activities throughout most of American history. The problems are recent, dating from World War II.

Article I grants Congress the power to "grant Letters of Marque and Reprisal." At a time when the United States lacked a standing army and a strong navy, Congress could authorize these letters to permit private individuals and privately-owned warships to make war against other nations. This power is given expressly to Congress, not to the President. As Jefferson noted in 1793, if reprisal is invoked "Congress must be called on to take it; the right of reprisal being expressly lodged with them by the constitution, & not with the executive."[1] In the Quasi-War with France in 1798, Congress authorized the President to grant to the owners of private armed ships special commissions, giving them "the same license and authority for the subduing, seizing and capturing any armed French vessel."[2] In the wars against Tripoli and the Barbary pirates, Congress frequently authorized the President to grant commissions to the owners of private armed vessels.[3]

Congress jealously guarded this power. An amendment in 1802 to give the President the power of granting letters of marque and reprisal was rejected.[4] In 1834, President Andrew Jackson asked Congress to delegate to him authority to issue letters of marque and reprisal for the purpose of redressing a debt owed by France to the United States. The repeated failure of France to appropriate funds to discharge this debt convinced Jackson that the United States should invoke a remedy sanctioned by the laws of nations:

> It is a well-settled principle of the international code that where one nation owes another a liquidated debt which it refuses or neglects to pay the aggrieved party may seize on the property belonging to the other, its citizens or subjects, sufficient to pay the debt without giving just cause of war.
>
> . . . I recommend that a law be passed authorizing reprisals upon French property in case provision shall not be made for the payment of the debt at the approaching session of the French Chambers. Such a measure ought not to be considered by France as a menace.[5]

The Senate Foreign Relations Committee concluded that Congress could not, and should not, delegate such power to any President. Al-

1. 6 The Writings of Thomas Jefferson 259 (P. Ford ed. 1895).
2. 1 Stat. 579, sec. 2 (1798).
3. 2 Stat. 130, sec. 3 (1802); 3 Stat. 230, sec. 3 (1815).
4. Annals of Cong., 7th Cong., 1st Sess. 431 (1802).
5. 3 Richardson 1325.

though reprisals "do not of themselves produce a state of public war . . . they are not unfrequently the immediate precursor of it." The committee believed that U.S. reprisals would provoke retaliation by France, plunging both nations into war. It noted that the authority to issue letters of marque and reprisal is associated in the same clause that grants Congress the power to declare war. Since that authority was specifically delegated to Congress, the legislative branch "ought to retain to itself the right of judging of the expediency of granting them, under all the circumstances existing at the time when they are proposed to be actually issued."[6] Nevertheless, from the 1940s on, the executive branch has used private citizens repeatedly for paramilitary operations.

A second source of covert authority lies in the Statement and Account Clause. In the interest of financial accountability, the Constitution requires that a regular statement and account of the receipts and expenditures of all public money shall be published "from time to time." Open budgeting permits accountability to citizens in a democratic society. But what is meant by the phrase "from time to time?" Does that allow for secrecy?

Toward the end of the Philadelphia convention, George Mason proposed that "an Account of the public expenditures should be annually published."[7] Gouverneur Morris and Rufus King objected that publication would be "impossible in many cases" and that periodic statements might be so general that they "would afford no satisfactory information."[8] James Madison proposed to strike "annually" from Mason's proposal and insert "from time to time." He thought this change would "enjoin the duty of frequent publications and leave enough to the discretion of the Legislature."[9] James Wilson, supporting Madison, remarked that many operations of finance "cannot be properly published at certain times."[10] The delegates unanimously adopted Madison's phrase "from time to time."

During the Virginia ratifying convention in 1788, George Mason objected that the phrase "from time to time" was too loose an expression, noting that one justification for this language was that "there might be some matters which require secrecy."[11] Although he conceded that secrecy was necessary sometimes for matters relative to military operations

---

6. S. Rept. No. 40, 23d Cong., 2d Sess. 21–22 (1835).
7. 2 Farrand 618.
8. Id.
9. Id. at 618–19.
10. Id.
11. 3 Elliot 459.

and foreign negotiations, he did not "conceive that the receipts and expenditures of the public money ought ever to be concealed." The people "had a right to know the expenditures of their money." Accounting from time to time "might afford opportunities of misapplying the public money, and sheltering those who did it." These statements suggest that Mason merely supported some delay in publishing sensitive material, rather than suppressing it entirely.

Madison also seemed to endorse full disclosure. By giving Congress the opportunity to publish from time to time, "they would be more full and satisfactory to the public, and would be sufficiently frequent."[12] Publication of governmental expenditures was essential for popular control. As Robert Livingston told his colleagues at the New York ratifying convention, the Statement and Account Clause operated as a check against political corruption: "Congress are to publish, from time to time, an account of their receipts and expenditures. These may be compared together; and if the former, year after year, exceed the latter, the corruption may be detected, and the people may use the constitutional mode of redress."[13]

James McHenry, a member of the constitutional convention, advised the Maryland House of Delegates that "the People who give their Money ought to know in what manner it is expended."[14] Notwithstanding this history and intent, covert spending in the 1990s for the Central Intelligence Agency and other elements of the intelligence community runs in the neighborhood of $30 billion a year.

Early Departures from Openness

Confidential spending began with a single statutory precedent in 1790, providing the President with a $40,000 account "for the support of such persons as he shall commission to serve the United States in foreign parts."[15] The President could account for such expenditures "as in his judgment may be made public, and also for the amount of such expenditures as he may think it advisable not to specify." Congress decided to give the President this discretion to avoid publicizing different salaries for foreign ministers and thereby make "invidious distinctions between foreign nations."[16] The statute was extended in 1793, allowing the President

12. Id. at 460.
13. 2 Elliot 345.
14. 3 Farrand 150.
15. 1 Stat. 128–29 (1790).
16. 1 Annals of Cong. 1089 (1790) (statement of Congressman Scott).

to use certificates instead of vouchers.[17] With certificates, Presidents simply state that funds have been spent appropriately; documents or vouchers are not needed.

Confidential funding provoked only three controversies in the nineteenth century. The first case of secret funding involved President Madison. Concerned that certain territory south of Georgia might pass from Spain to another foreign power, he asked Congress for authority to take temporary possession. Voting in secret session in 1811, Congress provided $100,000 for that purpose. The public did not know of this action until 1818, when Congress published the secret statute.[18]

The second controversy arose in 1846, when the House of Representatives asked President Polk to furnish an account of all payments made on presidential certificates for the contingent expenses of foreign intercourse from March 4, 1841, to May 8, 1843. Polk refused to release the information on the ground that Congress had given the President statutory authority to decide whether such expenditures should be made public.[19]

The last dispute in the nineteenth century, arising after the Civil War, involved the use of confidential funds by President Lincoln. The heirs of a spy who had served under Lincoln during the Civil War tried to recover compensation. The Supreme Court decided that Lincoln, as Commander in Chief, could properly employ secret agents to cross Confederate lines and obtain reconnaissance information. The Court, holding that the contract between Lincoln and the spy had to remain forever confidential, denied the claim for compensation.[20]

By the end of the nineteenth century, Congress had authorized and funded only one confidential account. Congress established three other confidential funds in the early decades of the twentieth century: a $25,000 travel fund for the President in 1906, $50,000 for the Secretary of the Navy in 1916 to obtain information from abroad, and $20,000 for the Federal Bureau of Investigation "to meet unforeseen emergencies."[21] In this lengthy period—from 1789 to 1935—Congress deviated from the Statement and Account Clause only four times and for relatively small amounts.

World War II triggered a sharp rise in confidential spending, decreasing the visibility of some parts of the federal budget. The President and other

17. 1 Stat. 300 (1793).
18. 3 Stat. 471–72 (1818). See David Hunter Miller, Secret Statutes of the United States (1918).
19. 5 Richardson 2283.
20. Totten v. United States, 92 U.S. 105 (1875).
21. 34 Stat. 454 (1906); 39 Stat. 557 (1916); 49 Stat. 78 (1935).

cabinet officials were given broad discretion in spending emergency and confidential funds.[22] The Roosevelt administration hid money in appropriations accounts during World War II to fund the Manhattan Project, which developed and produced the atomic bomb, and only a handful of legislators knew of the more than $2 billion spent on this project.[23]

Over the next few decades, confidential funds were created for a number of agencies and appropriations accounts: the Atomic Energy Commission, defense operation and maintenance, defense contingencies, the Attorney General, the Drug Enforcement Administration, the Food and Drug Administration, the U.S. Coast Guard, the Bureau of Customs, the U.S. Secret Service, the Immigration and Naturalization Service, the District of Columbia, and several accounts for the White House.[24] The dollar figures for these accounts were modest. The major portion of secret funding involved the various agencies that make up the intelligence community.

The Intelligence Community

During World War II, the Office of Strategic Services (OSS) engaged not only in intelligence gathering but also covert actions involving sabotage, assassination, and commando operations. Unlike contemporary practices for the intelligence community, the OSS appropriation was published in federal statutes.[25] The National Security Act of 1947 established the Central Intelligence Agency (CIA) to give advice on intelligence activities related to national security and to perform "such other functions and duties related to intelligence affecting the national security as the National Security Council may from time to time direct."[26]

The general phrase "other functions and duties" would be used later as legal authority for covert operations. A report to the National Security Council in 1948, "taking cognizance of the vicious covert activities of the USSR," stated that the overt foreign activities of the U.S. government "must be supplemented by covert operations." That responsibility was placed in the CIA under a new Office of Special Projects. Covert operations were supposed to be planned and conducted "in a manner consis-

22. 55 Stat. 682, 818 (1941); 56 Stat. 611, 704, 995–96 (1942).
23. Louis Fisher, "Confidential Spending and Governmental Accountability," 47 G.W. L. Rev. 347, 361–62 (1979).
24. Id. at 362–82.
25. 57 Stat. 526–27 (1943); 58 Stat. 534–35 (1944); 59 Stat. 483 (1945).
26. 61 Stat. 498, sec. 102(d)(5) (1947).

tent with US foreign and military policies." The report defined covert operations to mean activities conducted or sponsored by the U.S. government in such a way that its responsibility "is not evident to unauthorized persons and that if uncovered the US Government can plausibly disclaim any responsibility for them."[27] Other reports over the next few years amplified this policy.[28]

Statutory support for secret funding awaited the Central Intelligence Act of 1949, which contained extraordinary authority over the transfer and application of funds. Sums made available to the CIA "may be expended without regard to the provisions of law and regulations relating to the expenditure of Government funds." For objects of a confidential nature, expenditures can be accounted for solely on the certificate of the CIA Director, with each certificate deemed a sufficient voucher for the amount spent.[29] In addition, rather than appropriating directly to the CIA, Congress authorized the agency to transfer to and receive from other government agencies "such sums as may be approved" by the Bureau of the Budget (later the Office of Management and Budget [OMB]) for the performance of any functions or activities authorized by the National Security Act of 1947. Other agencies were authorized to transfer to or receive from the CIA such sums "without regard to any provisions of law limiting or prohibiting transfers between appropriations."[30]

Funds for the "intelligence community" (Central Intelligence Agency, National Security Agency, Defense Intelligence Agency, National Reconnaissance Office, and other agencies) are initially concealed in several appropriations bills, the main one being defense. Appropriations accounts must be artificially inflated to hide the amounts destined for the intelligence community. After enactment of these bills, the OMB transfers the appropriate amounts to the intelligence agencies.

Current criticism of the CIA results from its evolution from an intelligence-gathering agency, confined to foreign activities, to that of a participant/catalyst in military and political operations that often affect domestic affairs. Harry Howe Ransom, a leading scholar on the subject, concluded that nothing in the public record nor in public archives (for example, the Truman Library) "suggests that Congress ever intended to create or knew that it was creating an agency for para-military operations and a wide

27. A Report to the National Security Council by Executive Secretary on Office of Special Projects, NSC 10/1, June 15, 1948, secs. 1, 3a, 3e(1), 5.
28. NSC 10/2, June 18, 1948; NSC 5412/1, March 12, 1955.
29. 63 Stat. 213, sec. 10 (1949).
30. 63 Stat. 211, sec. 6 (1949); 50 U.S.C. 403 (1988).

range of foreign political interventions."[31] Certainly the use of an intelligence agency for domestic operations was never anticipated, but OSS precedents and the early documents creating the CIA looked to an intelligence agency capable of conducting subversive operations abroad.

Beginning in the late 1940s, some of the power to use private individuals for war-making purposes shifted from legislative to executive control, and the CIA used paramilitary troops against foreign governments on numerous occasions. In 1953, the CIA was instrumental in undermining the Mossadegh regime in Iran and returning the Shah to his throne. In such countries as Guatemala, Cuba, and Nicaragua, the Agency hired mercenaries and directed them to carry out U.S. foreign policy. In Guatemala the CIA helped oust the Arbenz government in 1954 and orchestrated the ill-conceived Bay of Pigs invasion in Cuba in 1961.

Although President Eisenhower sought congressional support in advance of possible military action in Formosa and the Middle East, relying on area resolutions for executive-legislative cooperation, he readily sanctioned covert operations in Iran and Guatemala without seeking legislative authority. Planning for the Bay of Pigs invasion was initiated by his administration. CIA activities in the 1950s reflected the attitudes of the Doolittle Committee, a special study group created by Eisenhower in 1954 to examine covert operations by the CIA. Its report cited the need for a gloves-off policy:

> . . . another important requirement is an aggressive covert psychological, political and paramilitary organization more effective, more unique and, if necessary, more ruthless than that employed by the enemy. No one should be permitted to stand in the way of the prompt, efficient and secure accomplishment of this mission.
>
> . . . It is now clear that we are facing an implacable enemy whose avowed objective is world domination by whatever means and at whatever cost. There are no rules in such a game. Hitherto acceptable norms of human conduct do not apply. If the United States is to survive, long-standing American concepts of "fair play" must be reconsidered.[32]

In the early 1970s, the CIA spent millions trying to discredit Salvador Allende, the Marxist-socialist leader in Chile, and from 1963 to 1973, the

31. Harry Howe Ransom, "Secret Intelligence Agencies and Congress," Society, March/April 1975, at 34.

32. Special Study Group on Covert Activities of the Central Intelligence Agency, September 30, 1954, at 6–7 (declassified in part in 1976).

Agency supported the Meo hill tribes of North Laos in a war against the Communist Pathet Lao. The CIA also sponsored guerrilla wars in the Ukraine, Poland, Albania, Hungary, Indonesia, China, Oman, Malaysia, Iraq, the Dominican Republic, Venezuela, North Korea, Bolivia, Thailand, Haiti, Greece, Turkey, Vietnam, Afghanistan, and Angola.[33]

The CIA has been involved in a number of plots to assassinate foreign leaders: Fidel Castro in Cuba, Patrice Lumumba in the Congo (now Zaire), Rafael Trujillo in the Dominican Republic, Ngo Dinh Diem in South Vietnam, and General Rene Schneider of Chile. The efforts against Castro failed, a rival Congolese faction murdered Lumumba before CIA operatives could carry out their plan, and the other murders were accomplished without full Agency control.[34] The Church Committee, established by the Senate to investigate abuses by intelligence agencies, recommended in 1975 that Congress enact legislation "making it a Federal crime to commit or attempt an assassination, or to conspire to do so."[35]

In 1976, President Ford issued Executive Order 11905 on "United States Foreign Intelligence Activities." One of the sections prohibited assassinations: "No employee of the United States Government shall engage in, or conspire to engage in, political assassination."[36] President Carter continued that ban in 1978 with Executive Order 12036,[37] as did President Reagan in 1981 with Executive Order 12333.[38] Nonetheless, in 1984 Congress learned of a CIA-approved manual that advocated that government officials in Nicaragua be "neutralized." As translated by the Congressional Research Service, the manual read:

> It is possible to neutralize carefully selected and planned targets, such as court judges . . . police and state security officials, CDA (Sandinista Defense Committee) chief, etc. For psychological purposes, it is necessary to take extreme precautions, and it is absolutely necessary to

---

33. Loch J. Johnson, America's Secret Power: The CIA in a Democratic Society 26 (1989); Jules Lobel, "Covert War and Congressional Authority: Hidden War and Forgotten Power," 134 U. Pa. L. Rev. 1035, 1056, 1076 n.178 (1986).

34. Johnson, America's Secret Power 27–28; John Ranelagh, The Agency: The Rise and Decline of the Agency 336–45 (1987); "Alleged Assassination Plots Involving Foreign Leaders," S. Rept. No. 465, 94th Cong., 1st Sess. 4–5 (1975).

35. S. Rept. No. 465, 94th Cong., 1st Sess. 281 (1975).

36. 41 Fed. Reg. 7733 (1976).

37. 43 Fed. Reg. 3687 [Sec. 2.305] (1978).

38. 46 Fed. Reg. 59952 [Sec. 2.11] (1981).

gather together the population affected, so that they will be present, take part in the act, and formulate accusations against the oppressor.[39]

The word "neutralize," especially in the context used, appeared to mean assassination. More charitable interpretations were offered, such as advocating "restraint" on certain officials. The CIA took sanctions against six employees for their role in producing the manual.[40]

Even with assassinations supposedly prohibited by executive order, military operations can "indirectly" kill the leader of a foreign country. In the air raids on Libya in 1986, the headquarters of Muammar el-Qaddafi was damaged in the attack, but administration officials denied that the intent was to kill the Libyan leader.[41] There have been reports that the Bush administration gave some consideration to a plan to kill Saddam Hussein during his travels between Baghdad and Kuwait City,[42] and the Clinton administration's plan to "capture" Mohamed Farah Aideed in Somalia came very close to killing him.[43]

Statutory Controls on the CIA

The War Powers Resolution of 1973 placed restrictions only on the President's power to dispatch *armed service personnel* into hostilities. Not covered are activities by civilian combatants and "paramilitary operations." The resolution does cover, however, instances in which military personnel are temporarily detailed to the CIA, but it does not cover the CIA's use of civilian or ex-military personnel.[44]

Senator Thomas Eagleton proposed that covert operations be explicitly covered by the War Powers Resolution. He had in mind the CIA advisers who organized indigenous Laotian forces to engage in hostilities to carry out the policy objectives established by the executive branch of the U.S. government.[45] Another example was the covert military operation, under the code name Operation Plan 34A, initiated by President Johnson in Feb-

39. Congressional Quarterly Almanac, 1984, at 91.
40. Id.
41. Congressional Quarterly Weekly Report, April 19, 1986, at 838.
42. "The Plan to Kill Saddam Hussein," Newsweek, January 10, 1994, at 31.
43. Patrick J. Sloyan, "How the Warlord Outwitted Clinton's Spooks," Washington Post, April 3, 1994, at C3.
44. 4A O.L.C. 197 (1983).
45. 119 Cong. Rec. 25079 (1973).

ruary 1964 to provoke the enemy and justify the bombing of North Vietnam.[46] Eagleton's amendment was defeated, 34 to 53.[47]

In 1974, Congress attempted to monitor covert operations by requiring timely reporting by the President. As a general limitation on intelligence activities, the Hughes-Ryan Amendment of 1974 provided that no funds appropriated may be expended by or on behalf of the CIA for operations in foreign countries, other than activities intended solely for obtaining necessary intelligence, "unless and until the President finds that each operation is important to the national security of the United States and reports, in a timely fashion, a description and scope of such operations" to the appropriate committees of Congress, including the Senate Committee on Foreign Relations and the House Committee on Foreign Affairs. The Armed Services and the Appropriations Committees also received the reports. This procedure would not apply during military operations initiated by the United States under a declaration of war approved by the Congress "or an exercise of powers by the President under the War Powers Resolution."[48]

The Hughes-Ryan Amendment responded to reports about the CIA's involvement in the overthrow of the Allende regime in Chile in 1973. The Amendment had several purposes. One was to provide some assurance that designated congressional committees would be notified of covert activities. However, the opportunity for executive evasion was evident in the vague language requiring that the President report to Congress "in a timely fashion." The second purpose was to require that the President be personally responsible for approving these operations. Instead of a system of "plausible denial," permitting the President to feign ignorance of actions taken by the executive branch, the Hughes-Ryan Amendment required the President to "find" that these operations were important to U.S. national security. Findings had to be signed by the President.

In 1975, Congress enacted legislation to prohibit a CIA operation in Angola. The Angolan civil war involved a Cuban-and-Soviet-supported faction fighting against an opposition force assisted by the CIA. The Agency spent an estimated $32 million for arms and equipment, communications gear, political action support, and other items.[49] Toward the end of 1975, Senator John Tunney offered an amendment to strike $33 million in CIA

---

46. Id. at 25080.

47. Id. at 25092. Senator Eagleton reintroduced his amendment two years later; 121 Cong. Rec. 40884 (1975).

48. 88 Stat. 1804, sec. 32 (1974); H. Rept. No. 1471, 93d Cong., 2d Sess. 43–44 (1974).

49. Stephen R. Weissman, "CIA Covert Action in Zaire and Angola: Patterns and Consequences," 94 Pol. Sci. Q. 263, 283–84 (1979).

money hidden in an account in the defense appropriations bill and to restrict CIA activities in Angola to intelligence gathering.[50] The reduction was not accepted, but the restriction on CIA actions in Angola became law in early 1976.[51] Having finally extricated the United States from Southeast Asia, Congress was in no mood to approve military involvement in Africa.

The Senate acted partly in response to duplicity within the Ford administration. During hearings held by the Senate Foreign Relations Committee, the CIA deputy director of operations admitted that the agency was sending arms to Angola. Shortly after he left the room, the deputy assistant secretary of state for African affairs testified that arms were not being sent to Angola (the administration's cover story). Confronted with the earlier admission by the CIA, the State Department witness switched his position. The committee then unanimously agreed to terminate U.S. military involvement in Angola.[52]

Also in 1976, Congress enacted what became known as the Clark Amendment (named after Senator Dick Clark) to place further restrictions on CIA activities in Angola. The legislative language provided that no assistance "of any kind may be provided for the purpose, or which would have the effect, of promoting or augmenting, directly or indirectly, the capacity of any nation, group, organization, movement, or individual to conduct military or paramilitary operations in Angola unless and until the Congress expressly authorizes such assistance by law."[53]

The Clark Amendment did not prohibit U.S. intervention in Angola. It merely required that U.S. assistance "be provided openly, through authorizations approved by Congress."[54] If the administration wanted to intervene in Angola it had to come to Congress, present its views, and answer questions. In 1976, Congress also used its power of the purse to deny funds to military activities in Angola: "None of the funds appropriated or made available pursuant to this Act shall be obligated or expended to finance directly or indirectly any type of military assistance to Angola."[55] The Clark Amendment was repealed in 1985.[56]

Following a series of disclosures in the 1970s about CIA violations and abuses, both at home and abroad, Congress created intelligence commit-

50. 121 Cong. Rec. 41141, 42213–19 (1975); 122 Cong. Rec. 1035–57 (1976).
51. 90 Stat. 166 (1976).
52. John Stockwell, In Search of Enemies: A CIA Story 230 (1978).
53. 90 Stat. 757, sec. 404 (1976).
54. S. Rept. No. 97–83, 97th Cong., 1st Sess. 79 (1981).
55. 90 Stat. 776, sec. 109 (1976).
56. 99 Stat. 264, sec. 811 (1985).

tees in each House to review and authorize Agency operations. Congress passed legislation in 1980 to regulate the President's power to engage in covert actions. The Intelligence Oversight Act of 1980 repealed Hughes-Ryan and reduced the number of congressional committees entitled to be notified of covert actions from eight to two.[57] The 1980 statute required the Director of Central Intelligence and the heads of all other agencies or entities of the United States involved in intelligence activities to keep the two intelligence committees "fully and currently informed" of all intelligence activities. If the President determined that it was essential to limit prior notice to meet "extraordinary circumstances affecting vital interests of the United States," he could limit notice to eight members of Congress: the chair and ranking minority members of the intelligence committees, the Speaker and Minority Leader of the House, and the Majority and Minority Leaders of the Senate.[58] This so-called Gang of Eight was never notified of the Iran-Contra operations. Under the 1980 statute, if the President did not give notice to Congress, he had to "fully inform" the intelligence committees "in a timely fashion" and explain the failure to provide notice, but President Reagan never notified the intelligence committees of the events, separate or combined, that became known as the Iran-Contra affair. After ten months had elapsed some of the facts spilled out in Lebanese and U.S. newspapers.

Covert Action in the Open

CIA involvement in Angola illustrates how often covert operations become the topic of public debate. So prevalent is this pattern that it suggests a basic principle: Covert operations should be conducted with the understanding that they will become public knowledge, probably within a short time. Policymakers need to act in ways that are defensible once the operation comes to light, and covert actions should be consistent with the declared policy of government and with the values of the nation.

A conspicuous example of a covert action that did not withstand public scrutiny is the Bay of Pigs. On April 7, 1961, the *New York Times* ran an article entitled "Anti-Castro Units Trained to Fight at Florida Bases," describing an effort by the Kennedy administration to train 5,000 to 6,000 Cuban exiles at camps located in Florida, Louisiana, and Guatemala to

---

57. 94 Stat. 1981, sec. 407(a) (1980).
58. Id. at 1981, sec. 407(b).

overthrow Premier Fidel Castro. A subhead in the lengthy story, supplying many details of the plan, read: "Invasion Reported Near."[59]

On April 12, President Kennedy was asked whether a decision had been made to invade Cuba. He dissembled: "First, I want to say that there will not be, under any conditions, an intervention in Cuba by the United States Armed Forces. This Government will do everything it possibly can, and I think it can meet its responsibilities, to make sure that there are no Americans involved in any actions inside Cuba."[60] Later in the news conference, when asked whether the U.S. government would "oppose any attempt to mount an offensive against Castro from this country," Kennedy responded: "If your phrase 'to mount an offensive' is as I understand it, I would be opposed to mounting an offensive."[61]

Undisclosed in these remarks, of course, was the administration's ongoing effort to use the CIA to train Cuban exiles, supply them with equipment and arms, and direct the planned invasion. At the news conference, Kennedy publicly tied his hands. Having pledged that the United States would not intervene in Cuba and would not be involved in any actions inside Cuba, he was in no position to provide key air support to the Cuban exiles when they went ashore at the Bay of Pigs. The result was a quick and humiliating defeat.

After the Soviet Union invaded Afghanistan in 1979, the United States gave weapons and support to the Afghan resistance, the Mujahedeen. A special emphasis was placed on building a rebel anti-aircraft capability to shoot down Soviet jet fighters and helicopters. The assistance was publicly debated in Congress, year in and year out.[62] Both Houses endorsed U.S. support for the Afghan rebels, even to the point of passing a sense of Congress resolution in 1984.[63] However, political and diplomatic factors prohibited official admission of American involvement. Denying the covert war, no matter how fictional, protected U.S. relations with Pakistan, which served as the conduit for assistance to Afghan rebels. Open acknowledgment would have threatened Pakistan's relationship with its northern neighbor, the Soviet Union.[64]

During the early 1980s, the Reagan administration conducted a supposedly secret war against the Sandinistas in Nicaragua. Legislation in 1981

59. The New York Times, April 7, 1961, at 2.
60. Public Papers of the Presidents, 1961, 256 (question 4).
61. Id. at 264 (question 20).
62. E.g., 130 Cong. Rec. 15526–28 (1984).
63. 130 Cong. Rec. 28983–85 (1984). See also 128 Cong. Rec. 26665–67 (1982).
64. Gregory F. Treverton, Covert Action: The Limits of Intervention in the Postwar World 213 (1987).

and 1982 provided covert assistance to the Contra rebels, but the operation was too large to remain hidden. By December 1982, Congressman Tom Harkin (D-Iowa) was able to introduce legislation to deny funds to the CIA and the Defense Department to furnish any military assistance to groups and individuals in Nicaragua.[65] Harkin could point to a variety of stories in newspapers and national magazines that publicly discussed military activities in Nicaragua.

During debate on the Harkin amendment, Congressman Edward Boland disclosed that the House Intelligence Committee had already put restrictive language in the classified annex that accompanies the intelligence authorization bill. The committee decided that no funds authorized by the intelligence bill should be used "to overthrow the Government of Nicaragua or to provoke a military exchange between Nicaragua and Honduras."[66] Congress enacted language prohibiting the CIA or the Defense Department from furnishing military equipment, military training or advice, or other support for military activities "to any group or individual, not part of a country's armed forces, for the purpose of overthrowing the Government of Nicaragua or provoking a military exchange between Nicaragua and Honduras."[67]

The 1982 curb proved ineffective. The insurgents in Nicaragua openly acknowledged their goal of overthrowing the Sandinistas and provoking a military confrontation.[68] In a May 1983 report, the House Intelligence Committee admitted: "this is no longer a covert operation. The public can read or hear about it daily. Anti-Sandinista leaders acknowledge U.S. aid."[69] Congress discovered early in 1984 that the administration, operating through the CIA, had mined the harbors of Nicaragua. Congress responded with this statutory language: "It is the sense of the Congress that no funds heretofore or hereafter appropriated in any Act of Congress shall be obligated or expended for the purpose of planning, directing, executing, or supporting the mining of the ports or territorial waters of Nicaragua."[70]

Later in 1984, Congress enacted the Boland Amendment to delete all funds for the Contras. The language was intended to be all-embracing to prevent any further evasion by executive officials:

65. 128 Cong. Rec. 29457 (1982).
66. Id. at 29466.
67. 96 Stat. 1865, sec. 793 (1982).
68. H. Rept. No. 122 (part 1), 98th Cong., 1st Sess. 11 (1983).
69. Id. at 12.
70. 98 Stat. 1210, sec. 2907 (1984).

During fiscal year 1985, no funds available to the Central Intelligence Agency, the Department of Defense, or any other agency or entity of the United States involved in intelligence activities may be obligated or expended for the purpose or which would have the effect of supporting, directly or indirectly, military or paramilitary operations in Nicaragua by any nation, group, organization, movement, or individual.[71]

Congress devised this tortured language because the Reagan administration had demonstrated a disposition to exploit every possible loophole. It was the intention of Congress to close them all.

Even with this explicit language, some legislators suspected that the Reagan administration might find some indirect way of assisting the Contras. During hearings on March 26, 1985, Senator Christopher Dodd (D-Conn.) said that there "have been a number of rumors or news reports around this town about how the administration might go about its funding of the contras in Nicaragua. There have been suggestions that it would be done through private parties or through funneling funds through friendly third nations, or possibly through a new category of assistance and asking the Congress to fund the program openly."[72]

The administration's spokesman, Ambassador Langhorne A. Motley, assured Senator Dodd that there would be no attempt to circumvent the Boland Amendment by soliciting funds from private parties or from foreign governments. He pledged that the Amendment would be complied with fully: "Nobody is trying to play games with you or any other Member of Congress. That resolution stands, and it will continue to stand; and it says no direct or indirect. And that is pretty plain English; it does not have to be written by any bright, young lawyers. And we are going to continue to comply with that."[73]

Ambassador Motley provided similar statements to the House Committee on Appropriations on April 18, 1985, testifying that the administration would not attempt to solicit funds from outside sources to assist the Contras.[74] When President Reagan signed the continuing resolution that contained the strict language of the Boland Amendment, he did not issue a

71. 98 Stat. 1935, sec. 8066(a) (1984).
72. "Security and Development Assistance," hearings before the Senate Committee on Foreign Relations, 99th Cong., 1st Sess. 908 (1985).
73. Id. at 910. At the time he testified, Ambassador Motley was Assistant Secretary of State for Inter-American Affairs.
74. "Department of Defense Appropriations for 1986" (part 2), hearings before the House Committee on Appropriations, 99th Cong., 1st Sess. 1092 (1985).

statement claiming that Congress had overstepped its powers and that the administration would pursue its course in Nicaragua. The Attorney General did not challenge the constitutionality of the Boland Amendment, and the Office of Legal Counsel in the Justice Department did not conclude in any internal memorandum or report that the amendment was invalid or nonbinding.

Nevertheless, at the very moment Ambassador Motley was testifying before two congressional committees, executive branch officials were actively soliciting funds from private parties and from foreign governments to assist the Contras. Working closely with the White House and the National Security Council, private citizens raised money from private contributors to provide military weapons and supplies to the Contras.[75] This subterfuge eventually degenerated into the Iran-Contra affair.

The Iran-Contra Affair

Illegal assistance to the Contras became linked with another Reagan initiative: supplying arms to Iran. The Reagan administration had issued a number of policy declarations covering the war between Iran and Iraq. Executive officials repeatedly told the American public and allies that all nations should remain neutral in the conflict. Weapons were not supposed to be sent to either country (Operation Staunch). The Reagan administration emphasized that it was firmly opposed to giving any concessions to terrorists, much less providing them arms in exchange for hostages.

In November 1986, the American public received the first details of the Iran-Contra affair from a newspaper in Beirut. The Reagan administration had sold arms to Iran (violating its declared policy) and had sent weapons to the Contras (violating the Boland Amendment). New twists and turns emerged, describing a complex covert operation carried out by a mixture of executive officials and private citizens. Some of the profits from the sale of arms to Iran had been diverted to the Contras. Congressional hearings added insights, as did investigation and prosecution by Independent Counsel Lawrence E. Walsh. The resulting picture cast a permanent shadow over the two terms of Ronald Reagan. Either he knew of the effort and deliberately defied the law and the Constitution, or he was unaware of a high-level national security initiative operating within his own office. Neither interpretation adds luster to his public service.

75. Report of the Congressional Committees Investigating the Iran-Contra Affair, H. Rept. No. 433 and S. Rept. No. 216, 100th Cong., 1st Sess. 85–103 (1987) (hereafter referred to as Iran-Contra Report).

Only one document from the administration asserted that the Boland Amendment permitted some executive officials to assist the Contras. Bretton G. Sciaroni, counsel to the President's Intelligence Oversight Board, issued a memorandum on September 12, 1985, concluding that the National Security Council (NSC) was not covered by the Amendment.[76] This memorandum was never made available to Congress or to the public. Its existence was revealed only after the Iran-Contra affair became public in November 1986. According to the legal analysis in the memorandum, John Poindexter, Robert McFarlane, Oliver North, and other members of the NSC staff could do what the intelligence community, the Defense Department, and "any other agency or entity" had been prohibited from doing by the Boland Amendment.

The Sciaroni memo is deficient in several respects. First, under the terms of the Boland Amendment, the NSC is an "entity . . . involved in intelligence activities." The National Security Act provides that there "is established under the National Security Council a Central Intelligence Agency."[77] If a subordinate body (the CIA) is involved in intelligence activities, so is the controlling body (the NSC). Second, the NSC-CIA relationship is elaborated in Executive Order 12333, issued by President Reagan in 1981. The order states that the NSC "shall act as the highest Executive Branch entity that provides review of, guidance for and direction to the conduct of all national foreign intelligence, counterintelligence, and special activities [covert operations], and attendant policies and programs."[78] This provides clear evidence that the NSC is "involved in intelligence activities" within the meaning of the Boland Amendment. Moreover, the Director of Central Intelligence "shall be responsible directly to the President and the NSC,"[79] and the CIA shall "conduct services of common concern for the Intelligence Community as directed by the NSC."[80] The principal responsibility for implementing the order, entitled "United States Intelligence Activities," falls to the NSC.[81] Finally, even if one were to reject this analysis, the plain fact is that the NSC under North and company *was* "involved in intelligence activities."

76. Memorandum from Bretton G. Sciaroni to Robert C. McFarlane, Assistant to the President for National Security Affairs, September 12, 1985, reprinted in "Iran-Contra Investigation," joint hearings by the Iran-Contra Committees, 100th Cong., 1st Sess., vol. 100–105, 1158 (hereafter referred tó as Iran-Contra Hearings).
77. 50 U.S.C. sec. 403(a) (1988).
78. 46 Fed. Reg. 59942 (Sec. 1.2) (1981).
79. Id. at 59943 (Sec 1.5).
80. Id. at 59946 (Sec. 1.8[f]).
81. Id. at 59952 (Sec. 3.2).

The idea that North and other members of the NSC could carry out a covert operation to assist the Contras is contrary to Section 1.8(e) of Executive Order 12333. No agency except the CIA "may conduct any special activity [covert operation] unless the President determines that another agency is more likely to achieve a particular objective." President Reagan never determined that the NSC should conduct a covert action to replace the CIA. Such a determination would have deliberately undermined the Boland Amendment, shifting the operating responsibility from an agency proscribed by law to one that attempts, by stealth and proxy, to achieve an end prohibited by Congress.

The NSC has a conflict of interest when called upon to present, in objective fashion, options to the President while it is conducting covert operations. It cannot be both analyst and advocate. An operational role undermines the NSC's function as a coordinating body and honest broker between the various departments that have responsibility for national security affairs. When Frank Carlucci became National Security Adviser after the Iran-Contra affair became public, he barred the NSC from conducting covert operations.[82] National Security Decision Directive 266, issued by President Reagan on March 31, 1987, stipulated that "the NSC staff itself will not undertake the conduct of covert activities."[83]

The Iran-Contra affair is an example of the executive branch usurping the power of Congress to use private parties for military purposes (marque and reprisal). Private citizens involved in the scandal included Carl R. "Spitz" Channell and Richard Miller, who helped raise money for the Contras. They pleaded guilty to tax fraud. Richard V. Secord, a former Air Force officer, pleaded guilty to making false statements to congressional investigators about assistance to the Contras. Thomas G. Clines, a former CIA agent who assisted with arms sales to the Contras, was convicted of tax violations. Another member recruited from the private sector was Albert Hakim, who assisted with arm sales to Iran. Hakim pleaded guilty to a misdemeanor charge of helping to supplement Oliver North's government salary by arranging to pay for his home security system.

Major administration figures included North, National Security Adviser Poindexter, and former National Security Adviser McFarlane. McFarlane pleaded guilty to four misdemeanor charges of withholding information from Congress. North was convicted of obstructing Congress, unlawfully mutilating government documents, and taking an illegal gratuity. Poindexter was convicted of conspiracy, making false statements to Congress, destroying and re-

---

82. 45 Cong. Q. Weekly Rep. 339, 349 (1987).
83. Reprinted in H. Doc. No. 58, 100th Cong., 1st Sess. 3 (1987).

moving records, and obstructing Congress. The convictions of North and Poindexter were later overturned by an appellate court, which ruled that new trials would have to demonstrate that evidence against them had not been tainted by the congressional hearings. The difficulty of this hurdle convinced Independent Counsel Walsh not to retry North and Poindexter. Elliott Abrams, former Assistant Secretary of State, pleaded guilty to withholding information from Congress about covert assistance to the Contras. Caspar W. Weinberger, former Secretary of Defense, was charged with four counts of false statements and perjury. He was pardoned before trial by President Bush.

The CIA was deeply involved. Before investigators could learn about the full influence of its Director, William Casey, he died of a brain tumor on May 6, 1987. Clair George, CIA deputy director for operations, was convicted of false statements and perjury before Congress. Alan D. Fiers, chief of the Agency's Central American Task Force, pleaded guilty to withholding information from Congress. Duane (Dewey) Clarridge, former chief of the CIA's Latin American Division, was indicted on seven counts of perjury and false statements, but he too was pardoned before trial by President Bush. The pardon also covered George and Fiers. Another CIA employee, Joseph Fernandez, was indicted on four counts of obstruction and making false statements relating to his assistance to the Contras. His case was dropped when Attorney General Dick Thornburgh refused to declassify information needed for the trial.

Precisely what happened in the Iran-Contra affair, and why, may never be determined. Administration officials destroyed documents, declined to tell the truth to investigators, and key trials (like Fernandez's') were aborted by executive branch decisions. When Independent Counsel Walsh brought indictments against former Secretary of Defense Caspar Weinberger, there was an opportunity to learn more about the responsibility of President Reagan and Vice President Bush for the Iran-Contra affair. Weinberger was scheduled to go on trial on January 5, 1993; a likely witness to be called was President Bush. Two weeks before the trial Bush issued pardons for Weinberger and five other federal officials involved in the Iran-Contra affair. Three had already pleaded guilty (Abrams, Fiers, and McFarlane), and the pardons of Clarridge and George eliminated any chance of discovering the full extent of CIA participation.

Congressional Reforms

Congress enacted legislation in 1991 to reduce the likelihood for future situations like the Iran-Contra affair. A key issue is presidential notification to Congress. The Intelligence Oversight Act of 1980 required Presidents to make a "finding" on the necessity of a covert operation. In the course of the Iran-Contra affair, President Reagan made an "oral" finding on one occasion and at another point issued a finding that tried to retroactively authorize what the CIA had done. At no time did he notify the Intelligence Committees. The 1991 statute requires that presidential findings must be in writing and cannot have retroactive effect. Moreover, findings may not authorize any action that violates federal law or the Constitution and must identify any third party (foreign nation) that is involved in the covert action.[84]

One of the most disturbing theories to emerge from the Iran-Contra affair was the claim that Presidents, denied funds by Congress, may finance foreign policy goals by using nonappropriated funds obtained from private citizens and foreign governments. In their effort to provide military assistance to the Contras after enactment of the Boland Amendment, officials in the Reagan administration sought funds from private individuals, Saudi Arabia, and other countries. At the congressional hearings, both Poindexter and North defended the constitutionality of these initiatives, claiming that these efforts did not violate the Boland Amendment because that amendment applied only to appropriations.[85]

The Poindexter-North theory raises two issues, one constitutional, the other political. As explained in Chapter 1, the framers took great pains to keep the legislative purse separate from the presidential sword. They did not want a single branch to both make and fund war. Allowing the President to carry out foreign policy with private or foreign contributions would create what the framers feared most: union of purse and sword. If President Reagan had authorized the theory propounded by Poindexter and North, he would have invited, and deserved, impeachment proceedings. He would have failed in his constitutional duty to see that the laws are faithfully executed and would have precipitated a major constitutional crisis by merging the power of the purse with the power of the sword.

Moreover, soliciting funds from foreign governments to promote U.S. foreign policy opens the door to widespread compromise and corruption. Accepting funds from foreign governments to sustain the Contras created an implicit quid pro quo, requiring the United States to reciprocate by giving donor countries special consideration in such tangible forms as foreign assistance, military assistance, arms sales, and trade con-

84. 105 Stat. 441–45 (1991).
85. Iran-Contra Hearings, vol. 100–108, 158, and vol. 100–107, part II, 37.

cessions.[86] Instead of national policy being articulated by Congress through an open legislative process, it became the net product of secret agreements. Government went underground.

Congress had passed legislation to stop these quid pro quos. The Pell Amendment in 1985 prohibited the use of any U.S. funds to provide "assistance of any kind, either directly or indirectly, to any person or group engaging in an insurgency or other act of rebellion against the Government of Nicaragua." The purpose was to prevent recipients of U.S. funds and materials from giving assistance to the Contras as a condition, or quid pro quo, for obtaining aid.[87] In 1989, President Bush vetoed a bill that contained criminal sanctions to punish quid pro quos.[88] In that same year he vetoed another bill establishing restrictions on quid pro quos, even though this measure omitted criminal sanctions.[89] In each of his veto messages Bush stated that he was "sensitive to the concerns" that prompted Congress to add such language.[90] The principle that Congress advocated merited presidential support. It was a matter of finding the right language.

Bush signed a revised bill aimed at quid pro quos. The new law states that appropriated funds for foreign assistance may not be provided to "any foreign government (including any instrumentality or agency thereof), foreign person, or United States person in exchange for that foreign government or person undertaking any action which is, if carried out by the United States Government, a United States official or employee, expressly prohibited by a provision of United States law."[91] In signing the legislation, Bush agreed that the section prohibited quid pro quo transactions "in which U.S. funds are provided to a foreign nation on the express condition that the foreign nation provide specific assistance to a third country, which assistance U.S. officials are expressly prohibited from providing by U.S. law."[92]

The House and Senate Iran-Contra Committees' joint report, released in November 1987, stresses that Congress as well as the President has important powers in the areas of foreign policy and national security. Foreign policy cannot be successful in the long run unless it has bipartisan congressional support.[93] The "misrepresentations, half-truths, and conceal-

---

86. Iran-Contra Hearings, vol. 100–101, 25, 201, 279–80.
87. 99 Stat. 254, sec. 722(d) (1985).
88. Public Papers of the Presidents, 1989, II, 1567–69.
89. Id. at 1546.
90. Id. at 1546, 1569.
91. 103 Stat. 1251, sec. 582 (1989).
92. Public Papers of the Presidents, 1989, II, 1573.
93. Iran-Contra Report 19, 20.

ment" employed by executive officials in the Iran-Contra affair reflected an attitude "based on a view of Congress' role in foreign policy that is without historical or legal foundation."[94]

Future Presidents may refuse to abide by statutory procedures that strengthen the ability of Congress to oversee covert operations, just as Presidents have not complied fully with the War Powers Resolution. Still, it is important for Congress to express its sense of prerogatives and constitutional duties. Otherwise, executive officials (and courts) are likely to interpret congressional passivity as support for the President's unilateral assertion of power.

The Iran-Contra affair was not an aberration. Given the attitudes within the executive branch, it was a disaster waiting to happen, and it progressed because of a series of carefully calculated, conscious choices, all designed to concentrate foreign policymaking within the presidency. Any impediments to that goal—the Constitution, Congress, opposition within the executive branch—were systematically swept aside by the individuals in charge of the operations and those at a higher level who assisted with winks and nods. The lesson from recent decades is that the temptation of executive officials to exceed constitutional limits in covert operations is ever-present, always pushing, and in constant need of checks from other institutions and the public.

94. Id. at 387.

9

RESTORING CHECKS AND BALANCES

The drift of the war power from Congress to the President after World War II is unmistakable. The framers' design, deliberately placing in Congress the decision to expend the nation's blood and treasure, has been radically transformed. Presidents now regularly claim that the commander-in-chief clause empowers them to send American troops anywhere in the world, including into hostilities, without first seeking legislative approval. Congress has made repeated efforts since the 1970s to restore legislative prerogatives, with only moderate success. Presidents continue to wield military power single-handedly, agreeing only to consult with legislators and notify them of completed actions. That is not the framers' model.

Many justifications are advanced to defend this fundamental shift in constitutional power. Champions of executive power cite the need for secrecy and prompt action, qualities supposedly associated in some unique fashion with the Executive. The framers knew about dangers and emergencies, and they understood the virtues of speed and secrecy. They lived at risk also but drafted a charter that vested in Congress the crucial responsibility for moving the nation from peace to war. Contemporary justifications for presidential dominance must be examined closely to discard, or at least qualify, explanations that initially may have superficial allure. Some have substance; most are shallow.

Contemporary Justifications

It is often argued that presidential power in the twentieth century must be defined more broadly than the model formulated by the framers. They agreed that the President could "repel sudden attacks," but advocates of executive power want more elbow room than that. The climate after World War II, they say, is far more dangerous and much more in need of decisive presidential action. Promptness, we are told, is a quality of the Executive, not the Legislature.

It is simplistic to claim that the conditions of the modern world make it necessary to vest in the President the crucial decision to go to war. If the

current risk to national security is great, so is the risk of presidential mis-
calculation and aggrandizement—all the more reason for insisting that
military decisions be thoroughly examined and approved by Congress.
Contemporary presidential judgments need more, not less, scrutiny.

The framers also lived at a dangerous time, possibly more hazardous
than today. After granting the President power to repel sudden attacks,
they relied for their safety primarily on Congress. In a succession of statutes, Congress authorized the President to respond to emergencies involving Indians, domestic rebellions, the Barbary conflicts, and other national security issues. Presidents acted on statutory, not inherent,
authority. As noted in one study:

> Despite glib assertions of the novelty and gravity of the post-Korean
> war period, the threats confronting the United States during the first
> quarter century of government under the Constitution imperiled the
> very independence and survival of the nation. The United States
> Government fought wars against France and England, the two great-
> est powers of that period, to protect its existence, preserve the bal-
> ance of power, and defend its commerce. Notably, both conflicts, the
> Franco-American War [the Quasi-War of 1798–1800] and the War of
> 1812, were authorized by statute.[1]

In the years following World War II, there has been more than enough
time to seek authorization in advance from Congress before committing
the nation to war. Even if one could argue that President Truman needed
to take immediate "police action" to respond to North Korea's provocation, he had time after that to ask Congress to authorize extended hostilities. Presidents find time to seek advice from executive officials, often
over a period of months, before acting. They even reach out to inform allies of planned attacks. Few uses of unilateral force by the President can
be explained by genuine emergencies. Contrived emergencies, perhaps,
but not real ones. In the period since World War II, only *one* situation justified presidential action in the absence of congressional authority: President Ford's evacuation of Americans and foreign nationals from Vietnam.

Does the specter of nuclear war—unknown to the framers—require
concentrating in the President the sole responsibility for launching missiles? That is a beguiling, but misleading, proposition. There is a difference between first use of nuclear weapons (any initiation of war requires

---

1. David S. Friedman, "Waging War Against Checks and Balances—The Claim of an Unlimited Presidential War Power," 57 St. John's L. Rev. 213, 228 (1983).

prior congressional authority) and retaliatory second strikes (a unilateral presidential power pursuant to the executive duty to repel sudden attacks). Policymakers generally assume that nuclear weapons would be used only after a conventional war escalates, over a period of weeks or months, to a nuclear confrontation. Time is available within the executive branch to debate and decide the use of nuclear weapons, permitting adequate opportunity for a congressional role.[2]

If Presidents decide that an emergency requires action without first obtaining approval from Congress, it is far better for them to use military force on suspect authority and come later to Congress to explain what they did, why they acted, and request Congress to provide retroactive authorization. The burden is wholly on the President to make the case. Congress is the only branch that can confer legitimacy on an emergency measure. That is the procedure Lincoln used in the Civil War. It is the model for all Presidents. Congress should not attempt to provide advance authority for every type of emergency action. Having been burned on the Tonkin Gulf Resolution, the Senate Foreign Relations Committee concluded in 1969:

> Finally, should the President find himself confronted with a situation of such complexity and ambiguity as to leave him without guidelines for constitutional action, it would be far better for him to take the action he saw fit without attempting to justify it in advance and leave it to Congress or the courts to evaluate his action in retrospect. A single unconstitutional act, later explained or pronounced unconstitutional, is preferable to an act dressed up in some spurious, precedent-setting claim of legitimacy.[3]

The concept of "defensive war" has expanded in recent decades beyond any definition familiar to the framers. During the nineteenth century, defensive war was confined to protective action along the borders of the United States and ships at sea. Twentieth-century notions of defensive war are far more ambitious. As a result of World War II, American military bases are now dispersed around the globe. By 1966, the legal adviser to the State Department, Leonard C. Meeker, could offer this open-ended concept of presidential power:

2. Peter Raven-Hansen, ed., First Use of Nuclear Weapons: Under the Constitution, Who Decides? (1987); Allan Ides, "Congressional Authority to Regulate the Use of Nuclear Weapons," 13 Hastings Const. L. Q. 233 (1986); Jeremy J. Stone, "Presidential First Use Is Unlawful," 56 Foreign Policy 94 (1984).

3. S. Rept. No. 129, 91st Cong., 1st Sess. 32 (1969).

In 1787 the world was a far larger place, and the framers probably had in mind attacks upon the United States. In the 20th century, the world has grown much smaller. An attack on a country far from our shores can impinge directly on the nation's security. In the SEATO treaty, for example, it is formally declared that an armed attack against Viet-Nam would endanger the peace and safety of the United States.[4]

That statement distorts the significance of SEATO and other mutual security pacts. Each nation, in accordance with its "constitutional processes," decides for itself the appropriate response. Nothing in those pacts defines constitutional processes to mean whatever the President wants to do. The Senate, in agreeing to those treaties, did not abandon its constitutional responsibilities or attempt to deny to the House of Representatives its constitutional role in authorizing war. A shrinking globe is no reason to shrink congressional power.

Defenders of presidential war power point to more than two hundred instances in which Presidents have used military force without an authorization from Congress. Those actions were minor adventures done in the name of protecting American lives or property, taken at a time when U.S. intervention in neighboring countries was considered routine and proper. Today, such invasions violate international law and regional treaties. Is the bombardment of Greytown, Nicaragua, in 1854 an acceptable "precedent" for the current use of American military power? Are we comfortable with citing America's occupation of Haiti from 1915 to 1934 or the repeated interventions in Nicaragua from 1909 to 1933? We should not speak nonchalantly about "more than 200 precedents," assuming that such numbers, by themselves, justify unilateral military action by the President. We need to examine the specific instances. Are they attractive precedents for the use of force today? None of the 200 incidents comes close to justifying military actions of the magnitude and risk of Korea in 1950, Panama in 1989, Iraq in 1990, or Bosnia and Haiti in 1994.

It has been proposed that the War Powers Resolution be replaced by a Use of Force Act, which would delegate to the President a number of authorities, including the right "to protect and extricate citizens and nationals of the United States located abroad in situations involving a direct and imminent threat to their lives, provided they are being evacuated as rap-

---

4. 54 Dep't of State Bull. 474, 484 (1966).

idly as possible."⁵ Such language could have been used to justify the U.S. invasions of the Dominican Republic, Grenada, and Panama. Americans abroad are abused and threatened every year. Concern about using military force improperly to protect Americans abroad led to legislation in 1868 (still in effect) that directs the President to take all *diplomatic* steps necessary to free American citizens. Presidential initiatives must be those "not amounting to acts of war."⁶

As another justification for executive power, Presidents Truman, Bush, and Clinton have told the American public that mutual defense treaties (like NATO) and resolutions passed by the UN Security Council provide sufficient legal support for presidential military actions. There is no basis for these claims. Treaties entered into by the President and the Senate— whether for NATO or the UN Charter—cannot strip from the House of Representatives its constitutional duties over military commitments.

The claim by the executive branch that President Bush was justified in invading Panama to stop drug trafficking is facially ludicrous. Under that theory, the United States would have a right to intervene militarily in South America, Mexico, Turkey, the Golden Triangle, and other regions of the world. Such arguments fail the straight-face test.

President Bush invaded Panama because he and his advisers concluded that Panama was too weak and isolated to resist American force. His action parallels President Wilson's invasion of Veracruz in 1914. At that time Felix Frankfurter was a young attorney working in the War Department. Enoch H. Crowder, the Judge Advocate General, asked for his advice after the White House requested a memorandum on whether Wilson's action should be treated as an act of war. Frankfurter had this conversation:

> General, I'm going to ask to be excused. I don't have to work on that. I know the answer to that.
> You do?
> Yes, I do.
> What is the answer?
> It would be an act of war against a great nation; it isn't against a small nation.
> I can't give him that.
> I know you can't but that's the answer.⁷

5. Joseph R. Biden, Jr., and John B. Ritch III, "The War Power at a Constitutional Impasse: A 'Joint Decision' Solution," 77 Geo. L. J. 367, 398 (1988).

6. 15 Stat. 223 (1868); 22 U.S.C. 1732 (1988). Legislation in 1989 inserted "and not otherwise prohibited by law" after "acts of war." 103 Stat. 1900, sec. 9 (1989).

7. Felix Frankfurter Reminisces 60 (1960).

Frankfurter's analysis has a cynical edge, but it captures a recurring fla-
vor of U.S. foreign policy. American troops have been used repeatedly
against small nations over incidents that would have been considered too
minor to justify the use of force against larger powers. Targets of American military power are typically weak and isolated nations, including
Cambodia, Libya, Grenada, Panama, Iraq, and Haiti.

Jackson's Zone of Twilight

In his concurring opinion in the Steel Seizure Case in 1952, Justice Jackson
identified three scenarios for presidential power. When the President acts
pursuant to an express or implied authorization of Congress, his authority
"is at its maximum, for it includes all that he possesses in his own right plus
all that Congress can delegate." The President's power is "at its lowest ebb"
when he takes measures incompatible with the expressed or implied will of
Congress, for then he relies only upon his own constitutional powers minus
any constitutional powers possessed by Congress.[8] Jackson's third scenario,
in which Congress neither grants nor denies power, is of special interest:

> When the President acts in absence of either a congressional grant
> or denial of authority, he can rely upon his own independent powers,
> but there is a zone of twilight in which he and Congress may have
> concurrent authority, or in which its distribution is uncertain. There-
> fore, congressional inertia, indifference or quiescence may some-
> times, at least as a practical matter, enable, if not invite, measures on
> independent presidential responsibility. In this area, any actual test of
> power is likely to depend on the imperatives of events and contem-
> porary imponderables rather than on abstract theories of law.[9]

In this same case, Justice Frankfurter also explored the impact of custom and practice on presidential power. Legislative and executive power
were not defined purely on the basis of textual grants. The behavior of
each branch added meaning to constitutional power:

> Deeply embedded traditional ways of conducting government can-
> not supplant the Constitution or legislation, but they give meaning to
> the words of a text or supply them. It is an inadmissibly narrow con-
> ception of American constitutional law to confine it to the words of

8. Youngstown Co. v. Sawyer, 343 U.S. 579, 635–37 (1952).
9. Id. at 637.

the Constitution and to disregard the gloss which life has written upon them. In short, a systematic, unbroken, executive practice, long pursued to the knowledge of the Congress and never before questioned, engaged in by Presidents who have also sworn to uphold the Constitution, making as it were such exercise of power part of the structure of our government, may be treated as a gloss on "executive Power" vested in the President by § 1 of Art. II.[10]

These observations by Jackson and Frankfurter seem innocent enough: Custom helps shape the Constitution. However, they also give some encouragement to presidential raids of power, done with the knowledge that the additional power seized will be successful and permanent unless Congress effectively defends itself. Jackson and Frankfurter provide an incentive for aggression similar to disputes between nations. When one nation expands its territory by violating surrounding borders, the burden is placed on neighboring countries to resist.

To a certain extent, this dynamic describes the U.S. constitutional system. If one branch encroaches, the branch under attack must respond. It must fight back out of a sense of institutional survival. However, in recognizing these struggles as part of the system of checks and balances, legitimacy should not be conferred on illegimate actions. Illegal and unconstitutional actions, no matter how often repeated, do not build a lawful foundation. If Presidents withdrew funds from the Treasury without an appropriation from Congress, those actions would have no constitutional legitimacy, regardless of the number of infractions. As Gerhard Casper has remarked: "unconstitutional practices cannot become legitimate by the mere lapse of time."[11] Justice Frankfurter noted: "Illegality cannot attain legitimacy through practice."[12] Presidential acts of war can never be accepted as constitutional or as a legal substitute for congressional approval.

Revisiting the War Powers Resolution

Critics of the War Powers Resolution argue that it has failed to work as planned and trenches upon the constitutional powers of the President. No doubt it does not function as planned. To repeal it, however, would send the wrong signal: a green light to presidential adventurism unchecked by the

10. Id. at 610–11.
11. Gerhard Casper, "Constitutional Constraints on the Conduct of Foreign and Defense Policy: A Nonjudicial Model," 43 U. Chi. L. Rev. 463, 479 (1976).
12. Inland Waterways Corp. v. Young, 309 U.S. 517, 524 (1940).

legislative branch. The core concept of the War Powers Resolution is sound. The decision to commit U.S. troops to hostilities should be a matter for "collective judgment" entered into by both branches. Only after Congress authorizes military action, reaching that decision through parliamentary deliberations, may the President as Commander in Chief order troops into combat. That principle was well-grounded in 1787. It remains so today.

Does the War Powers Resolution trench upon presidential authority? No one has identified a military initiative, desired by the President after 1973, that has been canceled or restricted because of this legislation. Where else did Presidents want to intervene? The historical record is silent. Presidents have generally done what they wanted to do, notwithstanding the War Powers Resolution. Their actions have been hurried in some instances (as in Grenada) and restricted in others (El Salvador).[13] If anything, the resolution recognizes too much latitude for presidential war power. An expansive reading implies that the President may use military force unilaterally for up to sixty days—anywhere, any time, for any reason. The framers would never have allowed that kind of open-ended discretion.

If the War Powers Resolution is revised, there is good reason to shorten or eliminate the sixty-day period. A grace period of two months allows such operations as the invasion of Grenada and of Panama, conducted without any congressional support or involvement. John Hart Ely recommends that the period be reduced to twenty days.[14] Restricting the scope of presidential latitude is wise (as well as constitutional), but even twenty days (or ten) exceeds the constitutional plan. Presidents need some emergency authority, as in evacuating Americans and foreign nationals from Vietnam, but not to the extent of invading other countries.

Congressional (and public) control would be greatly strengthened if tied to the power of the purse. A revised War Powers Resolution could prohibit the President from obligating or spending any funds to initiate military action unless Congress passes legislation appropriating funds. Such language would give the President some latitude in responding to an emergency, subject to the condition that Congress must provide funds and authority for military conflicts. The burden would be on the President, as it should be, to seek congressional authority.[15]

---

13. Ellen C. Collier, "Statutory Constraints: The War Powers Resolution." In Gary M. Stern and Morton H. Halperin, eds., The Constitution and the Power to Go to War 65–66 (1994).

14. John Hart Ely, War and Responsibility 120, 127–28, 136 (1993).

15. Michael J. Glennon, "Strengthening the War Powers Resolution: The Case for Purse-Strings Restrictions," 60 Minn. L. Rev. 1, 32 (1975); Cyrus R. Vance, "Striking the Balance: Congress and the President Under the War Powers Resolution," 133 U. Pa. L. Rev. 79, 93–94 (1984); Ely, War and Responsibility, 121.

As another option, Congress could pass a concurrent resolution disapproving of a presidential war, automatically triggering a point of order against any measure that contains funds to perpetuate the conflict. Operating as an internal mechanism (one part of Congress controlling another part), no constitutional objection can be raised that the concurrent resolution is a "legislative veto" prohibited by *INS* v. *Chadha*.[16] The legislative veto applies to congressional efforts to control the executive branch, not its own internal proceedings.

The consultation provision of the War Powers Resolution could be improved. Consultation is something more than getting in touch with legislators after the executive branch decides on a course of action. The process of consultation means talking to Congress when a policy is still open to change. As pointed out by the legislative history of the War Powers Resolution, consultation means that "a decision is pending on a problem and that members of Congress are being asked by the President for their advice and opinions and, in appropriate circumstances, their approval of action contemplated."[17] That understanding should be made explicit in law.

A second issue of consultation concerns the number of members of Congress that the President should contact. Obviously, the War Powers Resolution does not require the President to consult 535 legislators. Even for smaller numbers, Presidents complain about the impracticality of the consultation provision. President Ford said that during the evacuation of Vietnam in 1975, the leaders of Congress were spread around the world during an Easter recess. Two were in Mexico, three in Greece, one in the Middle East, another in Europe, two in the People's Republic of China, and the rest found in twelve widely scattered states of the Union.[18] A year later, when he began the first evacuation of American citizens from Lebanon, Congress had adjourned for the day and he discovered that one member of Congress had an unlisted telephone number that his press secretary refused to divulge. Ford even had the local police leave a note on another legislator's beach cottage door, instructing: "Please call the White House."[19] Ford exaggerated the problem. The record shows that Presidents can reach legislators when they want to. When Presidents need members of Congress to vote on an administration bill, they usually have

16. Louis Fisher, "The Legislative Veto: Invalidated, It Survives," 56 Law & Contemp. Prob. 273, 283–84 (1993).

17. H. Rept. No. 287, 93d Cong., 1st Sess. 6–7 (1973).

18. Gerald R. Ford, "Congress, the Presidency and National Security Policy," 16 Pres. Stud. Q. 200, 202 (1986).

19. Id.

no difficulty in locating them and even arranging for a quick flight back to Washington, D.C.

There is some merit in creating a congressional consultative group, consisting of perhaps eighteen members: Speaker of the House, House Majority Leader, House Minority Leader, President Pro Tempore of the Senate, Senate Majority Leader, Senate Minority Leader, and the chairman and ranking members of six committees: Senate Foreign Relations, House Foreign Affairs, the Senate and House Armed Services Committee, and the Senate and House Intelligence Committees.[20] This core group of eighteen should be expanded, depending on the issue, to include other members of Congress who have special expertise and experience. However, consultation is not a *legal substitute* for full congressional action. Congress cannot delegate to a subunit the constitutional decision to go to war. A House bill providing for a consultative group explains that consultations "shall not be construed as a grant of authority from the Congress to the President to conduct such military action."[21]

A Forbidden Legislative Veto?

Some critics of the War Powers Resolution argue that the concurrent resolution is unconstitutional. In 1975, the legal adviser to the State Department told a House committee that if the President has the power to put men into combat, "that power could not be taken away by concurrent resolution because the power is constitutional in nature."[22] The Justice Department reached the same conclusion in 1980.[23] Those positions appeared to be strengthened in 1983 when the Supreme Court, in *INS* v. *Chadha*, struck down the legislative veto as unconstitutional. The Court ruled that whenever Congress wants to alter the legal rights, duties, or relations outside the legislative branch, it must act by both Houses in a bill or joint resolution that is presented to the President for his signature or veto.[24] Concurrent resolutions are adopted by both Houses but are not presented to the President.

In response to *Chadha*, an amendment was offered to make the proce-

20. Biden and Ritch, "The War Power at a Constitutional Impasse: A 'Joint Decision' Solution" 402–3.

21. H.R. 3405, 103d Cong., 1st Sess (October 28, 1993), sec. 2.

22. "War Powers: A Test of Compliance," hearings before the House Committee on International Relations, 94th Cong., 1st Sess. 91 (1975).

23. 4A O.L.C. 185, 197 (1980).

24. 462 U.S. 919 (1983).

dure of the War Power Resolution conform to the Court's decision. Instead of acting by concurrent resolution, Congress would pass a joint resolution or bill and present that to the President. As enacted, however, this
amendment did not alter the War Powers Resolution. The amendment became a freestanding procedure available to Congress to act by joint resolution to require the President to withdraw troops.[25] The concurrent resolution remains in the War Powers Resolution.

During hearings in 1988, the legal adviser to the State Department testified that the concurrent resolution in the War Powers Resolution was
"clearly" unconstitutional and should be repealed.[26] In a committee report in 1987, the Senate Foreign Relations Committee also stated that the
concurrent resolution in the War Powers Resolution "has been effectively
nullified" by *Chadha*.[27]

Replacing the concurrent resolution in the War Powers Resolution with
a joint resolution is both unnecessary and undesirable. As used by the Supreme Court in *Chadha*, the term "legislative veto" should be restricted
to the following meaning: a condition placed on delegated authority, such
as the one-House legislative veto that accompanied the delegation of reor-
ganization power to the President, or the two-House veto attached to
rulemaking authority for the Federal Trade Commission. The War Powers
Resolution does not delegate legislative authority to the President. No legislative veto exists as a condition on that authority. Section 8(d)(2) expressly states that nothing in the War Powers Resolution "shall be construed as granting any authority to the President with respect to the
introduction of United States Armed Forces into hostilities or into situations wherein involvement in hostilities is clearly indicated by the circumstances which authority he would not have had in the absence of this
joint resolution."

The constitutional disadvantage of acting by joint resolution is pro-
found. If Congress passed a joint resolution ordering the President to
withdraw troops and the President exercised his veto, Congress would
need a two-thirds majority in each House to override the veto. In other
words, the President could continue to prosecute a war he started even if
a majority in each House is opposed. He would simply need one-third
plus one in a single House to prevent the override. It does violence to the
Constitution to place that burden on Congress.

25. 97 Stat. 1062–63, sec. 1013 (1983); 50 U.S.C. 1546a (1988). See 129 Cong. Rec.
28406–8, 28673–74, 28683–84, 28686–89, 33385, 33395–96 (1983).
26. "The War Power after 200 Years," hearings before the Senate Committee on Foreign
Relations, 100th Cong., 2d Sess. 1061 (1988).
27. S. Rept. No. 106, 100th Cong., 1st Sess. 6 (1987).

The issue can be more clearly understood by reviewing the specific situation in 1973 when Congress tried to use its power of the purse to end the war in Vietnam. President Nixon vetoed a bill directing that no appropriated funds could be used to support combat activities in Cambodia or Laos. Congress, unable to override the veto, agreed to give Nixon forty-five additional days to bomb Cambodia. Congresswoman Elizabeth Holtzman filed a suit asking a federal court to determine that the President could not engage in combat operations in Southeast Asia without express authorization from Congress. Judge Orrin G. Judd ruled that Congress had not authorized the bombing in Cambodia and that its inability to override the veto could not be interpreted as an affirmative grant of authority. Said Judd: "It cannot be the rule that the President needs a vote of only one-third plus one of either House in order to conduct a war, but this would be the consequence of holding that Congress must override a Presidential veto in order to terminate hostilities which it has not authorized."[28] His order was stayed and eventually reversed because Congress had entered into the compromise with Nixon.[29]

The concurrent resolution remains a useful and appropriate means for expressing congressional policy. If Congress passed such a resolution, the President might well argue that it was legally null and void because of *Chadha*. How would that fare politically? Would a President keep troops in hostilities after a majority in each House told him to bring the soldiers home? A majority vote should suffice, especially to rein in a war initiated by the President. Congress should not have to regain control by securing a two-thirds majority in both Houses.[30]

Even critics of the War Powers Resolution seem to concede that Congress does not need a two-thirds majority in each House to stop a presidential war. After leaving the White House, Gerald R. Ford said that it was the framers' intention that a President "could not initiate a war without the approval of both houses of Congress."[31] If a President needs the support of both Houses in advance, that means that either House can disap-

28. Holtzman v. Schlesinger, 361 F.Supp. 553, 565 (E.D. N.Y. 1973).

29. Holtzman v. Schlesinger, 414 U.S. 1304, 1316, 1321 (1973); Holtzman v. Schlesinger, 484 F.2d 1307 (2d Cir. 1973), cert. denied, 416 U.S. 936 (1974).

30. For those who support the constitutionality of the concurrent resolution in the War Powers Resolution, see Ely, War and Responsibility 119–20; G. Sidney Buchanan, "In Defense of the War Powers Resolution: *Chadha* Does Not Apply," 22 Houston L. Rev. 1155 (1985); Cyrus R. Vance, "Striking the Balance: Congress and the President Under the War Powers Resolution" 86–87; and Casper, "Constitutional Constraints on the Conduct of Foreign and Defense Policy: A Nonjudicial Model" 484–85.

31. Foreword to Robert F. Turner, Repealing the War Powers Resolution: Restoring the Rule of Law in U.S. Foreign Policy vii (1991).

prove and leave the President with no authority. In essence, the framers anticipated a one-House veto over the war power. Robert F. Turner, another critic of the War Powers Resolution, concludes that the concurrent resolution is invalid under *Chadha*.[32] Yet Turner also states that the Constitution, as intended by the framers, gives Congress a one-House veto over presidential wars. One of the checks "incorporated to protect against executive abuse [is] the power of either house of Congress to veto a decision to initiate a war."[33] That is the correct principle; a two-thirds majority in each House is constitutionally excessive.

In vetoing the War Powers Resolution, President Nixon objected that the procedure for a sixty-to-ninety-day limit meant that Congress did not have to vote. It could control by inaction: "No overt Congressional action would be required to cut off these powers—they would disappear automatically unless the Congress extended them. In effect, the Congress is here attempting to increase its policymaking role through a provision which requires it to take absolutely no action at all."[34] There is nothing unusual or unconstitutional about Congress controlling the President through inaction. If Congress doesn't want to vote funds or authority for something the President wants, there is no obligation to act. A failure by the President to persuade Congress that the proposal has merit means that it dies. Congress need not even report the proposal out of committee. Such are the hazards of the legislative process—perhaps unfortunate for the President but fully constitutional.

Compelling Court Action

In recent decades, federal courts have consistently refused to reach the merits in war power cases. Throughout the Vietnam period such cases were regarded as political questions to be resolved by the elected branches.[35] By the time of the Reagan and Bush years, federal judges offered other reasons to avoid a decision: the issue was moot,[36] it was not

32. Id. at 116–18.
33. Id. at xiv.
34. Public Papers of the Presidents, 1973, 894.
35. E.g., Luftig v. McNamara, 373 F.2d 664 (D.C. Cir. 1967); Velvel v. Johnson, 287 F.Supp. 846 (D. Kans. 1968); Berk v. Laird, 317 F.Supp. 715 (E.D. N.Y. 1970); Orlando v. Laird, 443 F.2d 1039 (2d Cir. 1971); Atlee v. Laird, 347 F.Supp. 689 (E.D. Pa. 1972); Gravel v. Laird, 347 F.Supp. 7 (D.D.C. 1972); DaCosta v. Laird, 471 F.2d 1146 (2d Cir. 1973); and Mitchell v. Laird, 488 F.2d 611 (D.D.C. 1973).
36. Conyers v. Reagan, 765 F.2d 1124 (D.C. Cir. 1985).

ripe,[37] plaintiffs lacked standing,[38] a variety of doctrines on judicial prudence and "equitable discretion,"[39] and a finding of nonjusticiability because judicial resolution would require fact-finding better done by Congress.[40]

Several proposals would try to force a judicial decision. One recommendation would authorize any member of Congress to bring an action in federal court for declaratory judgment and injunctive relief on the grounds that the President had violated statutory policy.[41] In such actions, courts "shall not decline to make a determination on the merits based upon the doctrine of political question, remedial discretion, equitable discretion, or any other finding of nonjusticiability, unless such declination is required by Article III of the Constitution."[42] Another variation of the court-forcing idea would give members of Congress standing to go to court whenever the President fails to start the clock by reporting under Section 4(a)(1). Under this proposal, judges could not invoke standing, political question, ripeness, or any other threshold to avoid deciding the matter.[43]

Federal courts have decided many cases involving foreign affairs and the war power. Depending on the circumstances, they can help clarify constitutional issues and monitor the relationships between Congress and the President. But efforts to *compel* judges to decide cases are unwise and unconstitutional. Most of the thresholds used by courts to avoid a decision (standing, mootness, ripeness, and so forth) are derived from the case-or-controversy test in Article III.[44] Judges must decide what is a case or controversy. Congress cannot compel them to decide a case, especially when it is not in their institutional interest to act. For any number of sound reasons (including lack of judicial competence), judges may properly conclude that disputes over the war power are best left to the elected branches.

As noted by Harold Koh, statutes cannot require federal judges to "sur-

37. Dellums v. Bush, 752 F.Supp. 1141, 1149–52 (D.D.C. 1990); Ange v. Bush, 752 F.Supp. 509, 515–17 (D,D.C. 1990).

38. Dornan v. U.S. Secretary of Defense, 851 F.2d 450 (D.C. Cir. 1988).

39. Lowry v. Reagan, 676 F.Supp. 333, 337–39 (D.D.C. 1987); Conyers v. Reagan, 578 F.Supp. 324 (D.D.C. 1984).

40. Crockett v. Reagan, 558 F.Supp. 893, 898 (D.D.C. 1982); Sanchez-Espinoza v. Reagan, 568 F.Supp. 596, 600 (D.D.C. 1983).

41. Biden and Ritch, "The War Power at a Constitutional Impasse: A 'Joint Decision' Solution" 409.

42. Id. at 410.

43. Ely, War and Responsibility, 60–63, 125, 135.

44. Louis Fisher, American Constitutional Law 97–98, 104, 126, 130 (1995).

render their discretion to dismiss those suits in which concerns about separation of powers proved particularly intense, for example, suits brought by constitutionally inappropriate plaintiffs."[45] Even for techniques of judicial abstention that supposedly lack an Article III basis, such as prudential consideration and equitable discretion, a judge's decision not to decide is rooted in an institutional judgment that abstention is necessary for the continued independence and health of the courts.

Furthermore, members of Congress (and the President) should not press for a judicial decision without knowing what it will be, and they cannot know that ahead of time. It is standard courtroom practice for attorneys not to ask a question of a witness unless they know that the answer will assist their case. Federal courts have generally expanded, not restricted, presidential power. If courts in a particular case decide that the President acted properly in initiating military action without first seeking congressional authority, the cause of Congress (and the Constitution) would be gravely compromised. It would now face not one branch, acting on suspect authority, but two branches agreed on the use of force.

The framers' basic theory, guiding us for two centuries, is that "ambition must be made to counteract ambition."[46] Each branch must protect its own territory. Congress cannot go to the courts, hat in hand, asking judges to do what legislators are fully capable of doing: Check the President. Congress should not entrust to the judiciary the duty of protecting legislative prerogatives. As Justice Jackson said in the Steel Seizure Case, "only Congress itself can prevent power from slipping through its fingers."[47]

Statutory Restrictions

Instead of relying on unpredictable court decisions, Congress must learn to invoke the powerful weapons at its command. Through its prerogative to authorize programs and appropriate funds, it can define and limit presidential power. In domestic as well as in foreign affairs, Congress can with-

---

45. Harold Hongju Koh, The National Security Constitution: Sharing Power After the Iran-Contra Affair 223 (1990).

46. James Madison, Federalist no. 51, The Federalist 356 (Benjamin Fletcher Wright ed. 1961).

47. Youngstown Co. v. Sawyer, 343 U.S. at 654.

hold all or part of an appropriation and may attach riders to appropriations measures to proscribe certain actions.[48]

Some claim that the power of the purse is ineffective in restraining presidential wars. Senator Jacob Javits said that Congress "can hardly cut off appropriations when 500,000 American troops are fighting for their lives, as in Vietnam."[49] The short answer is that Congress can, and has, used the power of the purse to restrict presidential war power. If members of Congress are worried about American troops fighting for their lives in a futile war, those lives are not protected by voting for continued funding. The proper and responsible action is to terminate appropriations and bring the troops home. Members need to make that case to their constituents. It can be done.

The Supreme Court has held that the President as Commander in Chief "is authorized to direct the movements of the naval and military forces placed by law at his command, and to employ them in the manner he may deem most effectual to harass and conquer and subdue the enemy."[50] The power to move forces "placed *by law*" at his command implies that Congress can, by statute, control the scope of the commander-in-chief powers. Many such restrictions have been enacted. Following are some contemporary examples.

In 1973, Congress used the power of the purse to end the war in Vietnam. Three years later it prohibited the CIA from operating in Angola other than to gather intelligence. Legislation also prohibited the Agency from conducting military or paramilitary operations in Angola and denied any appropriated funds to finance directly or indirectly any type of military assistance to Angola.[51]

In 1984, Congress adopted the Boland Amendment to prohibit assistance of any kind by the Reagan administration to support the Contras in Nicaragua. The all-embracing language read: "During fiscal year 1985, no funds available to the Central Intelligence Agency, the Department of Defense, or any other agency or entity of the United States involved in intelligence activities may be obligated or expended for the purpose or which would have the effect of supporting, directly or indirectly, military or

48. Eli E. Nobleman, "Financial Aspects of Congressional Participation in Foreign Relations," 289 The Annals 145 (1953); Louis Fisher, "How Tightly Can Congress Draw the Purse Strings?" 83 Am. J. Int'l L. 758 (1989).

49. Jacob K. Javits, "The War Powers Resolution and the Constitution: A Special Introduction," in The President's War Powers: From the Federalists to Reagan 3 (Demetrios Caraley ed. 1984).

50. Fleming v. Page, 50 U.S. (9 How.) 602, 614 (1850).

51. 90 Stat. 166 (1976); 90 Stat. 757, sec. 404 (1976); 90 Stat. 776, sec. 109 (1976).

paramilitary operations in Nicaragua by any nation, group, organization, movement, or individual."[52] No constitutional objection to this provision was ever voiced publicly by President Reagan, the White House, the Justice Department, or any other agency of the executive branch.

Two years later, Congress restricted the President's military role in Central America by stipulating that U.S. personnel "may not provide any training or other service, or otherwise participate directly or indirectly in the provision of any assistance, to the Nicaraguan democratic resistance pursuant to this title within those land areas of Honduras and Costa Rica which are within 20 miles of the border with Nicaragua."[53] The statute defined U.S. personnel to mean "any member of the United States Armed Forces who is on active duty or is performing inactive duty training" and any employee of any department, agency, or other component of the executive branch.[54] The clear purpose was to prevent military activities in Honduras and Costa Rica from spilling over into Nicaragua. The Reagan administration never offered any constitutional objections to this statutory restriction.

Also in 1986, Congress passed this prohibition on placing U.S. personnel in Nicaragua: "no member of the United States Armed Forces or employee of any department, agency, or other component of the United States Government may enter Nicaragua to provide military advice, training, or logistical support to paramilitary groups operating inside that country. Nothing in this title shall be construed as authorizing any member or unit of the Armed Forces of the United States to engage in combat against the Government of Nicaragua."[55]

In 1991, when Congress authorized President Bush to use military force against Iraq, the authority was explicitly linked to UN Security Council Resolution 678, which was adopted to expel Iraq from Kuwait.[56] Thus, the legislation did not authorize any wider action, such as using U.S. forces to invade and occupy Iraq. In 1993, Congress established a deadline for troops to leave Somalia. No funds could be used for military action after March 31, 1994, unless the President requested an extension from Congress and received legislative authority.[57]

52. 98 Stat. 1935, sec. 8066(a) (1984).
53. 100 Stat. 3341–307, sec. 216(a) (1986).
54. Id. at sec. 216(b).
55. 100 Stat. 1783–298, sec. 203(e) (1986).
56. 105 Stat. 3 (1991).
57. 107 Stat. 1476, sec. 8151(b)(2)(B) (1993).

Thinking National Interest

It is in the nature of the White House that Presidents will be surrounded by aides who advocate heavy reliance on executive powers and inherent authority, thus eliminating the need to build congressional support. Watergate and the Iran-Contra affair teach us that executive officials have great capacity for self-inflicted injuries. The loyalty of political appointees to the President gives them little stake in the long-term operations of government. Quick to bridle at the frustrations of orderly, constitutional procedures, executive officials are tempted to circumvent laws with interpretations they regard as clever.

Political appointees are often willing to initiate actions that come at great cost to Congress, the President, and the political system. Eager for results and ignorant of constitutional processes, they seek immediate action regardless of long-term damage. By the time the offense is uncovered they are likely to be back in the private sector. Contemptuous of government, they make government contemptible by their conduct. The task of cleaning up the debris is then left to careerists and professionals in Congress and the executive branch. They have done it before and can do it again, but the political system is inevitably poisoned. Afterwards there is less good faith, trust, and confidence between the branches—qualities indispensable in a government of divided powers, general grants of constitutional authority, and broadly drawn statutes that demand sound judgment from administrators.

Power has been shifting from career executives to short-term political appointees. The latter are more loyal to the President than to the federal policies that Congress enacts into law, and they have less of a stake in healthy executive-legislative relations. Political appointees "have enough time to make mistakes, but not enough time to learn from them."[58] Increased numbers of political appointees pose serious risks: a layer of inexperienced policymakers subject to frequent turnover, the exclusion of many career professionals from agency deliberations, and greater administrative instability and incompetence. The result is that Congress enacts legislation but has less confidence that laws will be carried out faithfully.

In its report released in 1989, the Volcker Commission studied the relationship between political appointees and career executives and recommended that the number of political appointees be reduced by about one-

---

58. James P. Pfiffner, "Political Appointees and Career Executives: The Democracy-Bureaucracy Nexus in the Third Century," 47 Pub. Adm. Rev. 57, 63 (1987). See also Patricia W. Ingraham, "Building Bridges or Burning Them? The President, the Appointees, and the Bureaucracy," 47 Pub. Adm. Rev. 425 (1987).

third.[59] Unfortunately, that proposal was not adopted, and the reforms pushed by the Clinton administration, particularly the National Performance Review (the Gore Report on "reinventing government"), will make the ratio worse. Careerists will be reduced by about 252,000 over five years without any decrease in political appointees. Congress later increased the personnel cut to 272,900.

This climate will invite short-term political appointees to augment presidential war power and ignore congressional controls. Democrats eager to support President Clinton as Commander in Chief, pressing those powers to the limit, should review earlier experiences with that strategy. President Wilson's entry into World War I cost the Democrats control of Congress in the 1918 elections and the loss of the White House in 1920. Truman's war in Korea resulted in the election of Eisenhower, ending twenty years of Democratic control of the White House. Lyndon Johnson's entanglement in Vietnam set the stage for Richard Nixon's victory in 1968. This is not a winning pattern.

Republicans, especially those with monarchical leanings, should also reflect on the costs to their party when presidential war power is unchecked. Dwight Eisenhower understood the need to share the war power with Congress. He served for two full terms. Under Richard Nixon, exaggerated notions of national security and a refusal to recognize congressional prerogatives led to Watergate and Nixon's resignation. The Iran-Contra fiasco discredited the Reagan administration and the Republicans' traditional claim that they can manage the executive branch. President Reagan said he did not know what was being done within his own National Security Council. Even George Bush's "popular" actions in Panama and Iraq yielded no benefits for his reelection effort in 1992. Activists in both parties need to rethink the merits of presidential wars.

For its part, Congress needs to rediscover its institutional and constitutional duties. Legislators must be prepared, and willing, to use the ample powers at their disposal. Too often members make careless remarks that the President "makes foreign policy," is "preeminent" in foreign affairs, and that, as Commander as Chief, he may send troops wherever he likes. During hearings in 1983 on covert operations, the chairman of the House Intelligence Committee, Edward P. Boland, remarked: "We do not meet today to dispute the President's pre-eminence in foreign affairs."[60] Such

59. Task Force Reports to the National Commission on the Public Service, Leadership in America: Rebuilding the Public Service 158–90 (1989).

60. "Congressional Oversight of Covert Activities," hearings before the House Permanent Select Committee on Intelligence," 98th Cong., 1st Sess. 1 (1983).

comments undermine constitutional checks and feed executive arrogance. Even the most cursory glance at the Constitution and American history demonstrates the solid base of congressional responsibilities in foreign policy and the war power.

Much of the imbalance between executive and legislative power lies in the disparate defense measures available to the President and to Congress. Presidents and their assistants are quick to react to congressional initiatives they see as invasive. The Justice Department, the White House, and other centers of the executive branch are ready to challenge and fight off legislative actions. That is as it should be. Congressional leaders, on the other hand, are often at cross-purposes: partly inclined to protect their institution, but just as disposed to defend the President's powers and interests. That is especially so when congressional leaders are of the same party as the President, but this pattern is evident even when the President is from the opposite party. Thus, the executive branch has a defense mechanism that is fairly central and unified, while Congress is decentralized and divided in purpose. This is a major institutional deficiency for Congress, and legislative leaders (as well as the rank and file) need to be sensitive about this imbalance. For all that is written about the "Imperial Congress" with its penchant for "micromanagement," there is too great a temptation on the part of Congress to let down its guard and fail to defend its prerogatives.

The post-Vietnam years offer many constructive lessons on the need for Presidents to reach an accommodation with Congress in foreign policy and national defense. Unilateral executive claims of military power are counterproductive for Congress, the President, and the country. To sustain a successful policy, the executive branch needs the support and cooperation of Congress. After championing executive power for years, in 1975 Secretary of State Henry Kissinger observed:[61]

> Comity between the executive and legislative branches is the only possible basis for national action. The decade-long struggle in this country over executive dominance in foreign affairs is over. The recognition that the Congress is a coequal branch of government is the dominant fact of national politics today. The executive accepts that the Congress must have both the sense and the reality of participation: foreign policy must be a shared enterprise.[61]

In testimony before the Senate Foreign Relations Committee in 1988, Abraham Sofaer, legal adviser to the State Department, said that the

61. 73 Dept. of State Bull. 562 (1975).

Reagan administration recognized that Congress has "a critical role" to play in determining when the United States commits armed forces to actual or potential hostilities. No presidential policy in this area can have "any hope of success in the long term unless Congress and the American people concur in it and are willing to support its execution."[62] Robert F. Turner, who recognizes a greater latitude for presidential war power than I do, nevertheless appreciates the need for executive-legislative cooperation. In testimony before the House Foreign Affairs Committee in 1988, he expressed this position very eloquently. Although from "a purely constitutional perspective" the President possesses a great deal of independent power in the making and conduct of foreign policy, "in the long run those policies are almost guaranteed to fail if the Congress and the American people do not understand and support them." Regardless of legal analysis, Turner said it is a "political imperative" that Congress and the President cooperate in a spirit of mutual respect and comity.[63]

Members of Congress need to participate in the daily grind of overseeing administration policies, passing judgment on them, and behaving as a coequal, independent branch. When Presidents overstep constitutional barriers or threaten to do so, Congress must respond with solid statutory checks, not floor speeches and "sense of Congress" resolutions. Action by statute is needed to safeguard the legislative institution, maintain a vigorous system of checks and balances, and fulfill the role of Congress as the people's representatives. Members do more than represent districts and states; they represent popular control. Citizens entrust to Congress the safekeeping of their powers, especially over matters of war and peace. Legislators act as custodians of the people. If they neglect that function, citizens, scholars, and interest groups must apply constant pressure on Congress to discharge the constitutional duties assigned to it.

Congress may stand against the President or stand behind him, but it should not stand aside as it did year after year during the Vietnam War, looking the other way and occasionally complaining about executive usurpation. Members have to participate actively in questions of national policy, challenging Presidents and contesting their actions. Military issues need the thorough exploration and ventilation that only Congress can provide.

Justice Robert H. Jackson, whose entire career with the federal govern-

62. "The War Power After 200 Years: Congress and the President at a Constitutional Impasse," hearings before the Senate Committee on Foreign Relations, 100th Cong., 2d Sess. 144 (1988).

63. "War Powers: Origins, Purposes, and Applications," hearings before the House Committee on Foreign Affairs, 100th Cong., 2d Sess. 56 (1988).

ment lay outside the legislative branch, serving first as Attorney General and later as Associate Justice of the Supreme Court, urged us to hold fast to essentials: "With all its defects, delays and inconveniences, men have discovered no technique for long preserving free government except that the Executive be under the law, and that the law be made by parliamentary deliberations."[64]

64. Youngstown Co. v. Sawyer, 343 U.S. at 655.

APPENDICES

Appendix A

FRAMERS' DEBATE ON THE WAR POWER
(August 17, 1787; 2 Farrand 318–19)

"To make war"

Mr Pinkney opposed the vesting this power in the Legislature. Its proceedings were too slow. It wd. meet but once a year. The Hs. of Reps. would be too numerous for such deliberations. The Senate would be the best depositary, being more acquainted with foreign affairs, and most capable of proper resolutions. If the States are equally represented in Senate, so as to give no advantage to large States, the power will notwithstanding be safe, as the small have their all at stake in such cases as well as the large States. It would be singular for one authority to make war, and another peace.

Mr Butler. The Objections agst the Legislature lie in a great degree agst the Senate. He was for vesting the power in the President, who will have all the requisite qualities, and will not make war but when the Nation will support it.

Mr. M ⟨adison⟩ and Mr Gerry moved to insert *"declare,"* striking out *"make"* war; leaving to the Executive the power to repel sudden attacks.

Mr Sharman thought it stood very well. The Executive shd. be able to repel and not to commence war. "Make" better than "declare" the latter narrowing the power too much.

Mr Gerry never expected to hear in a republic a motion to empower the Executive alone to declare war.

Mr. Elseworth. there is a material difference between the cases of making *war,* and making *peace.* It shd. be more easy to get out of war, than into it. War also is a simple and overt declaration. peace attended with intricate & secret negociations.

Mr. Mason was agst giving the power of war to the Executive, because not ⟨safely⟩ to be trusted with it; or to the Senate, because not so constructed as to be entitled to it. He was for clogging rather than facilitating war; but for facilitating peace. He preferred *"declare"* to *"make."*

On the Motion to insert *declare*—in place of *Make,* ⟨it was agreed to.⟩

N. H. no. Mas. abst. Cont. no.* Pa ay. Del. ay. Md. ay. Va. ay. N. C. ay. S. C. ay. Geo- ay. [Ayes—7; noes—2; absent—1.]

Mr. Pinkney's motion to strike out the whole clause, disagd. to without call of States.

Mr Butler moved to give the Legislature power of peace, as they were to have that of war.

Mr Gerry 2ds. him. 8 Senators may possibly exercise the power if vested in that body, and 14 if all should be present; and may consequently give up part of the U. States. The Senate are more liable to be corrupted by an Enemy than the whole Legislature.

On the motion for adding "and peace" after "war"

N. H. no. Mas. no. Ct. no. Pa. no. Del. no. Md. no. Va. no. N. C. ⟨no⟩ S. C. no. Geo. no. [Ayes–0; noes–10.]

Adjourned

---

*On the remark by Mr. King that *"make"* war might be understood to "conduct" it which was an Executive function, Mr. Elseworth gave up his objection ⟨and the vote of Cont was changed to—ay.⟩

Appendix B

CONSTITUTIONAL ALLOCATION OF
FOREIGN AFFAIRS AND THE WAR POWER

Legislative

"All legislative Powers herein granted shall be vested in a Congress."
Power to provide for the common defense
To regulate foreign commerce
"To define and punish Piracies and Felonies committed on the high Seas, and Offenses against the Law of Nations."
"To declare War, grant Letters of Marque and Reprisal, and make rules concerning Captures on Land and Water
Raise and support armies
Provide and maintain a navy
Make rules and regulations of the land and naval forces
"To provide for calling forth the Militia to execute the Laws of the Union, suppress Insurrections, and repel Invasions."
"To provide for organizing, arming, and disciplining, the Militia, and for governing such Part of them as may be employed in the Service of the United States."
"To make all Laws which shall be necessary and proper for carrying into Execution the foregoing Powers and all other Powers vested by this Constitution in the government of the United States, or in any Department or Officer thereof."
Power of the purse ("No money shall be drawn from the Treasury, but in Consequence of Appropriations made by Law.")

Executive

"The executive Power shall be vested in a President."
"The President shall be Commander in Chief of the Army and Navy of the United States, and of the Militia of the several States, when called into the actual Service of the United States."
"[The President] shall receive Ambassadors and other public Ministers."

Shared Powers

"[The President] shall have Power, by and with the Advice and Consent of the Senate, to make Treaties, provided two thirds of the Senators present concur; and he shall nominate, and by and with the Advice and Consent of the Senate, shall appoint Ambassadors, other public Ministers and Consuls, Judges of the supreme Court, and all other Officers of the United States, whose Appointments are not herein otherwise provided for, and which shall be established by Law: but the Congress may by Law vest the Appointment of such inferior Officers, as they think proper, in the President alone, in the Courts of Law, or in the Heads of Departments."

[The Constitution also provides that "The Privilege of the Writ of Habeas Corpus shall not be suspended, unless in Cases of Rebellion or Invasion the public Safety may require it." This provision appears in Article I, defining the powers of Congress, but the writ was suspended by President Lincoln in 1861 while Congress was adjourned. Uncertain of his legal authority, he asked Congress to sanction what he had done. Congress passed legislation retroactively authorizing his action.]

Appendix C

UN PARTICIPATION ACT OF 1945
(59 Stat. 621)

SEC. 6. The President is authorized to negotiate a special agreement or agreements with the Security Council which shall be subject to the approval of the Congress by appropriate Act or joint resolution, providing for the numbers and types of armed forces, their degree of readiness and general location, and the nature of facilities and assistance, including rights of passage, to be made available to the Security Council on its call for the purpose of maintaining international peace and security in accordance with article 43 of said Charter. The President shall not be deemed to require the authorization of the Congress to make available to the Security Council on its call in order to take action under article 42 of said Charter and pursuant to such special agreement or agreements the armed forces, facilities, or assistance provided for therein: *Provided,* That nothing herein contained shall be construed as an authorization to the President by the Congress to make available to the Security Council for such purpose armed forces, facilities, or assistance in addition to the forces, facilities, and assistance provided for in such special agreement or agreements.

Appendix D

1949 AMENDMENTS TO UN PARTICIPATION ACT
(63 Stat. 735)

SEC. 5. Such Act is hereby amended by inserting after section 6 the following new section:

"SEC. 7. (a) Notwithstanding the provisions of any other law, the President, upon the request by the United Nations for cooperative action, and to the extent that he finds that it is consistent with the national interest to comply with such request, may authorize, in support of such activities of the United Nations as are specifically directed to the peaceful settlement of disputes and not involving the employment of armed forces contemplated by chapter VII of the United States Charter—

"(1) the detail to the United Nations, under such terms and conditions as the President shall determine, of personnel of the armed forces of the United States to serve as observers, guards, or in any noncombatant capacity, but in no event shall more than a total of one thousand of such personnel be so detailed at any one time: *Provided,* That while so detailed, such personnel shall be considered for all purposes as acting in the line of duty, including the receipt of pay and allowances as personnel of the armed forces of the United States, credit for longevity and retirement, and all other perquisites appertaining to such duty: *Provided further,* That upon authorization or approval by the President, such personnel may accept directly from the United Nations (a) any or all of the allowances or perquisites to which they are entitled under the first proviso hereof, and (b) extraordinary expenses and perquisites incident to such detail;

"(2) the furnishing of facilities, services, or other assistance and the loan of the agreed fair share of the United States of any supplies and equipment to the United Nations by the National Military Establishment, under such terms and conditions as the President shall determine;

"(3) the obligation, insofar as necessary to carry out the purposes of clauses (1) and (2) of this subsection, of any funds appropriated to the National Military Establishment or any department therein, the procurement of such personnel, supplies, equipment, facilities, services, or other assistance as may be made available in accordance with the request of the United Nations, and the replacement of such items, when necessary, where they are furnished from stocks.

"(b) Whenever personnel or assistance is made available pursuant to the authority contained in subsection (a) (1) and (2) of this section, the President shall require reimbursement from the United Nations for the expense thereby incurred by the United States: *Provided,* That in exceptional circumstances, or when the President finds it to be in the national interest, he may waive, in whole or in part, the requirement of such reimbursement: *Provided further,* That when any such reimbursement is made, it shall be credited, at the option of the appropriate department of the National Military Establishment, either to the appropriation, fund, or account utilized in incurring the obligation, or to an appropriate appropriation, fund, or account currently available for the purposes for which expenditures were made.

"(c) In addition to the authorization of appropriations to the Department of State contained in section 8 of this Act, there is hereby authorized to be appropriated to the National Military Establishment, or any department therein, such sums as may be necessary to reimburse such Establishment or department in the event that reimbursement from the United Nations is waived in whole or in part pursuant to authority contained in subsection (b) of this section.

"(d) Nothing in this Act shall authorize the disclosure of any information or knowledge in any case in which such disclosure is prohibited by any other law of the United States."

Appendix E

WAR POWERS RESOLUTION OF 1973
(87 Stat. 555)

Concerning the war powers of Congress and the President.

*Resolved by the Senate and House of Representatives of the United States
of America in Congress assembled,*

Short Title

SECTION 1. This joint resolution may be cited as the "War Powers Resolution."

Purpose and Policy

SEC. 2. (a) It is the purpose of this joint resolution to fulfill the intent of
the framers of the Constitution of the United States and insure that the
collective judgment of both the Congress and the President will apply to
the introduction of United States Armed Forces into hostilities, or into situations where imminent involvement in hostilities is clearly indicated by
the circumstances, and to the continued use of such forces in hostilities or
in such situations.

(b) Under article I, section 8, of the Constitution, it is specifically provided that the Congress shall have the power to make all laws necessary
and proper for carrying into execution, not only its own powers but also
all other powers vested by the Constitution in the Government of the
United States, or in any department or officer thereof.

(c) The constitutional powers of the President as Commander-in-Chief to
introduce United States Armed Forces into hostilities, or into situations
where imminent involvement in hostilities is clearly indicated by the circumstances, are exercised only pursuant to (1) a declaration of war, (2) spe-

cific statutory authorization, or (3) a national emergency created by attack upon the United States, its territories or possessions, or its armed forces.

Consultation

SEC. 3. The President in every possible instance shall consult with Congress before introducing United States Armed Forces into hostilities or into situations where imminent involvement in hostilities is clearly indicated by the circumstances, and after every such introduction shall consult regularly with the Congress until United States Armed Forces are no longer engaged in hostilities or have been removed from such situations.

Reporting

SEC. 4. (a) In the absence of a declaration of war, in any case in which United States Armed Forces are introduced—
(1) into hostilities or into situations where imminent involvement in hostilities is clearly indicated by the circumstances;
(2) into the territory, airspace or waters of a foreign nation, while equipped for combat, except for deployments which relate solely to supply, replacement, repair, or training of such forces; or
(3) in numbers which substantially enlarge United States Armed Forces equipped for combat already located in a foreign nation;
the President shall submit within 48 hours to the Speaker of the House of Representatives and to the President pro tempore of the Senate a report, in writing, setting forth—
(A) the circumstances necessitating the introduction of United States Armed Forces;
(B) the constitutional and legislative authority under which such introduction took place; and
(C) the estimated scope and duration of the hostilities or involvement.
(b) The President shall provide such other information as the Congress may request in the fulfillment of its constitutional responsibilities with respect to committing the Nation to war and to the use of United States Armed Forces abroad.
(c) Whenever United States Armed Forces are introduced into hostilities or into any situation described in subsection (a) of this section, the President shall, so long as such armed forces continue to be engaged in such hostilities or situation, report to the Congress periodically on the status

of such hostilities or situations as well as on the scope and duration of such hostilities or situation, but in no event shall he report to the Congress less often than once every six months.

Congressional Action

Sec. 5. (a) Each report submitted pursuant to section 4(a)(1) shall be transmitted to the Speaker of the House of Representatives and to the President pro tempore of the Senate on the same calendar day. . . .

(b) Within sixty calendar days after a report is submitted or is required to be submitted pursuant to section 4(a)(1), whichever is earlier, the President shall terminate any use of United States Armed Forces with respect to which such report was submitted (or required to be submitted), unless the Congress (1) has declared war or has enacted a specific authorization for such use of Unites States Armed Forces, (2) has extended by law such sixty-day period, or (3) is physically unable to meet as a result of an armed attack upon the United States. Such sixty-day period shall be extended for not more than an additional thirty days if the President determines and certifies to the Congress in writing that unavoidable military necessity respecting the safety of United States Armed Forces requires the continued use of such armed forces in the course of bringing about a prompt removal of such forces.

(c) Notwithstanding subsection (b), at any time that United States Armed Forces are engaged in hostilities outside the territory of the United States, its possessions and territories without a declaration of war or specific statutory authorization, such forces shall be removed by the President if the Congress so directs by concurrent resolution.

Congressional Priority Procedures for Joint Resolution
or Bill

Sec. 6 *[Provides for expedited consideration of a joint resolution or bill introduced pursuant to Section 5(b). Deadlines are established for committee and floor action, unless the House or Senate determine otherwise by yeas and nays. The objective is to complete action not later than the expiration of the sixty-day period.]*

Congressional Priority Procedures for Concurrent
Resolution

Sec. 7. *[Provides for expedited consideration of a concurrent resolution introduced pursuant to Section 5(c). Deadlines are established for committee and floor action, unless the House or Senate determine otherwise by yeas and nays. The objective is to complete action within forty-eight days.]*

Interpretation of Joint Resolution

SEC. 8. (a) Authority to introduce United States Armed Forces into hostilities or into situations wherein involvement in hostilities is clearly indicated by the circumstances shall not be inferred—

(1) from any provision of law (whether or not in effect before the date of the enactment of this joint resolution), including any provision contained in an appropriation Act, unless such provision specifically authorizes the introduction of United States Armed Forces into hostilities or into such situations and states that it is intended to constitute specific statutory authorization within the meaning of this joint resolution; or

(2) from any treaty heretofore or hereafter ratified unless such treaty is implemented by legislation specifically authorizing the introduction of United States Armed Forces into hostilities or into such situations and stating that it is intended to constitute specific statutory authorization within the meaning of this joint resolution.

(b) Nothing in this joint resolution shall be construed to require any further specific statutory authorization to permit members of United States Armed Forces to participate jointly with members of the armed forces of one or more foreign countries in the headquarters operations of high-level military commands which were established prior to the date of enactment of this joint resolution and pursuant to the United Nations Charter or any treaty ratified by the United States prior to such date.

(c) For purposes of this joint resolution, the term "introduction of United States Armed Forces" includes the assignment of members of such armed forces to command, coordinate, participate in the movement of, or accompany the regular or irregular military forces of any foreign country or government when such military forces are engaged, or there exists an imminent threat that such forces will become engaged, in hostilities.

(d) Nothing in this joint resolution—

(1) is intended to alter the constitutional authority of the Congress or of the President, or the provisions of existing treaties; or

(2) shall be construed as granting any authority to the President with respect to the introduction of United States Armed Forces into hostilities or into situations wherein involvement in hostilities is clearly indi-

cated by the circumstances which authority he would not have had in the absence of this joint resolution.

Separability Clause

SEC. 9. If any provision of this joint resolution or the application thereof to any person or circumstance is held invalid, the remainder of the joint resolution and the application of such provision to any other person or circumstance shall not be affected thereby.

Effective Date

SEC. 10. This joint resolution shall take effect on the date of its enactment.

Appendix F

INTELLIGENCE OVERSIGHT ACT OF 1991
(105 Stat. 441–45)

General Congressional Oversight Provisions

"SEC. 501. (a)(1) The President shall ensure that the intelligence committees are kept fully and currently informed of the intelligence activities of the United States, including any significant anticipated intelligence activity [covert action] as required by this title.

"(2) As used in this title, the term 'intelligence committees' means the Select Committee on Intelligence of the Senate and the Permanent Select Committee on Intelligence of the House of Representatives.

"(3) Nothing in this title shall be construed as requiring the approval of the intelligence committees as a condition precedent to the initiation of any significant anticipated intelligence activity.

"(b) The President shall ensure that any illegal intelligence activity is reported promptly to the intelligence committees, as well as any corrective action that has been taken or is planned in connection with such illegal activity.

"(c) The President and the intelligence committees shall each establish such procedures as may be necessary to carry out the provisions of this title.

"(d) The House of Representatives and the Senate shall each establish, by rule or resolution of such House, procedures to protect from unauthorized disclosure all classified information, and all information relating to intelligence sources and methods, that is furnished to the intelligence committees or to Members of Congress under this title. Such procedures shall be established in consultation with the Director of Central Intelligence. In accordance with such procedures, each of the intelligence committees shall promptly call to the attention of its respective House, or to any appropriate committee or committees of its respective House, any matter relating to intelligence activities requiring the attention of such House or such committee or committees.

"(e) Nothing in this Act shall be construed as authority to withhold information from the intelligence committees on the grounds that providing the information to the intelligence committees would constitute the unauthorized disclosure of classified information or information relating to intelligence sources and methods.

"(f) As used in this section, the term 'intelligence activities' includes covert actions as defined in section 503(e).

"Reporting of Intelligence Activities Other Than Covert Actions

"SEC. 502. To the extent consistent with due regard for the protection from unauthorized disclosure of classified information relating to sensitive intelligence sources and methods or other exceptionally sensitive matters, the Director of Central Intelligence and the heads of all departments, agencies, and other entities of the United States Government involved in intelligence activities shall—

"(1) keep the intelligence committees fully and currently informed of all intelligence activities, other than a covert action (as defined in section 503(e)), which are the responsibility of, are engaged in by, or are carried out for or on behalf of, any department, agency, or entity of the United States Government, including any significant anticipated intelligence activity and any significant intelligence failure; and

"(2) furnish the intelligence committees any information or material concerning intelligence activities, other than covert actions, which is within their custody or control, and which is requested by either of the intelligence committees in order to carry out its authorized responsibilities.

"Presidential Approval and Reporting of Covert Actions

"SEC. 503. (a) The President may not authorize the conduct of a covert action by departments, agencies, or entities of the United States Government unless the President determines such an action is necessary to support identifiable foreign policy objectives of the United States and is important to the national security of the United States, which determination shall be set forth in a finding that shall meet each of the following conditions:

"(1) Each finding shall be in writing, unless immediate action by the United States is required and time does not permit the preparation of a written finding, in which case a written record of the President's decision shall be contemporaneously made and shall be reduced to a written finding as soon as possible but in no event more than 48 hours after the decision is made.

"(2) Except as permitted by paragraph (1), a finding may not authorize or sanction a covert action, or any aspect of any such action, which already has occurred.

"(3) Each finding shall specify each department, agency, or entity of the United States Government authorized to fund or otherwise participate in any significant way in such action. Any employee, contractor, or contract agent of a department, agency, or entity of the United States Government other than the Central Intelligence Agency directed to participate in any way in a covert action shall be subject either to the policies and regulations of the Central Intelligence Agency, or to written policies or regulations adopted by such department, agency, or entity, to govern such participation.

"(4) Each finding shall specify whether it is contemplated that any third party which is not an element of, or a contractor or contract agent of, the United States Government, or is not otherwise subject to United States Government policies and regulations, will be used to fund or otherwise participate in any significant way in the covert action concerned, or be used to undertake the covert action concerned on behalf of the United States.

"(5) A finding may not authorize any action that would violate the Constitution or any statute of the United States.

"(b) To the extent consistent with due regard for the protection from unauthorized disclosure of classified information relating to sensitive intelligence sources and methods or other exceptionally sensitive matters, the Director of Central Intelligence and the heads of all departments, agencies, and entities of the United States Government involved in a covert action—

"(1) shall keep the intelligence committees fully and currently informed of all covert actions which are the responsibility of, are engaged in by, or are carried out for or on behalf of, any department, agency, or entity of the United States Government, including significant failures; and

"(2) shall furnish to the intelligence committees any information or material concerning covert actions which is in the possession, custody, or control of any department, agency, or entity of the United States Government and which is requested by either of the intelligence committees in order to carry out its authorized responsibilities.

"(c)(1) The President shall ensure that any finding approved pursuant to subsection (a) shall be reported to the intelligence committees as soon as possible after such approval and before the initiation of the covert action authorized by the finding, except as otherwise provided in paragraph (2) and paragraph (3).

"(2) If the President determines that it is essential to limit access to the finding to meet extraordinary circumstances affecting vital interests of the United States, the finding may be reported to the chairmen and ranking minority members of the intelligence committees, the Speaker and minority leader of the House of Representatives, the majority and minority leaders of the Senate, and such other member or members of the congressional leadership as may be included by the President.

"(3) Whenever a finding is not reported pursuant to paragraph (1) or (2) of this section, the President shall fully inform the intelligence committees in a timely fashion and shall provide a statement of the reasons for not giving prior notice.

"(4) In a case under paragraph (1), (2), or (3), a copy of the finding, signed by the President, shall be provided to the chairman of each intelligence committee. When access to a finding is limited to the Members of Congress specified in paragraph (2), a statement of the reasons for limiting such access shall also be provided.

"(d) The President shall ensure that the intelligence committees, or, if applicable, the Members of Congress specified in subsection (c)(2), are notified of any significant change in a previously approved covert action, or any significant undertaking pursuant to a previously approved finding, in the same manner as findings are reported pursuant to subsection (c).

"(e) As used in this title, the term 'covert action' means an activity or activities of the United States Government to influence political, economic, or military conditions abroad, where it is intended that the role of the United States Government will not be apparent of acknowledged publicly, but does not include—

"(1) activities the primary purpose of which is to acquire intelligence, traditional counterintelligence activities, traditional activities to improve or maintain the operational security of United States Government programs, or administrative activities;

"(2) traditional diplomatic or military activities or routine support to such activities;

"(3) traditional law enforcement activities conducted by United States Government law enforcement agencies or routine support to such activities; or

"(4) activities to provide routine support to the overt activities (other than activities described in paragraph (1), (2), or (3) of other United States Government agencies abroad.

"(f) No covert action may be conducted which is intended to influence United States political processes, public opinion, policies, or media."

• • •

Appendix G

THE CLINTON ADMINISTRATION'S POLICY ON REFORMING
MULTILATERAL PEACE OPERATIONS
(May 1994)

EXECUTIVE SUMMARY

Last year, President Clinton ordered an inter-agency review of our nation's peacekeeping policies and programs in order to develop a comprehensive policy framework suited to the realities of the post-Cold War period. This policy review has resulted in a Presidential Decision Directive (PDD). The President signed this directive, following the completion of extensive consultations with Members of Congress. This paper summarizes the key elements of that directive.

As specified in the "Bottom-Up Review," the primary mission of the U.S. Armed Forces remains to be prepared to fight and win two simultaneous regional conflicts. In this context, peacekeeping can be one useful tool to help prevent and resolve such conflicts before they pose direct threats to our national security. Peacekeeping can also serve U.S. interests by promoting democracy, regional security, and economic growth.

• • •

VII. *Congress and the American People*

To sustain U.S. support for UN peace operations, Congress and the American people must understand and accept the potential value of such operations as tools of U.S. interests. Congress and the American people must also be genuine participants in the processes that support U.S. decision-making on new and on-going peace operations.

Traditionally, the Executive branch has not solicited the involvement of Congress or the American people on matters related to UN peacekeeping. This lack of communication is not desirable in an era when peace operations have become more numerous, complex and expensive. The Clinton Administration is committed to working with Congress to improve and regularize communication and consultation on these important issues. Specifically, the Administration will:

—Regularize recently-initiated periodic consultation with bipartisan Congressional leaders on foreign policy engagements that might involve U.S. forces, including possible deployments of U.S. military units in UN peace operations.

—Continue recently-initiated monthly staff briefings on the UN's upcoming calendar, including current, new and expanded peace operations.

—Inform Congress as soon as possible of unanticipated votes in the UNSC on new or expanded peace operations.

—Inform Congress of UN command and control arrangements when U.S. military units participate in UN organizations.

—Provide UN documents to appropriate committees on a timely basis.

—Submit to Congress a comprehensive annual report on UN peace operations.

—Support legislation along the lines of that introduced by Senators Mitchell, Nunn, Byrd and Warner to amend the War Powers Resolution to introduce a consultative mechanism and to eliminate the 60-day withdrawal provisions.

• • •

SUGGESTED READINGS

Constitutional Framework

Adler, David Gray. "The Constitution and Presidential Warmaking: The Enduring Debate," 103 Political Science Quarterly 1 (1988).

Banks, William C., and Peter Raven-Hansen. National Security Law and the Power of the Purse (1994).

Berdahl, Clarence A. War Powers of the Executive in the United States (1921).

Caraway, Demetrios, ed. The President's War Powers (1984).

Corwin, Edward S. Total War and the Constitution (1947).

Fisher, Louis. "Historical Survey of the War Powers and the Use of Force." In Gary M. Stern and Morton H. Halperin, eds., The U.S. Constitution and the Power to Go to War 11–28 (1994).

Franck, Thomas M., ed. The Tethered Presidency: Congressional Restraints on Executive Power (1981).

Henkin, Louis. Constitutionalism, Democracy, and Foreign Affairs (1990).

_____, et al., eds. Foreign Affairs and the U.S. Constitution (1990).

Javits, Jacob K. Who Makes War: The President Versus Congress (1973).

Levy, Leonard W. Original Intent and the Framers' Constitution 30–53 (1988).

Lofgren, Charles A. "War-Making Under the Constitution: The Original Understanding," 81 Yale Law Journal 672 (1972).

Moore, John N. "The National Executive and the Use of the Armed Forces Abroad," 21 Naval War College Review 28 (1969).

Muskie, Edmund S., Kenneth Rush, and Kenneth W. Thompson, eds. The President, the Congress and Foreign Policy (1986).

Note. "Congress, the President, and the Power to Commit Forces to Combat," 81 Harvard Law Review 1771 (1968).

Pusey, Merlo J. The Way We Go to War (1969).

Reveley, W. Taylor III. War Powers of the President and Congress: Who Holds the Arrows and Olive Branch? (1981).

Shuman, Howard E., and Walter R. Thomas, eds. The Constitution and National Security (1990).

Stern, Gary M., and Morton H. Halperin, eds. The U.S. Constitution and the Power to Go to War: Historical and Current Perspectives (1994).

Thomas, Ann Van Wynen, and A. J. Thomas, Jr. The War-Making Powers of the President: Constitutional and International Law Aspects (1982).

Wormuth, Francis P., and Edwin B. Firmage. To Chain the Dog of War: The War Powers of Congress in History and Law (1986).

Declared and Undeclared Wars

Baldwin, Simeon E. "The Share of the President of the United States in a Declaration of War," 12 American Journal of International Law 1 (1918).

Blechman, Barry M., and Stephen S. Kaplan. Force Without War: U.S. Armed Forces as a Political Instrument (1978).

Eagleton, Clyde. "The Form and Function of the Declaration of War," 32 American Journal of International Law 19 (1938).

Emerson, J. Terry. "Making War Without a Declaration," 17 Journal of Legislation 23 (1990).

Fenwick, C. G. "War Without a Declaration," 31 American Journal of International Law 694 (1937).

Keynes, Edward. Undeclared War: Twilight Zone of Constitutional Power (1982).

Leckie, Robert. The Wars of America (1968).

Maurice, J. F. Hostilities Without Declaration of War: From 1700 to 1870 (1883).

Ronan, William J. "English and American Courts and the Definition of War," 31 American Journal of International Law 642 (1937).

Sidak, J. Gregory. "To Declare War," 41 Duke Law Journal 27 (1991).

Power of Commander in Chief

Carter, Clarence E. "The Office of Commander in Chief: A Phase of Imperial Unity on the Eve of the Revolution." In Richard B. Morris, ed., The Era of the American Revolution (1971).

Dawson, Joseph G., ed. Commanders in Chief: Presidential Leadership in Modern Wars (1993).

Deutsch, Eberhard P. "The President as Commander in Chief," 57 American Bar Association Journal 27 (1971).

Fairman, Charles. "The President as Commander-in-Chief," 11 Journal of Politics 145 (1949).

Fisher, Louis. "The Power of Commander in Chief." In Marcia Lynn Whicker et al., eds., The Presidency and the Persian Gulf War, 45–61 (1993).

Hassler, Warren W., Jr. The President as Commander in Chief (1971).

Heller, Francis H. "The President as the Commander in Chief," 42 Military Review 5 (1962).

Hollander, Bennet N. "The President and Congress—Operational Control of the Armed Forces," 27 Military Law Review 49 (1965).

Hoxie, R. Gordon. "The Office of Commander in Chief: An Historical and Projective View," 6 Presidential Studies Quarterly 10 (1976).

May, Ernest R., ed. The Ultimate Decision: The President as Commander in Chief (1960).

Raven-Hansen, Peter, and William C. Banks. "Pulling the Purse Strings of the Commander in Chief," 80 Virginia Law Review 833 (1994).

Rossiter, Clinton. The Supreme Court and the Commander in Chief (1951).

Timbers, Edwin. "The Supreme Court and the President as Commander in Chief," 16 Presidential Studies Quarterly 224 (1986).

U.S. Congress. The Powers of the President as Commander in Chief of the Army and Navy of the United States, H. Doc. No. 443, 84th Cong., 2d Sess. (1956).

Early Precedents (1789–1900)

Anderson, William G. "John Adams, the Navy, and the Quasi-War with France," 30 The American Neptune 117 (1970).

Baldwin, Leland D. Whiskey Rebels: The Story of a Frontier Uprising (1939).

Casper, Gerhard. "An Essay in Separation of Powers: Some Early Versions and Practices," 30 William and Mary Law Review 211 (1989). (Analyzes the Washington administration's handling of the Algiers problem.)

Coles, Harry L. The War of 1812 (1965).

DeConde, Alexander. "The Quasi-War," 12 American History Illustrated 4 (1977).

_____. The Quasi-War: The Politics and Diplomacy of the Undeclared War with France, 1797–1801 (1966).

Dupuy, R. Ernest, and William H. Baumer. The Little Wars of the United States (1968).

Hickey, Donald R. The War of 1812 (1989).

McClellan, Major Edwin N. "The Naval War with France," 7 The Marine Corps Gazette 339 (1922).

Mahon, John K. The War of 1812 (1972).

Millis, Walter. The Martial Spirit: A Study of Our War with Spain (1931).

Morgan, H. Wayne. William McKinley and His America (1963).

Pomeroy, William. American Neo-Colonialism: Its Emergence in the Philippines and Asia (1970).

Singletary, Otis A. The Mexican War (1960).

Slaughter, Thomas P. The Whiskey Rebellion: Frontier Epilogue to the American Revolution (1986).

Sofaer, Abraham D. "The Presidency, War, and Foreign Affairs: Practice Under the Framers," 40 Law and Contemporary Problems 12 (1976).

_____. War, Foreign Affairs and Constitutional Power: The Origins (1976). (Focuses on the 1789–1829 period.)

Stagg, J. C. A. Mr. Madison's War: Politics, Diplomacy, and Warfare in the Early American Republic, 1783–1830 (1983).

Sword, Wiley. President Washington's Indian War: The Struggle for the Old Northwest, 1790–1795 (1985).

Trask, David F. The War with Spain in 1898 (1981).

Ward, Townsend. "The Insurrections of the Year 1794, in the Western Counties of Pennsylvania," 6 Pennsylvania Historical Society Memoirs 117 (1858).

Whiting, William. War Powers Under the Constitution of the United States (1864).

Williams, T. Harry. Lincoln the Commander in Chief, Historical Bulletin no. 15 (Lincoln Fellowship of Wisconsin, 1957)

Precedents from 1900 to 1945

Calder, Bruce J. The Impact of Intervention: The Dominican Republic during the U.S. Occupation of 1916–1924 (1984).

Cox, Isaac Joslin. Nicaragua and the United States, 1909–1927. World Peace Foundation Pamphlets, vol. 10, no. 7 (1927).

Denny, Harold Norman. Dollars for Bullets: The Story of American Rule in Nicaragua (1929).

DeWeerd, Harvey A. President Wilson Fights His War: World War I and the American Intervention (1968).

Dupuy, R. Ernest, and William H. Baumer. The Little Wars of the United States (1968).

Garcia, Rogelio. Opposition Within the Senate to the American Military Intervention in Nicaragua, 1926–1933. Ph.D. diss., Columbia University, 1973.

Koenig, Louis William. The Presidency and the Crisis: Powers of the Office from the Invasion of Poland to Pearl Harbor (1944).

Langer, William L., and S. Everett Gleason. The Challenge to Isolation: The World Crisis of 1937–1940 and American Foreign Policy (1952).

————. The Undeclared War, 1940–1941 (1953).

Larrabee, Eric. Commander in Chief: Franklin Delano Roosevelt, His Lieutenants, and Their War (1987).

Martin, Charles E. The Policy of the United States as Regards Intervention. Ph.D. diss., Columbia Univ., 1921.

Munro, Dana G. Intervention and Dollar Diplomacy in the Caribbean, 1900–1921 (1964).

Offutt, Milton. The Protection of Citizens Abroad by the Armed Forces of the United States. Johns Hopkins University Studies in Historical and Political Science, ser. 46, no. 4 (1928).

Quirk, Robert E. An Affair of Honor: Woodrow Wilson and the Occupation of Veracruz (1962).

Rogers, James Grafton. World Policing and the Constitution (1945).

Schmidt, Hans. The United States Occupation of Haiti, 1915–1934 (1971).

Stuart, Graham H. Latin America and the United States (1943).

Tansill, Charles Callan. America Goes to War (1938).

————. Back Door to War: The Roosevelt Foreign Policy, 1933–1941 (1952).

Williams, William Appleman. "American Intervention in Russia: 1917–1920." In David Horowitz, ed., Containment and Revolution (1968).

Wood, Bryce. The Making of the Good Neighbor Policy (1961).

The UN Charter and Korea

"Authority of the President to Repel the Attack in Korea," 23 Department of State Bulletin 173 (July 31, 1950).

Caridi, Ronald, Jr. The Korean War and American Politics: The Republican Party as a Case Study (1968).

Fehrenbach, T. R. This Kind of War (1963).

George, Alexander L. "American Policy-making and the North Korean Aggression," 7 World Politics 209 (1955).

Gross, Leo. "The Charter of the United Nations and the Lodge Reservations," 41 American Journal of International Law 531 (1947).

Haynes, Richard F. The Awesome Power: Harry S. Truman as Commander in Chief (1973).

Hoyt, Edwin C. "The United States Reaction to the Korean Attack: A Study of the Principles of the United Nations Charter as a Factor in American Policy-Making," 55 American Journal of International Law 45 (1961).

Kirkendall, Richard S. Harry S Truman, Korea and the Imperial Presidency (1975).

Lofgren, Charles A. "Mr. Truman's War: A Debate and Its Aftermath," 33 Review of Politics 223 (1969).

May, Ernest R. "Korea, 1950: History Overpowering Calculation." In "Lessons" of the Past: The Use and Misuse of History in American Foreign Policy 52–86 (1973).

Paige, Glenn D. The Korean Decision (1968).

Pollack, Samuel. "Self Doubts on Approaching Forty: The United Nations' Oldest and Only Collective Security Enforcement Army, The United Nations Command in Korea," 6 Dickinson Journal of International Law 1 (1987).

Pye, A. Kenneth. "The Legal Status of the Korea Hostilities," 45 Georgetown Law Journal 45 (1956).

Schick, F. B. "Videant Consules," 3 Western Political Quarterly 311 (1950).

Spanier, John W. The Truman-MacArthur Controversy and the Korea War (1965).

Watkins, Arthur W. "War by Executive Order," 4 Western Political Quarterly 539 (1951).

Wright, Quincy. "Collective Security in the Light of the Korean Experience," In Proceedings of the American Society of International Law, April 26–28, 1951, at 165–182.

Taking Stock (1951–1964)

Abel, Elie. The Missiles of October: The Story of the Cuban Missile Crisis (1969).

Allison, Graham T. Essence of Decision: Explaining the Cuban Missile Crisis (1971).

Banks, Robert F. "Steel, Sawyer, and the Executive Power," 14 University of Pittsburgh Law Review 467 (1953).

Briggs, Philip J. "Congress and the Cold War: U.S.-China Policy 1955," 85 China Quarterly 80 (1981).

———. "Congress and the Middle East: The Eisenhower Doctrine, 1956." In Joann P. Krieg, ed., Dwight D. Eisenhower: Soldier, President, Stateman (1987).

Central Intelligence Agency. The Secret Cuban Missile Crisis Documents (1964).

Corwin, Edward S. "The Steel Seizure Case: A Judicial Brick Without Straw," 53 Columbia Law Review 53 (1953).

Glennon, Michael J. "United States Mutual Security Treaties: The Commitment Myth," 24 Columbia Journal of International Law 509 (1986).

Grimmett, Richard F. The Politics of Constraint: The President, the Senate, and American Foreign Policy, 1947–1956. Ph.D. diss., Kent State Univ., 1973.

Heindel, Richard H., et al. "The North Atlantic Treaty in the United States Senate," 43 American Journal of International Law 633 (1949).

Kauper, Paul G. "The Steel Seizure Case: Congress, the President and the Supreme Court," 51 Michigan Law Review 141 (1952).

Kennedy, Robert F. Thirteen Days: A Memoir of the Cuban Missile Crisis (1969).

Marcus, Maeva. Truman and the Steel Seizure Case: The Limits of Presidential Power (1977; reissued in 1994).

Reichard, Gary W. "Divisions and Dissent: Democrats and Foreign Policy, 1952–1956," 93 Political Science Quarterly 51 (1978).

Richberg, Donald R. "The Steel Seizure Cases," 38 Virginia Law Review 713 (1952).

Schubert, Glendon A., Jr. "The Steel Case: Presidential Responsibility and Judicial Irresponsibility," 6 Western Political Quarterly 61 (1953).
Tanenhaus, Joseph. "The Supreme Court and Presidential Power," 307 The Annals 106 (1956).
Thompson, Robert Smith. The Missiles of October: The Declassified Story of John F. Kennedy and the Cuban Missile Crisis (1992).
Westin, Alan F. The Anatomy of a Constitutional Law Case [The Steel Seizure Case] (1958).
Williams, Phil. The Senate and US Troops in Europe (1985).

The Vietnam War

Anderson, David L., ed. Shadow on the White House: Presidents and the Vietnam War, 1945–1975 (1993).
Austin, Anthony. The President's War: The Story of the Tonkin Gulf Resolution and How the Nation was Trapped in Vietnam (1971).
Barrett, David M. Uncertain Warriors: Lyndon Johnson and His Vietnam Advisers (1993).
Berman, Larry. Lyndon Johnson's War: The Road to Stalemate in Vietnam (1989).
_____. Planning a Tragedy: The Americanization of the War in Vietnam (1982).
Burke, John P., and Fred I. Greenstein. How Presidents Test Reality: Decisions on Vietnam, 1954 and 1965 (1989).
D'Amato, Anthony A., and Robert M. O'Neil. The Judiciary and Vietnam (1972).
Eagleton, Thomas F. "The August 15 Compromise and the War Powers of Congress," 18 Saint Louis University Law Journal 1 (1973).
Friedman, Leon, and Burt Neuborne. Unquestioning Obedience to the President: The ACLU Case Against the Legality of the War in Vietnam (1972).
Gibbons, William Conrad. The U.S. Government and the Vietnam War: Executive and Legislative Roles and Relationships (3 vols., 1986, 1989).
Goulden, Joseph C. Truth Is the First Casualty: The Gulf of Tonkin Affairs—Illusion and Reality (1969).
Graff, Henry F. The Tuesday Cabinet: Deliberation and Decision on Peace and War under Lyndon B. Johnson (1970).
Henkin, Louis. "Viet-Nam in the Courts of the United States: 'Political Questions'," 63 American Journal of International Law 284 (1969).
Karnow, Stanley. Vietnam: A History (1991).
Malawer. "The Vietnam War Under the Constitution: Legal Issues Involved in the United States Military Involvement in Vietnam," 31 University of Pittsburgh Law Review 205 (1969).
Newman, John M. JFK and Vietnam: Deception, Intrigue, and the Struggle for Power (1992).
Robertson, David W. "The Debate Among American International Lawyers About the Vietnam War," 46 Texas Law Review 898 (1968).
Schandler, Herbert Y. The Unmaking of a President: Lyndon Johnson and Vietnam (1977).
Schwartz, Warren F., and Wayne McCormack. "The Justiciability of Legal Objections to the American Military Effort in Vietnam," 46 Texas Law Review 1033 (1968).

Velvel, Lawrence R. "The War in Viet Nam: Unconstitutional, Justiciable, and Jurisdictionally Attackable," 16 University of Kansas Law Review 449 (1968).

The War Powers Resolution of 1973

Allison, Graham T. "Making War: The President and Congress," 40 Law and Contemporary Problems 86 (1976).

Berger, Raoul. "War-Making by the President," 121 University of Pennsylvania Law Review 29 (1972).

Clark, Robert D., Andrew M. Egeland, Jr., and David B. Sanford. The War Powers Resolution (1985).

Collier, Ellen C. "Statutory Constraints: The War Powers Resolution." In Gary M. Stern and Morton H. Halperin, eds., The U.S. Constitution and the Power to Go to War 55–82 (1994).

Eagleton, Thomas F. War and Presidential Power: A Chronicle of Congressional Surrender (1974).

Fisher, Louis. "War Powers: The Need for Collective Judgment." In James A. Thurber, ed., Divided Democracy 199–217 (1990).

Franck, Thomas M. "After the Fall: The New Procedural Framework for Congressional Control Over the War Power," 71 American Journal of International Law 605 (1977).

Glennon, Michael J. "The War Powers Resolution Ten Years Later: More Politics Than Law," 78 American Journal of International Law 571 (1984).

Ratner, Leonard G. "The Coordinated Warmaking Power: Legislative, Executive, and Judicial Tools," 44 Southern California Law Review 461 (1971).

Robbins, Patrick D. "The War Powers Resolution After Fifteen Years: A Reassessment," 38 American University Law Review 141 (1988).

Rostow, Eugene V. "Great Cases Make Bad Law: The War Powers Act," 50 Texas Law Review 833 (1972).

————. " 'Once More Unto the Breach': The War Powers Resolution Revisited," 21 Valparaiso University Law Review 1 (1986).

Rushkoff, Bennett C. "A Defense of the War Powers Resolution," 93 Yale Law Journal 1330 (1984).

Schlesinger, Arthur M., Jr. The Imperial Presidency (1973).

Spong, William B., Jr. "The War Powers Resolution Revisited: Historic Accomplishment or Surrender?" 16 William and Mary Law Review 823 (1975).

Turner, Robert F. Repealing the War Powers Resolution: Restoring the Rule of Law in U.S. Foreign Policy (1991).

Zablocki, Clement J. "War Powers Resolution: Its Past Record and Future Promise," 17 Loyola of Los Angeles Law Review 579 (1984).

Military Initiatives from Ford to Carter

Brzezinski, Zbigniew. "The Failed Mission: The Inside Account of the Attempt to Free the Hostages in Iran," New York Times Magazine, April 18, 1982, at 28–31, 61–62, 64, 69–70, 72, 78–79.

Carlile, Donald E. "The Mayaguez Incident: Crisis Management," 56 Military Review 3 (1976).

D'Angelo, John R. "Resort to Force by States to Protect Nationals: The U.S. Rescue Mission to Iran and Its Legality Under International Law," 21 Va. J. Int'l L. 485 (1981).

Jeffery, Anthea. "The American Hostages in Tehran: The I.C.J. and the Legality of Rescue Missions," 30 Int'l and Comp. L. Q. 717 (1981).

Kelley, Michael F. "The Constitutional Implications of the Mayaguez Incident," 3 Hastings Constitutional Law Quarterly 301 (1976).

Lamb, Chris. "Belief Systems and Decision Making in the *Mayaguez* Crisis," 99 Political Science Quarterly 681 (1984–85).

Paust, Jordan J. "More Revelations About Mayaquez (and its Secret Cargo)," 4 Boston Coll. Int'l & Comp. L. Rev. 61 (1981).

———. "The Seizure and Recovery of the *Mayaguez*," 85 Yale Law Journal 774 (1976).

Rowan, Roy. The Four Days of *Mayaguez* (1975).

Ryan, Paul B. The Iranian Rescue Mission: Why It Failed (1985).

Smith, Steve. "Policy Preferences and Bureaucratic Position: The Case of the American Hostage Rescue Mission," 61 International Affairs 9 (1984).

Stein, Ted L. "Contempt, Crisis, and the Court: The World Court and the Hostage Rescue Attempt," 76 Am. J. Int'l L. 499 (1982).

U.S. Congress. "Seizure of the Mayaguez," hearings before the House Committee on International Relations, 94th Cong., 1st Sess. (1975).

Zutz, Robert. "The Recapture of the S.S. Mayaguez: Failure of the Consultation Clause of the War Powers Resolution," 8 New York University Journal of International Law and Politics 457 (1976).

Military Initiatives by Reagan

Beck, Robert J. "International Law and the Decision to Invade Grenada: A Ten-Year Retrospective," 33 Virginia Journal of International Law 765 (1993).

Blum, Zehuda Z. "The Gulf of Sidra Incident," 80 American Journal of International Law 668 (1986).

Bostdorff, Denise. "The Presidency and Promoted Crisis: Reagan, Grenada, and Issue Management," 21 Presidential Studies Quarterly 737 (1991).

Congressional Digest. "The War Powers Act and the Persian Gulf: Pro & Con" (December 1987).

Davis, Brian L. Quaddafi, Terrorism, and the Origins of the U.S. Attack on Libya (1990).

Haerr, Roger Cooling. "The Gulf of Sidra," 24 San Diego Law Review 751 (1987).

Kaldor, Mary, and Paul Anderson, eds. Mad Dogs: The US Raids on Libya (1986).

Rubner, Michael. "Antiterrorism and the Withering of the 1973 War Powers Resolution," 102 Political Science Quarterly 193 (1987).

———. "The Reagan Administration, the 1973 War Powers Resolution, and the Invasion of Grenada," 100 Political Science Quarterly 627 (1985–1986).

Torricelli, Robert G. "The War Powers Resolution After the Libya Crisis," 7 Pace L. Rev. 661 (1987).

Turndorf, David. "The U.S. Raid on Libya: A Forceful Response to Terrorism," 14 Brooklyn Journal of International Law 187 (1988).

U.S. Congress. "War Powers, Libya, and State-Sponsored Terrorism." Hearings before the House Committee on Foreign Affairs, 99th Cong., 2d Sess. (1986).

Military Initiatives from Bush to Clinton

Berger, Matthew D. "Implementing a United Nations Security Council Resolution: The President's Power to Use Force Without the Authorization of Congress," 15 Hastings International and Comparative Law Review 83 (1991).

Bogus, Carl T. "The Invasion of Panama and the Rule of Law," 26 International Lawyer 781 (1992).

Burgin, Eileen. "Congress, the War Powers Resolution, & the Invasion of Panama," 25 Polity 217 (1992).

D'Amato, Anthony. "The Invasion of Panama Was a Lawful Response to Tyranny," 84 American Journal of International Law 516 (1990).

Farer, Tom J. "Panama: Beyond the Charter Paridigm," 84 American Journal of International Law 503 (1990).

Friedman, Alan. Spider's Web: The Secret History of How the White House Illegally Armed Iraq (1993).

Glennon, Michael J. "The Gulf War and the Constitution," 70 Foreign Affairs 84 (1991).

Henkin, Louis. "The Invasion of Panama Under International Law: A Gross Violation," 29 Columbia Journal of Transnational Law 293 (1991).

Lehman, John. Making War: The 200-Year-Old Battle Between the President and Congress over How America Goes to War (1992).

Maechling, Charles, Jr. "Washington's Illegal Invasion [Panama]," 79 Foreign Policy 113 (1990).

Nanda, Ved P. "The Validity of United States Intervention in Panama Under International Law," 84 American Journal of International Law 494 (1990).

Quigley, John. "The Legality of the United States Invasion of Panama," 15 Yale Journal of International Law 276 (1990).

Schachter, Oscar. "United Nations Law in the Gulf Conflict," 85 American Journal of International Law 452 (1991).

Sifry, Michael L., and Christopher Cerf, eds. The Gulf War Reader: History, Documents, Opinions (1991).

Sofaer, Abraham D. "The Legality of the United States Action in Panama," 29 Columbia Journal of Transnational Law 281 (1991).

Swan, George Steven. "Presidential Undeclared Warmaking and Functionalist Theory: *Dellums* v. *Bush* and Operations Desert Shield and Desert Storm," 22 California Western International Law Journal 75 (1991).

Tiefer, Charles. The Semi-Sovereign Presidency: The Bush Administration's Strategy for Governing Without Congress (1994).

Whicker, Marcia Lynn, James P. Pfiffner, and Raymond A. Moore, eds. The Presidency and the Persian Gulf War (1993).

White, N. D., and H. McCoubrey. "International Law and the Use of Force in the Gulf," 10 International Relations 347 (1991).

Woodward, Bob. The Commanders (1991).

Covert Operations and the Iran-Contra Affair

Adler, Emanuel. "Executive Command and Control in Foreign Policy: The CIA's Covert Activities," 23 Orbis 671 (1979).

Ambrose, Stephen E. Ike's Spies: Eisenhower and the Espionage Establishment (1981).

Draper, Theodore. A Very Thin Line: The Iran-Contra Affairs (1991).

Fisher, Louis. "Congressional Access to Executive Branch Information: Lessons from the Iran-Contra Affair," 6 Government Information Quarterly 383 (1989).

_____. "The Foundations of a Scandal [Iran-Contra]," 3 Corruption and Reform 157 (1988).

Gumina, Paul. "Title VI of the Intelligence Authorization Act, Fiscal Year 1991: Effective Covert Action Reform or 'Business as Usual?'," 20 Hastings Constitutional Law Quarterly 149 (1992).

Highsmith, Newell L. "Policing Executive Adventurism: Congressional Oversight of Military and Paramilitary Operations," 19 Harvard Journal on Legislation 327 (1982).

Immerman, Richard H. The CIA in Guatemala (1982).

Jeffrey-Jones, Rhodri. The CIA & American Democracy (1989).

Johnson, Loch. America's Secret Power: The CIA in a Democratic Society (1989).

Lobel, Jules. "Covert War and Congressional Authority: Hidden War and Forgotten Power," 134 University of Pennsylvania Law Review 1035 (1986).

Prados, John. President's Secret Wars: CIA and Pentagon Covert Operations Since World War II (1986).

Reisman, W. Michael, and James Baker. Regulating Covert Action (1992).

Richman, Peter. "For the Want of a Nail . . . the War was Lost: Separation of Powers and United States Counter-Terrorism Policy During the Reagan Years," 17 Hastings Constitutional Law Quarterly 609 (1990).

Silverberg, Marshall. "The Separation of Powers and Control of the CIA's Covert Operations," 68 Texas Law Review 575 (1990).

Steele, Douglas L. "Covert Action and the War Powers Resolution: Preserving the Constitutional Balance," 39 Syracuse Law Review 1139 (1988).

Stockwell, John. In Search of Enemies: A CIA Story [Angola] (1978).

Treverton, Gregory F. Covert Action: The Limits of Intervention (1987).

U.S. Court of Appeals for the District of Columbia Circuit. Final Report of the Independent Counsel for Iran/Contra Matters (3 vols. 1993).

Van Cleve, George W. "The Constitutionality of the Solicitation or Control of Third-Country Funds for Foreign Policy Purposes by United States Officials Without Congressional Approval," 11 Houston Journal of International Law 69 (1988).

Whiting, Alex. "Controlling Tin Cup Diplomacy," 99 Yale Law Journal 2043 (1990).

Wyden, Peter. Bay of Pigs (1979).

Restoring Checks and Balances

Biden, Joseph R., Jr., and John B. Ritch III. "The War Power at a Constitutional Impasse: A 'Joint Decision' Solution," 77 Georgetown Law Journal 367 (1988).

Buchanan, G. Sidney. "In Defense of the War Powers Resolution: *Chadha* Does Not Apply," 22 Houston Law Review 1155 (1985).

Edgar, Charles Ernest. "United States Use of Armed Force Under the United Nations . . . Who's In Charge?" 10 Journal of Law & Politics 299 (1984).

Ely, John Hart. "Suppose Congress Wanted a War Powers Act That Worked," 88 Columbia Law Review 1379 (1988).

———. War and Responsibility: Constitutional Lessons of Vietnam and Its Aftermath (1993).

Fisher, Louis. "How Tightly Can Congress Draw the Purse Strings?" 83 American Journal of International Law 758 (1989).

Friedman, David S. "Waging War Against Checks and Balances—The Claim of an Unlimited Presidential War Power," 57 St. John's Law Review 213 (1983).

Glennon, Michael J. Constitutional Diplomacy (1990).

———. "Strengthening the War Powers Resolution: The Case for Purse-Strings Restrictions," 60 Minnesota Law Review 1 (1975).

Halperin, Morton H. "Lawful Wars," 72 Foreign Policy 173 (1988).

Katzmann, Robert A. "War Powers: Toward a New Accommodation." In Thomas E. Mann, ed., A Question of Balance: The President, the Congress, and Foreign Policy (1990).

Kelly, Major Michael P. "Fixing the War Powers," 141 Military Law Review 83 (1993).

Koh, Harold Hongju. The National Security Constitution: Sharing Power After the Iran-Contra Affair (1990).

May, Christopher N. In the Name of War: Judicial Review and the War Powers Since 1918 (1989).

Nathan, James A. "Revising the War Powers Act," 17 Armed Forces & Society 513 (1991).

———. "Salvaging the War Powers Resolution," 23 Presidential Studies Quarterly 235 (1993).

Note. "Applying *Chadha*: The Fate of the War Powers Resolution," 24 Santa Clara Law Review 697 (1984).

Prober, Joshua Lee. "Congress, the War Powers Resolution, and the Secret Political Life of 'a Dead Letter,' " 7 Journal of Law & Politics 177 (1990).

Raven-Hansen, Peter, and William C. Banks. "Pulling the Purse Strings of the Commander in Chief," 80 Virginia Law Review 833 (1994).

Smyrl, Marc E. Conflict or Codetermination? Congress, the President, and the Power to Make War (1988).

Stromseth, Jane E. "Rethinking War Powers: Congress, the President, and the United Nations," 81 Georgetown Law Journal (1993).

"The President's Powers as Commander-in-Chief Versus Congress' War Power and Appropriations Power," 43 University of Miami Law Review 17 (1988). (Observations by Charles Bennett, Arthur B. Culvahouse, Jr., Geoffrey P. Miller, William Bradford Reynolds, and William Van Alstyne.)

Vance, Cyrus R. "Striking the Balance: Congress and the President Under the War Powers Resolution," 133 University of Pennsylvania Law Review 79 (1984).

INDEX OF CASES

SUBJECT INDEX